Data Analytics and Psychometrics

A volume in
The MARCES Book Series
Robert W. Lissitz and Hong Jiao, *Series Editors*

Data Analytics and Psychometrics

Informing Assessment Practices

edited by

Hong Jiao
University of Maryland

Robert W. Lissitz
University of Maryland

Anna Van Wie
University of Maryland

IAP

INFORMATION AGE PUBLISHING, INC.
Charlotte, NC • www.infoagepub.com

Library of Congress Cataloging-in-Publication Data

A CIP record for this book is available from the Library of Congress
http://www.loc.gov

ISBN: 978-1-64113-326-5 (Paperback)
978-1-64113-327-2 (Hardcover)
978-1-64113-328-9 (ebook)

Printed and bound by CPI Group (UK) Ltd, Croydon, CR0 4YY

CONTENTS

CHAPTER 1

ON INTEGRATING PSYCHOMETRICS AND LEARNING ANALYTICS IN COMPLEX ASSESSMENTS

Robert J. Mislevy
Educational Testing Service

ABSTRACT

Over the past century, psychometricians have developed an armamentarium of methods for reasoning about students' capabilities from their performances in familiar forms of assessment. This chapter discusses how key concepts underlying these tools can be reconceived and extended to play a valuable role for reasoning from performances in new forms of assessment with more complex data. It describes complementary roles for learning-analytic methods to *identify* evidence in performances and for modular probability-based latent-variable models to *integrate* evidence into a cross-task metric and to quantify its value. In addition to practical benefits, probability models with latent variables provide ways of conceptualizing and characterizing the assessment principles of reliability, validity, comparability, and fairness. Ideas are illustrated with excerpts from two assessments that address systems thinking: a scenario-based task using more familiar data forms and the game-based assessment SimCityEDU: Pollution Challenge!

Data Analytics and Psychometrics, pages 1–52

THESIS

The psychometric models used in educational measurement evolved to support inferences framed in trait and behavioral psychology, from tests composed of distinct tasks such as preconstructed multiple-choice questions and written answers scored by raters, each providing an independent nugget of evidence about the trait. This assemblage might be called the standard educational measurement paradigm (SEMP).

Over the years, psychometricians have developed methods to significantly improve practice and strengthen the inferential foundations of assessment practices that originated under SEMP (Lewis, 1986). This line of work introduced latent-variable probability models such as item response theory into the procedures, and led to practices under the standard paradigm that were at once more flexible and better grounded. A second critical line was viewing assessment applications as social practices. This line produced conceptions and practical tools for investigating validity, reliability, comparability, and fairness—which, as Messick (1994) points out, are not just measurement principles, but "*social values* that have meaning and force outside of measurement wherever evaluative judgments and decisions are made" (p. 13; emphasis in original).

Recent advances in psychology, technology, and analytic methods have generated interest in new forms of assessment that look very different from the traditional tests. They can go beyond standard forms in any of several ways, such as interactivity, digital environments, use of simulations or games, requiring complex products or processes, involving collaboration, or fostering learning during the course of assessment.

At first blush, the psychometric methods developed for familiar tests seem poorly suited to the challenges of designing such assessments, evaluating performances, and managing and using the evidence they produce. Many researchers have thus begun to explore alternative methods from learning analytics and data mining to produce meaningful inference from the rich data of complex digital assessments (e.g., Loh, Sheng, & Ifenthaler, 2015; Romero, Ventura, Pechenizkiy, & Baker, 2010). This chapter argues that the question is not, "Should we use psychometric methods *or* learning analytics to analyze complex digital assessments?"; but rather, "How can we integrate complementary advantages of psychometric methods *and* learning analytics to our advantage?"

Although methods such as IRT address inferences about traits or proficiency in task domains that address data that come in standard formats or elaborations of them, they can be viewed as special applications of more general principles of probability-based inference. By reconceiving existing models, extending them to a broader range of inferences and data, or augmenting them with additional evidentiary-reasoning structures, we can obtain practical and conceptual benefits analogous to those they provide in SEMP. This chapter focuses on two:

1. Managing evidence at the interface between learning-analytic methods for making sense of complex performances from rich performance data within assessment episodes (e.g., successive challenges in a game, or multiple troubleshooting problems in an interactive simulation).
2. Addressing issues of reliability, validity, comparability, and fairness.

The discussion in this chapter is conceptual. For recent literature reviews and examples of applications of psychometric modeling in game and simulation-based assessment, see de Klerk, Veldkamp, and Eggen (2015); Ifenthaler, Eseryel, and Ge (2012); Loh, Sheng, and Ifenthaler (2015); and Jaffal and Wloka (2015).

ROADMAP

The next section of this chapter provides background for the discussion. It describes two assessments that will be used to help fix ideas. Both address systems thinking. They are a scenario-based task that uses familiar data forms, and the game-based assessment SimCityEDU: Pollution Challenge! Some additional information on the SEMP that is needed in the following sections is provided. A graphic structure of assessment arguments is reviewed. It will prove useful to pinpoint a key juncture between bottom-up reasoning from performances and bidirectional reasoning in an overarching probability model.

The section entitled "Probability-Based Reasoning in the SEMP" describes probability-based reasoning in the SEMP, mainly with the IRT as one of the simpler and most widely used latent-variable models used in educational assessment. A variety of elaborations of task formats have been developed beyond the ones discussed here, as have a variety of latent-variable models. This discussion focuses on familiar task types and IRT because their role here is to illustrate the underlying concepts that make IRT work in SEMP, and can be generalized to more complex forms of assessment. The key ideas are modularity, bidirectional reasoning, expression of knowledge through probability distributions, metrics for evidence, and latent variables and conditional independence—not as psychological concepts but as machinery for managing knowledge and uncertainty. Also in this section, the terminology of *evidence identification* and *evidence accumulation* are described (Mislevy, Steinberg, & Almond, 2003). These terms simplify to "item scoring" and "test scoring" in the SEMP, and their easy-to-distinguish roles will be noted there. However, they highlight distinctions that are critical in the interface between analogous forms of reasoning that interact in assessments with continuous performances, continuous evaluations of performance, and continuous integration of knowledge about students.

The section entitled, "Implications of Situative/Sociocognitive Psychology" begins by reviewing key ideas from a situative/sociocognitive perspective on psychology, which is needed to design assessments, evaluate performances, and construct probability models in interactive environments. Implications of this perspective are noted for assessment in general and for task design in particular. The ideas are illustrated with SimCityEDU: Pollution Challenge!

Next, "Probability-Based Reasoning in Complex-Assessments" describes a paradigm for the interplay of probability-based reasoning and learning analytics methods as evidence identification and evidence accumulation in an assessment argument. It is not the only paradigm possible, but it is one that is a natural generalization of the form of reasoning underlying the SEMP to very different forms of performance and data.

"On Integrating Psychometric and Learning Analytics" summarizes the practical benefits that are obtained from the paradigm described in the preceding section, and points to how one uses the probability models to address measurement principles. Finally, the "Conclusion" sums up the central ideas of the chapter.

BACKGROUND

Two Illustrative Assessments

Systems thinking is an understanding of how components of a system influence each other, incorporating concepts such as feedback, adaptation, emergent behavior, and unintended consequences. Two enhanced assessments that address systems thinking are described in this section, the Burmese Python Task and the Jackson City challenge in SimCityEDU: Pollution Challenge! Both reflect principles of the Next Generation Science Standards (NGSS; NGSS Lead States, 2013), in engaging students in activities that involve not only disciplinary content, but also scientific practices such as *developing and using models* and cross-cutting concepts such as *systems and system models.* They differ primarily in a way that emphasizes the points about evidentiary reasoning we want to make: The Python task was constrained in its project to using familiar forms of assessment data, namely multiple-choice items, figural responses that could be automatically scored, and short constructed responses, while the SimCityEDU: Pollution Challenge! tasks take place in an interactive simulation environment adapted from the commercial game SimCity.

The Burmese Python Task

The Burmese Python task was developed in the project "Application of Evidence-Centered Design to State Large-Scale Science Assessment"[1] with support from the National Science Foundation. It is an example of a scenario-based task of the kind being developed at the time in the Minnesota Comprehensive Assessment (MCA-II). MCA-II science tasks were computer delivered, with sets of tasks embedded in a scenario that enabled greater context and higher-level thinking. Each scenario consisted of a series of four to six screens that addressed aspects of a theme, an inquiry, or a problem. Screens could present graphic material, simulations, and video clips. Responses could be multiple choice items, short constructed responses, or graphic responses such as "hot spots," drag-and-drop constructions, or filling in charts, which would be scored dichotomously.

This task is discussed more fully in Snow, Fulkerson, Feng, and Nichols (2011) and Mislevy et al. (2013). It suffices here to say the task consists of five screens concerning the impact of an invasive species, the Burmese python, into the Florida Everglades. Each screen presents stimulus materials and one or more items of varying types. Earlier screens present information and items concerning the habitat, the original food web, and results of investigations of python population and diet. Figure 1.1 shows the graphics and items on a later screen that includes items that involve systems thinking and modeling, namely how the system would change with the new species.

In order to perform well in the Python task, a student would need to use information about the ecological system comprising the habitat and its dwellers, reason through the relationships, and produce a representation of the food web in the new system including pythons. Much of the cognition and much of the understanding of interaction of elements within systems would be required in the Python task, just as it is required in the Jackson City challenge discussed next.

The key difference is that the work product that results will be a vector of (almost) conditionally independent dichotomous item responses, to be analyzed using IRT. In the course of a student's activity through the scenario, certain points have been preconstructed at which opportunities for obtaining evidence necessarily arise (the items) and preplanned procedures are in place for identifying and evaluating the nuggets of evidence (answer keys or rubrics). To introduce a term we will have further use for, the set of *evidence-bearing opportunities* (EBOs) is fully preconstructed into the assessment.

SimCityEDU: Pollution Challenge

GlassLab's game-based formative assessment SimCityEDU: Pollution Challenge! presents a series of challenges in which players tackle a city's problems that require balancing environmental impact, infrastructure

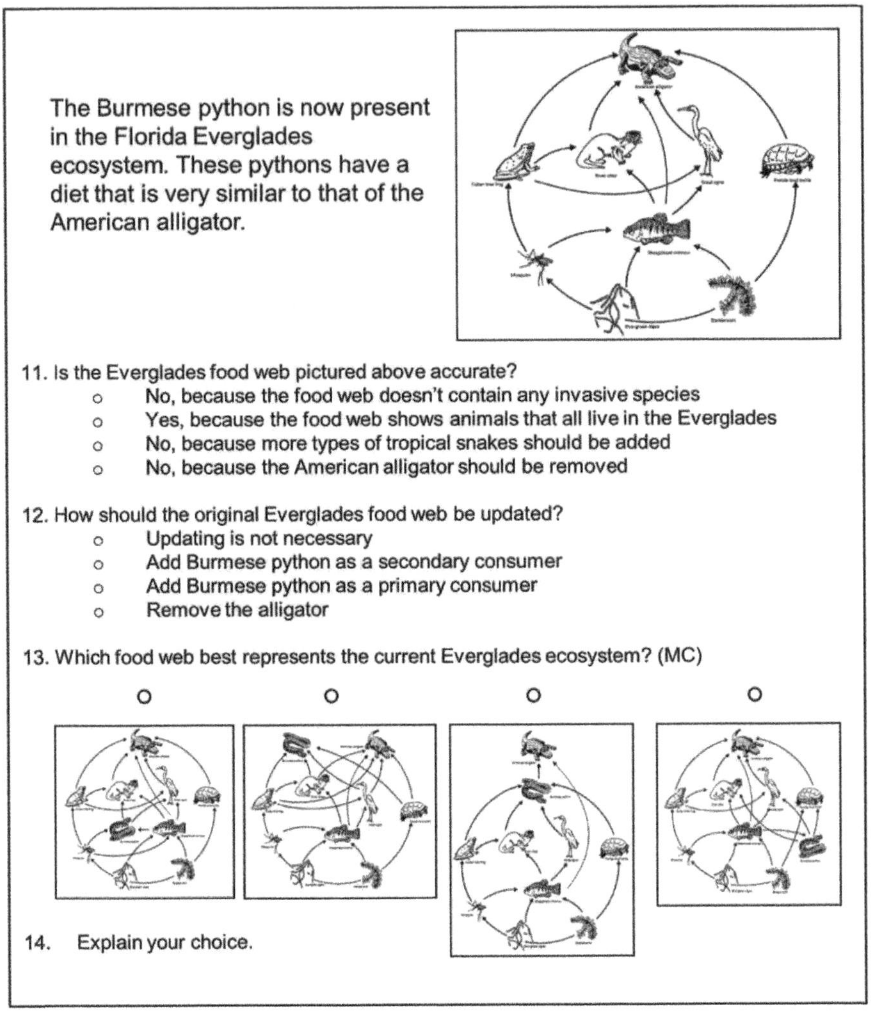

Figure 1.1 A screen from the Burmese python task. (Adapted with permission from SRI International from Snow, Fulkerson, Feng & Nichols, 2011).

needs, and employment (http://www.playfully.org/games/SC). The assessment is built on a learning progression, which is a framework for the development of student understanding in an area. The game's challenges reflect successive levels in Brown's (2005) learning progression for systems thinking (from Mislevy et al., 2014).

In the Jackson City challenge, the player (in the role of mayor) learns the residents seem unhappy and are leaving. Interaction with the Sim characters reveals that they are troubled by air pollution. Players can explore

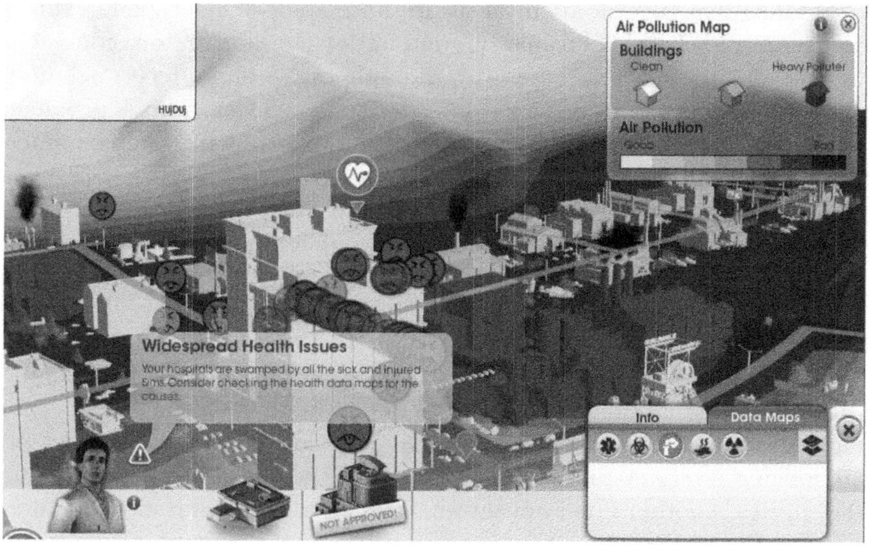

Figure 1.2 Use of a tool to monitor amounts and locations of pollution production. (Used with permission from the Institute of Play.)

data maps that show which buildings are polluting (Figure 1.2), how power is dispersed in the city, and how various areas are zoned. They can discover that coal plants are the biggest cause of pollution in the city. However, coal plants also provide much of the power in the city. Power impacts both residents' happiness and jobs, since unpowered businesses shut down.

Players can bulldoze buildings, place new power structures (wind, solar, or coal generated), build new roads to expand their city, and zone and de-zone residential, commercial, and industrial areas in order to achieve their goals. They can monitor the effects of their actions on pollution and jobs with on-screen thermometers. The player experience is one of tackling a troubleshooting challenge. At the same time, however, players' actions are captured and provide evidence about their level of systems thinking.

For example, a player might focus solely on the relationship between the coal plants and pollution, then simply bulldoze all the coal plants. This action is consistent with Level 2 in the learning progression: an elemental understanding of some aspects of systems (Brown, 2005, p. 7). They can use their models to represent simple, single cause and effect relations, but are prone to common misconceptions such as only relating macro-level, directly observable causes and effects rather than identifying hidden variables and factors.

Another player may instead recognize multiple effects of coal plants, both causing pollution and providing power. This player would be observed placing alternative energy options and bulldozing coal plants, but taking no actions that suggest attention to the unemployment problem. This is consistent with Level 3, locally coherent understanding. Actions consistent with Level 4 require reasoning with multiple causes and effects, including negative feedback. This is the level needed to solve Jackson City's problem, in addressing pollution and power tradeoffs and also creating new commercial zones to help increase available jobs.

There are some important similarities and differences between SimCityEDU! and the Python task. A key similarity is that both assessments address systems thinking, and the situations and performances can be coded into the systems-thinking learning progression. As described above, in SimCityEDU! the necessary features were designed into the challenges and evaluation procedures. In the Python task, the items can be coded in terms of the progression levels after the fact. For example, Items 13 and 14 as shown in Figure 1.1 require at least Level 2 thinking, in order to choose and defend an updated food web that correctly reflects the binary relationships among the species. Another item, not shown, is an open-ended question that asks a student to predict the effect on the ecosystem if the python population increases. Human raters could score students in terms of the level of thinking reflected in their written responses, all the way up to a Level 4 response that would incorporate multiple causes, multiple effects, and cause-effect chains that emerge from the network of links.

A critical difference between the two assessments, however, is that in SimCityEDU! not all specific points of information about students' thinking or procedures of identifying and characterizing them have been preplanned. Some have; for example, students are asked to construct systems diagrams like Figure 1.3 before and after the challenge. But for the most part, the "data" look like Figure 1.4, a log file of time-stamped actions and indicators of the game state. Procedures for evoking evidence and ways of identifying it are constructed iteratively. They begin with designers' theories about features of task situations that will manifest students' thinking, ways of recognizing them, and machinery to characterize them from the rich log of actions that students can take as they approach the challenge.

The Standard Educational Measurement Paradigm

What Is SEMP?

These are the basic features of the SEMP:

1. The aim is "*measuring a construct*," framed in trait or behavioral psychology.
2. Usually a *single measure* is desired.

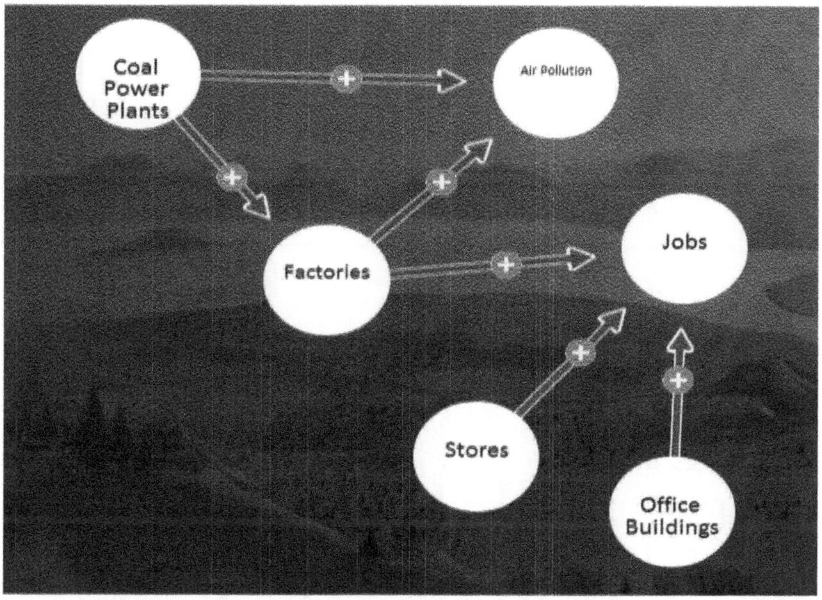

Figure 1.3 Example of a Jackson City system diagram. From Mislevy et al. (2014); used with permission from the Institute of Play.

3. *Each task (item) is a self-contained situation* that evokes a response which provides evidence about the construct.
4. Each response is evaluated to provide an *item score.*
5. *A test score accumulates item scores,* usually just summing them to produce a total score, but sometimes with a latent-variable model such as IRT.

The SEMP overlays a tradition of examinations stretching back 2 millennia to the Han dynasty in China and then the medieval universities of Europe, with scientific ideas of controlled observation and measurement from the Renaissance (Wilbrink, 1997). Each task is an instance of a situation requiring some socially-valued knowledge or skill. It can be administered to different people at different times and different places. A performance can be evaluated in a manner, whether automatically as with multiple choice or with shared rubrics and trained raters.

For a SEMP assessment cast in trait psychology, each task is designed to evoke the targeted construct, some "relatively stable characteristic of a person—an attribute, enduring process, or disposition—which is consistently manifested to some degree when relevant, despite considerable variation in the range of settings and circumstances" (Messick, 1989, p. 15). For a SEMP assessment cast in behavioral psychology, the targeted construct is

```
GL_Scenario_Loaded	{"name":"Medusa A3 - Large City.txt","scenarioTime":"00:00"}
00:04	GL_Scenario_Accepted	{"name":"Medusa A3 - Large City.txt","scenarioTime":"00:04"}
00:11	GL_Set_Speed	{"speed":"pause","scenarioTime":"00:11"}
06:23	GL_Set_Speed	{"speed":"resume","scenarioTime":"06:23"}
06:27	GL_Action_Building	{"action":"selected","name":"Coal Plant","scenarioTime":"06:27"}
06:28	GL_Action_Building	{"action":"viewed","name":"Coal Plant","scenarioTime":"06:28"}
06:31	GL_Action_Building	{"action":"deselected","name":"Coal Plant","scenarioTime":"06:31"}
06:33	GL_Action_Building	{"action":"view-hidden","name":"Moth Shop","scenarioTime":"06:33"}
06:41	GL_Challenge_Heartbeat	{"jobs":"5924","name":"Medusa A3 - Large City.txt","pollution":"67283140","simoleons":"35655","scenarioTime":"06:41"}

06:46	GL_Mayor_Rating	{"Resource":"-1965801614","Value":"74","scenarioTime":"06:46"}
06:46	GL_Jobs	{"Resource":"606764013","Value":"5728","scenarioTime":"06:46"}
06:46	GL_Power_Consumed	{"Resource":"522916859","Value":"30209","scenarioTime":"06:46"}
06:46	GL_Happiness	{"Resource":"-863362202","Value":"1367","scenarioTime":"06:46"}
06:46	GL_Expenses	{"Resource":"-308716970","Value":"14915","scenarioTime":"06:46"}
06:46	GL_Power_Produced	{"Resource":"416922972","Value":"33600","scenarioTime":"06:46"}
06:46	GL_Workers	{"scenarioTime":"06:46"}
06:46	GL_Sims	{"Resource":"681686445","Value":"4688","scenarioTime":"06:46"}
06:46	GL_Simoleons	{"Resource":"932594546","Value":"35655","scenarioTime":"06:46"}
06:46	GL_Income	{"Resource":"276811212","Value":"15570","scenarioTime":"06:46"}
06:46	GL_Solar_Power_Produced	{"Resource":"-1067234240","Value":"0","scenarioTime":"06:46"}
06:46	GL_Power_Wasted	{"Resource":"-665414129","Value":"0","scenarioTime":"06:46"}
06:46	GL_Wind_Power_Produced	{"Resource":"-626004793","Value":"0","scenarioTime":"06:46"}
06:46	GL_Coal_Power_Produced	{"Resource":"1467018548","Value":"34650","scenarioTime":"06:46"}
06:47	GL_Action_ToolCategory	{"action":"opened","tool":"power","scenarioTime":"06:47"}
06:46	GL_Air_Pollution	{"Resource":"295846734","Value":"43135844","scenarioTime":"06:46"}
07:00	GL_Unit_Plop	{"UGuid":"0x9122c84d","name":"","Pos":"-237.33, 233.38, 146.93","scenarioTime":"07:00"}
07:01	GL_Dezone	{"type":"commercial","scenarioTime":"07:01"}
07:02	GL_Action_Building	{"action":"selected","name":"Solar Power Plant","scenarioTime":"07:02"}
07:02	GL_Action_Building	{"action":"viewed","name":"Solar Power Plant","scenarioTime":"07:02"}
07:03	GL_Action_Building	{"action":"deselected","name":"Solar Power Plant","scenarioTime":"07:03"}
07:03	GL_Action_ToolCategory	{"action":"closed","tool":"power","scenarioTime":"07:03"}
07:04	GL_Action_Building	{"action":"view-hidden","name":"Solar Power Plant","scenarioTime":"07:04"}
07:08	GL_Unit_Plop	{"UGuid":"0xa230f2dc","name":"","Pos":"-147.38, 327.56, 146.93","scenarioTime":"07:08"}
07:15	GL_Challenge_Heartbeat	{"jobs":"6062","name":"Medusa A3 - Large City.txt","pollution":"86402071","simoleons":"9310","scenarioTime":"07:15"}
```


Figure 1.4 A clip from a SimCityEDU: Pollution Change! log file. (Used with permission from the Institute of Play.)

proficiency in a domain of tasks, each reflecting an aspect of a socially-defined constellation of capabilities, knowledge of plumbing concepts and procedures for a licensure test, for example, or mixed-number subtraction problems of the kind addressed in an instructional unit. In either case, the construct is operationalized as the overall tendency to perform well individual item by individual item (Green, 1978).

The Python task illustrates some critical points about the data in the SEMP. A student may engage rather sophisticated thinking, many aspects of knowledge and skill, and multiple processes of analysis and comparison to produce a response. The engaging scenario context, the multiple sources of information, and the various aspects of reasoning being addressed all work together to make the Python task a good example of a high quality task—created under the constraint of evaluation limited to objective-response item formats and human-scored open-ended, short-answer, written responses. All that appears in the data file is the evaluation of the work product, usually 0 or 1.

Historically, the most common way to get to 0/1 was to have a performance evaluated by a human rater. The last item in the Python example requires the student to explain the modified system diagram she has selected. Interactive, complex, and constructive performances can be elicited in this way, yet in operation might be limited to still producing a bit of data that is 0/1, or perhaps a rating on a scale with more levels. Such tasks are beneficial in local learning contexts, but scaling human scoring is costly and hard to keep reliable. Objectively scored formats such as the multiple-choice items do scale efficiently, but the constrained work product does not favor more interactive and constructive performances.

Classical Test Theory in SEMP

Researchers in the first half of the 20th century began to apply rigorous techniques to analyze such data. Spearman, Thurstone, Cattell, and many others were working at the joint frontiers of psychology, observational methods, and statistical modeling. A key insight from Spearman (1904) opened the door to probability-based reasoning: Conceiving of a test score not as the object of inference itself, but as "noisy" evidence of it. An analogue of measurement error in the physical sciences, true-score test theory or classical test theory (CTT) decomposes a test score X as the sum of two components, a "true score" T and an "error" e:

$$X = T + e. \tag{1.1}$$

With errors assumed uncorrelated, this simple formula is the basis of a surprisingly powerful armamentarium of practical tools for testing (Gulliksen, 1950/1987). In particular, reliability could be defined as the proportion of variance in the observed scores of a population of students that was due to their true scores. It could be estimated as the correlation between two parallel forms of a test;[2] that is, for each student, two observed scores with the same underlying true score and uncorrelated errors. Reliability provided a quantitative metric for the evidence scores contained, albeit restricted to the particular test and population. Most CTT tools used only first and second moments of scores and true scores—means, variances, correlations, linear regressions, and so on. Novick's (1966; also Novick, Jackson, & Thayer, 1971) full probability framework for CTT set the stage for IRT and further extensions as discussed in following sections.

Assessment Arguments

Figure 1.5 adapts Toulmin's (1958) schema for informal arguments for designing and interpreting assessments (Mislevy, 2016). It addresses a single, static, task; extensions to multiple tasks and to interactive assessments

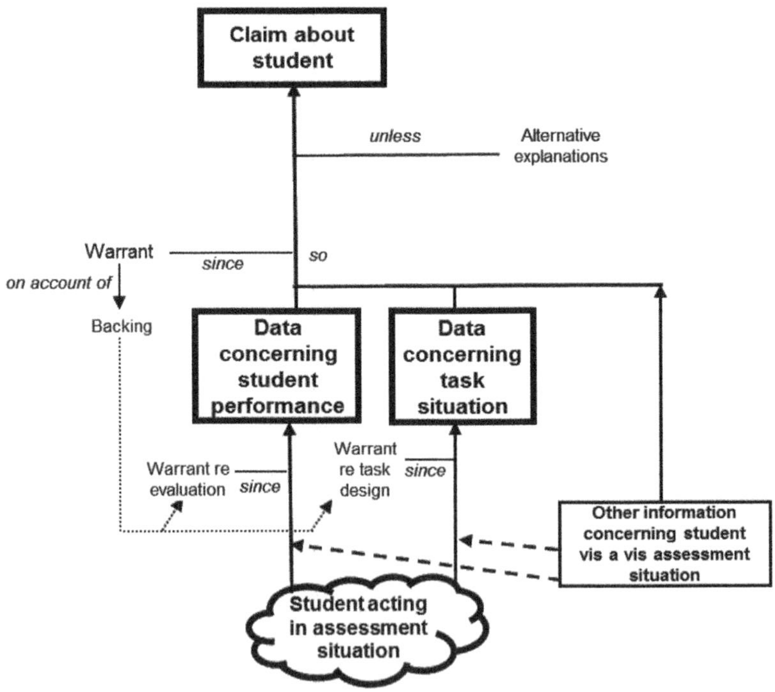

Figure 1.5 Assessment Design/Interpretation Argument Structure for a Single Task. (Adapted with permission (Adapted with permission from The Regents of the University of California.)

will be provided below. This brief overview focuses on the elements that are important to the present chapter and describes them in terms of familiar SEMP interpretations, again to be extended along the way.

The claim we want to make is at the top. In assessment, it is some aspect(s) of a student's capabilities, usually expressed in terms of a (possibly multifaceted) construct. The warrant, to the left, is a generalization about how persons with certain levels, kinds, or configurations of capability are likely to act in certain kinds of situations. The direction of reasoning in a warrant is "a person with such-and-such standing on the construct is likely to act in such-and-such ways in such-and-such kinds of situations." The warrant will be the justification for reasoning back from an examinee's performance to claims about her capabilities. Note that the direction of reasoning will have to be reversed. We ultimately want to say "a person who has acted in such-and-such ways in such-and-such kinds of situations is likely to have such-and-such standing on the construct." This is where probability-based reasoning through a psychometric model will play a role. The alternative explanations are ways other than the warranted explanation that a student's data could have come about, which weaken the force of the claim.

The cloud at the bottom of Figure 1.5 represents a student's performance in an assessment situation, from which we wish to identify what is meaningful. The two boxes just above it and the one to its right represent three kinds of data are involved in supporting an assessment claim. The first is most familiar, namely, features of the student's performance. This would be the 0/1 response to a task. Equally necessary, however, are data of the second kind, namely, features of the assessment situation. These two forms of data must be considered jointly to make sense of a performance.

The arrows that rise from the performance to these boxes represent the reasoning from the unique human event that constitutes performance in the task. These are straightforward and familiar in SEMP:

- The arrow from the cloud to data about student performance is the *evidence identification process*, by which features of the unique performance are recognized and evaluated into a 0 or 1. For a multiple choice item, it is determining whether the response-choice the student selects is the one keyed as correct. For a constructed response item, it is the cognitive processing of the human following a rubric or the rationale of the computer program as applied to the work product to assign a score.
- The arrow from the cloud to data about the situation ascertains that the features of the situation intended to elicit performances that provide information about the construct. In SEMP, these are the features of the stimulus, the directive, available tools, and so on, which are designed in by the test developer.

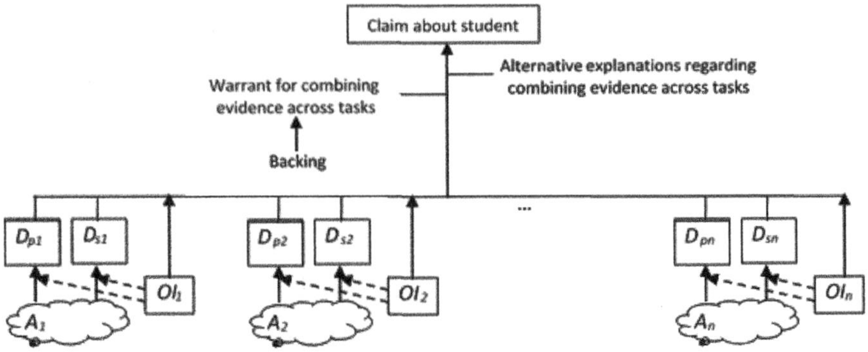

Figure 1.6 Assessment argument with multiple tasks. The figure does not depict task-level warrants, backing, and alternative explanations, and uses the abbreviations: A_j is the student's performance in Task j, D_{pj} is performance-features data, D_{sj} is situation-features data for Task j, and OI_j is "other information" concerning the relationship between the student and the task. (Adapted with permission from Mislevy, 2016)

The third kind of data, "other information about the student vis á vis the assessment situation," as well as the alternative explanations, do not appear in the visible machinery of an assessment but they are also integral to interpreting a performance as evidence for the claim. This is where tacitly presumed resources that are needed for performance can be explicated. These argument elements are critical for validity and fairness. Lacking knowledge or skills that needed to perform well but are not central to the intended construct is an alternative explanation for poor performance—an example of a threat to validity that Messick (1994) calls construct-irrelevant sources of variance. SimCityEDU! heads off some potential problems of this kind with practice problems to get students accustomed to the interface, tools, and language they will see in the challenges.

For assessments consisting of multiple tasks, Figure 1.6 shows that each task performance has its own subargument, which may share warrants, backing, and task features. The evidence across tasks is synthesized in some way to support a claim about the student. This is the evidence accumulation process. This synthesis could be an intuitive human judgment, but in SEMP applications it is accomplished with a psychometric model along the lines discussed in the following section.

PROBABILITY-BASED REASONING IN THE SEMP

This section describes how probability models have been developed for SEMP assessment, using IRT as a paradigmatic example. The nature and applications of IRT are briefly described in a manner that lends itself to the generalizations to more complex models and assessments, as discussed in the sections entitled, "Probability-Based Reasoning in Complex-Assessments" and "On Integrating Psychometric and Learning Analytics."

Probability-Based Reasoning

Despite its usefulness for practical applications of assessment under SEMP, CTT was largely limited to working with intact tests[3] and student groups. IRT cracked many problems that were intractable under CTT, such as adaptive testing, matrix sampling of items, and constructing tests to targeted levels of accuracy (Lord, 1980). The following description of how this was accomplished brings out more underlying ideas that can be extended beyond SEMP.

As prologue, we note that probability has been developed as a framework to express knowledge and uncertainty since Pascal's and Fermat's initial investigations of gambling problems in the mid-1600s. A major leap was sparked by the question of how to deal with uncertainty in computer-based expert systems being developed in the 1970s (Schum, 1994). These advances made it possible to extend probability-based reasoning to large networks of interrelated variables that could represent a variety of kinds of information. Such networks could include variables that characterize underlying, possibly inherently unobservable, states of a complex systems. Variables for observable evidence that could come in any form, containing information about aspects of the system or about the qualities of other elements of evidence. Parametric forms could be used to characterize the relationships among variables. The essential ideas are summarized below. We then see how they play out in IRT for SEMP.

1. Represent what is known about a variable X in terms of a probability distribution $p(X)$. Probability is viewed as an expression of belief. Different people may use different probabilities to express their belief about the same event, because they have different information or are using a different model to structure their reasoning (de Finetti, 1974).
2. Represent what is known about a variable given other information in terms of conditional probability distributions, $p(X|Y=y)$. This says what our belief about X would be if we knew that another Y took the particular value y. Conditional probability is the basis of evidentiary reasoning in the probability framework, because it tells us how to adjust our belief in light of new information.

3. Use Bayes Theorem to reverse the direction of reasoning. Suppose theory or experience gives us the relationship between two variables X and Y as in terms of $p(X|Y=y)$ for all possible values of Y. What we learn however is that X takes the particular value x, and we want to know how our belief about Y should change. Bayes Theorem says if our previous belief for a given y was $p(Y=y)$, then the updated belief is $p(Y=y|X=x) \propto p(X=x|Y=y)\ p(Y=y)$. Initial values of $p(Y=y)$ constitute the prior distribution for Y, $p(X=x|Y=y)$ is the likelihood function for values of X given a particular value of Y, and the posterior distribution for Y is given by the values of $p(Y=y|X=x)$ for a given observed value of X.
4. Use conditional independence relationships to account more simply for associations within and among groups of variables. Two variables are conditionally independent if they are independent when the value of some other variables are known; that is, if X and Y are conditionally independent given Z, then $p(X,Y|Z) = p(X|Z)\ p(Y|Z)$.

The key to a successful application of probability-based reasoning is mapping a real-world problem into this probability framework. The probability machinery then provides powerful tools for managing evidence and inference and for critiquing and improving models, but the quality of inference depends on the fidelity of the model to the important aspects of the real-world problem at hand. A probability model is always an approximation at best. Understanding the substance of a problem remains essential.

Conditional independence (#4) in particular is a matter of organizing knowledge about a problem and a domain, including the device of creating intervening variables to "explain" associations and thereby simplify calculations and explanations (Pearl, 1988). Medical applications, for example, use "syndromes" to account more simply for clusters of symptoms that tend to occur together.

Item Response Theory

Item response theory differs from CTT by modeling performance at the level of individual item responses rather than test scores. Scores to individual items are strongly associated, as people who do well on one are likely to perform well on others, and vice versa. IRT introduces an intervening variable, a number on $(-\infty,+\infty)$ usually denoted θ, and models the 0/1 response to each Item j as a function of θ. Each item has one or more parameters we will denote generically as β_j describing its relationship to θ, such as its difficulty. Each Student i's item responses are then modeled as conditionally independent given θ_i, so the conditional probability of Student i's response vector for n items is

$$p\left((x_{i1},\ldots,x_{in})\middle|\theta_i,\beta_1,\ldots,\beta_n\right)=\prod_j p(x_{ij}|\theta_i,\beta_j). \tag{1.2}$$

The IRT model does not address the nature of the performances, or the evidence identification procedures that led to the values of the *x*s. Nor does it address the interpretation of θ. Formally, it just quantifies probabilities of correct response—higher probabilities for higher values of θ, lower probabilities for lower values, with the exact probabilities depending on the values of the items' βs and the form of the link functions $p(x_{ij}|\theta_i,\beta_j)$.

Figure 1.7 overlays the assessment argument with a directed acyclic graph, or DAG, for an IRT model. A DAG indicates dependence and conditional independence relationships among variables. The student variable θ is represented by an open circle, which indicates it is inherently unobservable, or latent. The item responses x_j are indicated by squares, which indicates they are observable as far as the model is concerned—that is, the fact that it is an interpretation of a unique human performance, however it was arrived at, are below the level the model addresses. The arrows, or edges, from θ to each x_j indicate that they depend on θ (through $p(x_{ij}|\theta_i,\beta_j)$) but the fact that there are no edges among the x_js indicates that they are conditionally independent given θ. Note also that the features of the items and the other information are not addressed in the IRT model (although they are incorporated into some extensions discussed below). They are indispensable for the interpretation of θ, but they are the responsibility of the modeler, not of the model. For a behavioral construct, for example, θ represents proficiency in the domain of tasks.

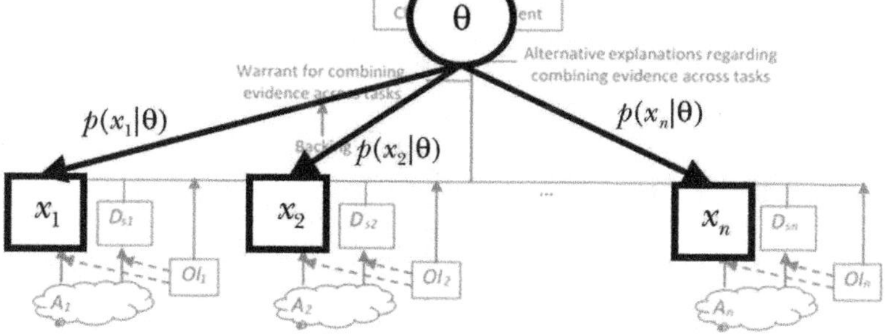

Figure 1.7 Directed graph for IRT overlaying an assessment argument with multiple tasks. (Adapted with permission from Mislevy, 2016)

An IRT model could be fit to students' response in the Python task, for example, as the items are predefined and encapsulated, and the evaluation procedures are defined so as to provide 0/1 item scores on each item.[4]

Adaptive Testing and Modularity

Computerized adaptive testing (CAT; van der Linden & Glas, 2000; Wainer et al., 2000) is an application that makes full use of IRT's item-level modeling and probability-based reasoning in SEMP. Figure 1.8 first illustrates how the four principles of probability-based reasoning are employed in inference about θ one item at a time, under the assumptions that IRT provides a satisfactory approximation to the capability of interest. Assume that the item parameters β_j are known for all the items. (In practice, they are estimated from a previous calibration study with a large sample of people to estimate them with sufficient accuracy, or a study that gives satisfactory estimates of their βs from the features of the items [Embretson, 2017; Mislevy, Sheehan, & Wingersky, 1993]. The latter approach

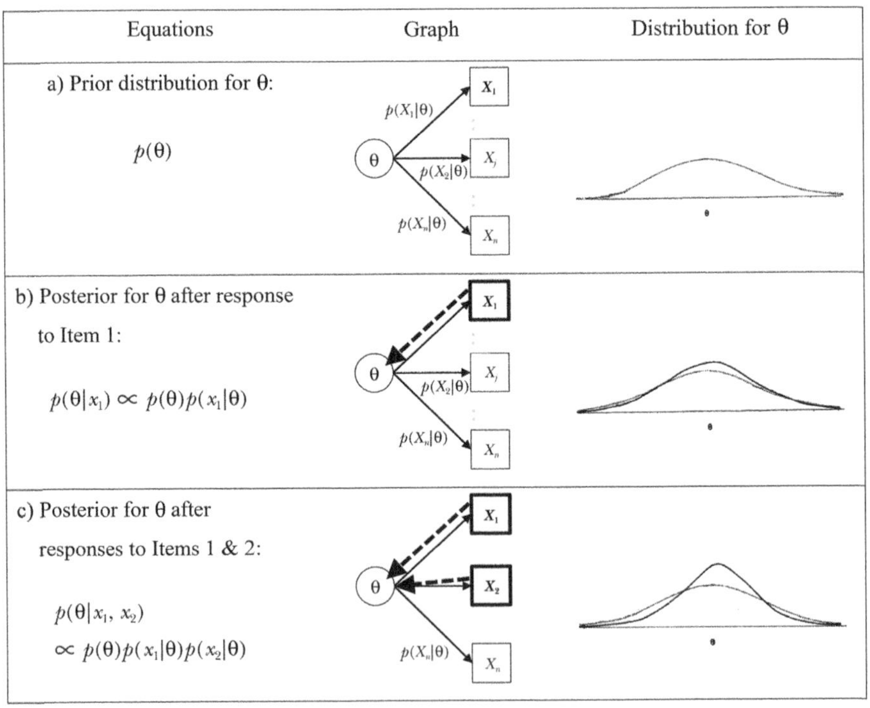

Figure 1.8 Adaptive testing with IRT.

becomes important in the section entitled, "Probability-Based Reasoning in Complex-Assessments.")

Panel (a) is an initial condition in which there is little knowledge about a given student's θ, expressed as the diffuse distribution $p(\theta)$. The initial status of the DAG is in the middle: The conditional independence structure, showing probabilities conditional on θ for responses to three as-yet-unadministered item.

Panel (b) depicts the situation after having administered Item 1 and acquiring the response x_1: An updated distribution for θ, obtained by Bayes theorem and displayed at the right. The DAG reflects that the response to Item 1 has now been observed, and the dashed line from X_1 to θ represents the reverse reasoning through Bayes theorem. The evidence in the response to Item 1 has been "absorbed" into belief about the latent variable θ. Not only has its distribution updated—in particular, yielding a bit more concentrated posterior, $p(\theta|x_1) \propto p(\theta)p(x_1|\theta)$—but expectations for the items that have not been administered also changed in response. A CAT algorithm then selects an item that is informative to administer about this student in light of her response. Typically, a correct response would lead to administering a harder item and an incorrect response would lead to administering an easier one.[5]

Panel (c) depicts the situation after another item has been administered, the responses observed, and belief about θ further updated. Students who responded differently would have been administered different items, yet for all students, a posterior distribution is obtained on the same θ scale. By tailoring item selection to be informative about students in light of their unfolding pattern of responses, testing is more efficient.

Three features of this scheme enabled by the conditional independence structure and probability-based reasoning will become important. First, the updating coherently converts and accumulates information about performance into quantifiable evidence about θ, in the form of a probability distribution at any point along the way. Second, the belief updating and the item selection are taking place in real time as the assessment situation unfolds. Third, the reasoning structure is *modular* with respect to items; that is, the probability model is assembled in response to the features of the evolving situation, an approach that knowledge engineers call "knowledge-based model construction" (Breese, Goldman, & Wellman, 1994). What makes it possible is structuring of the link functions $p(x|\theta)$, *from* a variable of pervasive interest, θ, *to* variables of transient interest, *x*s, within the reversible probability framework.

Most operational adaptive tests using IRT start with a bank of preconstructed items with (essentially) known βs—that is, a collection of items j and accompanying link functions, as suggested in Figure 1.9. After Student i has responded to the first k items that have been selected and administered

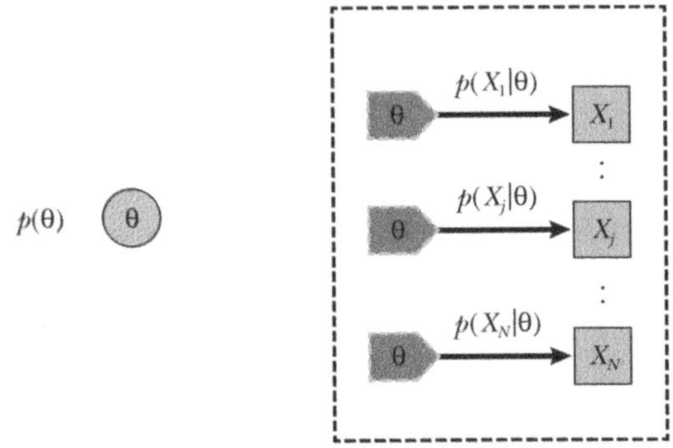

Figure 1.9 IRT latent variable θ and item bank containing link functions that can be connected with a distribution for θ for updating via Bayes theorem when a response to an item is observed, or for projecting current expected performance on an item. (Adapted with permission from Educational Testing Service)

to her, belief about her θ is $p(\theta_i|x_{i1},\ldots,x_{ik})$. The CAT algorithm calculates the expected response distribution to each of the not-yet-administered items and selects the $k+1$st item for her to be informative in light of current belief (for example, the one that is expected to provide the greatest reduction in the resulting posterior deviation for her θ). The testing system then administers that item, evaluates the student's response, and hooks up its link function with her response as the likelihood to apply Bayes theorem and obtain the updated belief $p(\theta_i|x_{i1},\ldots,x_{ik},x_{i,k+1})$.

Generalizations

Extensions

There are many grounds for objecting to the IRT-based adaptive testing scheme described above. It assumes a θ that does not change during the test (although our knowledge about its unknown value will continue to improve). It assumes that item responses are conditionally independent given θ, whereas certain items may in practice use shared stimuli, representations, or background knowledge that are not central to the intended construct. It uses a real-valued scale for θ, where latent variable(s) with ordered or unordered categories may be more appropriate for a given application. It assumes there is only a single dimension of θ. It addresses only dichotomous items, whereas other types of data may be desired, such as counts, response times, several ordered or unordered categories, and vectors of multiple aspects of a performance. There may be uncertainty in the evaluations to account for.

All of these departures from basic IRT assumptions are indeed possible. A large variety of extensions of IRT models and other psychometric models such as those of multivariate IRT, latent class analysis, cognitive diagnosis modeling, dynamic models, Bayesian inference network psychometric models, and mixtures of these have been developed (see, for example, Almond, Mislevy, Steinberg, Williamson, & Yan, 2015; de Boeck & Wilson, 2004; Rupp, Templin, & Henson, 2010; van der Linden, 2017). They can all be viewed as variations on the same themes described above for IRT, with latent variable types and structures motivated by substantive and theoretical concerns, and link functions determined by the properties of the kinds of data at issue. The point is that they all build on the fundamental structures and properties described in "Probability-Based Reasoning," "Item Response Theory," and "Adaptive Testing and Modularity," with elaborations of SEMP task types. It is these same fundamental structures and properties that will be further extended to deal with more complex and interactive assessments.

Building Task Features Into the Model

A brief description of one particular extension will be mentioned here explicitly, because it will be further extended to deal with the situations as they arise in interactive tasks. That extension is IRT models in which the link functions are modeled in terms of item features. The essential idea is to model the link function of Item j in terms of its salient features, say $(q_{j1},\ldots,q_{jK})$; then $\beta_j = f(q_{j1},\ldots,q_{jK})$. This idea can be useful for the articulation between evidence accumulation and evidence identification game-based and simulation-based tasks, as we will see in "Probability-Based Reasoning in Complex-Assessments."

As an example, the simplest such model is the linear logistic test model (LLTM; Fischer, 1973). It is an extension of the Rasch IRT model for dichotomous items, in which the item parameter for Item j is a single number, a difficulty parameter that indicates its location on the θ scale. In the LLTM, β_j is modeled as the sum of effects that are associated with its features:

$$\beta_j = \sum_k q_{jk}\eta_k, \tag{1.3}$$

where q_{jk} indicates the extent to which Feature k is represented in Item j and η_k is the contribution of Feature k to an item's difficulty. The matrix of the q-vectors for all the items in a test is called a Q-matrix (Tatsuoka, 1983), where each item's row q_j encodes its salient features.

When sufficient cognitive theory is available, it is possible to generate items around their salient features and model their difficulties using a model such as the LLTM (Embretson, 2017). This approach breaks one of the constraints of standard testing practice, wherein tests, even CATs, are assembled from preconstructed items. Assessment in such applications is still largely in the SEMP paradigm, but exploiting substantive theory in a way that will allow us to break further beyond it.

Structured item response models (de Boeck & Wilson, 2004), cognitive diagnosis models (Rupp et al., 2010) and Bayesian inference networks (Almond et al., 2015) can incorporate task features in the same manner, using Q-matrices or appropriate generalizations of them. An example of a simple cognitive diagnosis model called the binary skills model (Haertel, 1989) illustrates some ideas for which we will have further use.

A binary skills model posits a structure for characterizing both students and items in terms of *K* binary attributes (a term that can be broadly interpreted and implemented). Associated with Student *i* is a vector of 0/1 *latent* variables $\phi_i = (\phi_{i1}, \ldots, \phi_{iK})$, indicating the student's standing on each. Associated with Item j is a vector of *known* 0/1 variables $q_j = (q_{i1}, \ldots, q_{jK})$, indicating whether the item does or does not require each attribute. If Student *i* has all the attributes Item *j* requires, she is likely to answer correctly, with the "true positive" probability π_{j+}. If she lacks one or more attributes the item requires, she is less likely to get it right, with "false positive" probability π_{j-}. There may also be some structure among the attributes (Leighton, Gierl, & Hunka, 2004). This is a multidimensional model. Figure 1.10 shows a DAG for such a model, broken into fragments for the pervasive ϕs and the transient item responses x_j. There is an edge from Attribute *k* to the response for Item *j* only if $q_{ik} = 1$.

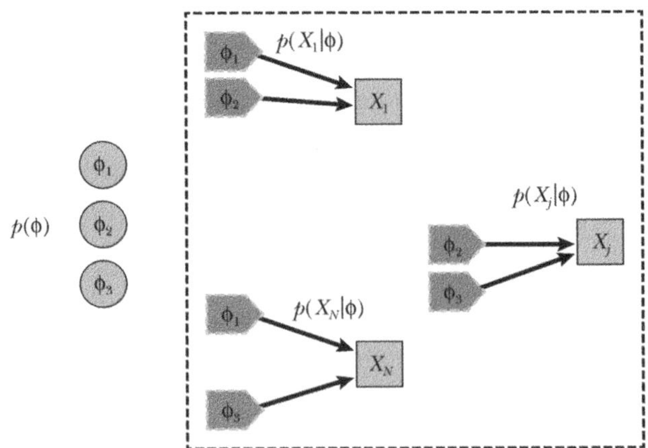

Figure 1.10 Cognitive diagnosis model with 3-dimensional latent variable ϕ and item bank containing link functions that can be connected with a distribution for ϕ for updating via Bayes theorem when a response to an item is observed, or for projecting current expected performance on an item.

Practical Advantages

Applying probability-based reasoning and latent variable models in the evidence accumulation process of SEMP provides several practical advantages. This section lists four that are important in CAT. Our aim will be to attain them in new forms of assessment as well.

What makes these benefits possible is the latent-variable model framework, in which students' actual complex and individuated capabilities are approximated as if they were values on a single measured variable. Note that this is not a claim about the psychological nature of capabilities, and it holds no necessary implications about the philosophical character of θ. Rather, θ is a piece of an evidentiary-reasoning machine. The adequacy of a given model for the domain, the tasks, and the population is the task developers' and analysts' responsibility. The situated meaning of θ in any given application depends on the domain, the tasks, and the population; fleshing out that meaning is the realm of validation, as noted in the next section.

Four important benefits of using probability-based reasoning and IRT in SEMP for adaptive testing, test construction, and item sampling in large-scale assessments can be described in more general terms:

1. *A common framework* for synthesizing from different observations for different students. Even though different students are administered different items, the evidence about their proficiency in the domain is expressed on the same θ scale.
2. *A metric for quantifying evidence.* Knowledge of a student's θ at a given point in time is expressed by a probability distribution, which expresses the weight of evidence for every possible value. It can be summarized by a mean or mode as a point estimate, and its standard deviation indicates how concentrated or diffuse the knowledge is. The probability framework supports rigorous methods for comparing the information contributions of items, or different versions of items, or different procedures for evaluating performances that produce *x*s.
3. *Knowledge-based model construction.* In light of #1 and #2, an assessor is not bound to intact tests, but can assemble tests flexibly, to suit the characteristics of individuals and populations and the intended use of an assessment (e.g., different test construction schemes are better for comparing students with one another as opposed to comparing them all against a fixed criterion).
4. *Model critiquing tools* to investigate how well the patterns the model can express accord with the patterns that are in the data. Benefits 1–3 involve reasoning through a model. If a given model does not conform well to the data of interest, inferences can be distorted

on the whole or for individuals. Probability provides a great array of techniques for critiquing and improving models. They are all based on the fact that a probability model, once fit to data, can be used in reverse to give probabilities for the data that were actually observed, for future data, or for some parts of the data based on fitting other parts. How surprising are actual observations given the predictions? Are there patterns in departures that suggest ways to improve the model, the data-gathering methods, or the underlying theory that motivates the assessment?

Measurement Issues Reflect Social Values

As noted in the introduction, Messick (1994) argued that validity, reliability, comparability, and fairness are social values that have force wherever we are making evaluative judgments and decisions. Psychometricians and educational measurement practitioners have developed over the years many ways to operationalize and investigate these values, to the end of improving practice. Latent-variable models and probability-based reasoning aid in this quest.

Reliability

Early psychometricians, notably Charles Spearman, moved assessment from "a score is a score is a score" to a measurement paradigm: the key idea is that the information we are working with is imperfect information about what we would really like to know. Classical reliability were based on test correlations, either literally correlations between parallel tests or approximations based on correlations among individual items. Latent-variable models provide better indications of accuracy, in terms of the posterior distributions for individuals. It is still possible to look at aggregated figures for assessments and groups of students if desired. It is more useful, however, to think in terms of *weight of evidence* rather than reliability per se, to characterize the value of information. That is, to directly characterize the weight and direction of evidence for inference in the latent-variable metric.

Comparability

Comparability is related to reliability, in that if different students were being assessed with different test forms, could we assure they were being compared fairly? At first this issue was solved under CTT in a limited way: Parallel test forms contained different items but were written to the same specifications and scores were fine-tuned with equating studies. Evidence was being made comparable by making the specific forms and procedures of observations comparable.

IRT opened further possibilities, still under SEMP, but by making it possible to quantify evidence on the same latent proficiency variable(s) even though different students took different items. The weights of evidence could be made comparable if desired, but one could intentionally obtain different amounts of evidence for different students or different purposes if need be. Comparability can be addressed in the space of inferences rather than limited to the space of observations. Comparability now focuses on to *what* inference is primary and *how much* evidence is derived, rather than conflated the *what* and the *how much*.

Validity

At the beginning of psychometrics in SEMP, validity was the correlation between scores and predicted outcomes of whatever decision they were being put to. This is useful, but it is not good enough. Contemporary theories of validity address the strength of theoretical and empirical evidence for the interpretations of assessment results and the uses to which they are put (Messick, 1989). When a latent-variable model is the basis of score interpretations and uses, the estimates and quantifications of their accuracy can be used to study not only predictions, but relationships with other measures and background variables to examine the degree to which expected patterns hold, and where they depart.

Validation studies below the level of score are now routinely carried out to determine whether students actually perform through knowledge, skills, and strategies that are consistent with the intended construct. Further, cognitive theories are increasingly used in item development, in order to improve the chances that students' will in fact perform in ways that are consistent with the intended interpretations, regardless of their level of performance (Ercikan & Pellegrino, 2017). All of these strategies are available for more complex assessments, as noted later in "Measurement Issues Reflect Social Values Revisited."

Fairness

IRT provided an approach for investigating an important aspect of fairness, namely, differential item functioning (DIF; Holland & Wainer, 1993). Under the usual IRT assumptions of unidimensionality and conditional independence, the relationship of all items to θ is the same regardless of other information about students, such as their gender, ethnicity, and previous experiences. This is equivalent to saying the items' link functions and β parameters are the same in all groups. If they are not, the same overall score, whether total score or estimated through the IRT model, has a different meaning for members of different affected groups. Probability machinery provides tools for detecting DIF in many ways, for groups known a priori or discovered from patterns in response data, and for individual items or with respect to features of items.

IMPLICATIONS OF SITUATIVE/SOCIOCOGNITIVE PSYCHOLOGY

To design, model, and analyze assessments that are more interactive requires working with the ways people learn and act moment-by-moment, and the milieu of social and cultural patterns that give meaning to learning and acting. An emerging situative, sociocognitive perspective that suits this purpose encompasses many strands of cognitive and social research (Greeno, Collins, & Resnick, 1997). The topic is too large to summarize here, but the ideas discussed in this section are important for understanding assessment, and crucial for understanding interactive assessment (Mislevy, 2016).

Some Key Ideas

The "socio-" in "sociocognitive" highlights the knowledge and activity patterns that structure individuals' interactions with the world and others. These include the structures and ways of using language, knowledge representations, and cultural models, and the patterns of activities of families, communities, personal interactions, classrooms, workplaces, and so on (Wertsch, 1994). Collectively we will call them linguistic, cultural, and substantive (LCS) patterns. There are LCS patterns of many kinds, grain sizes, and at different levels, which in various combinations and recurring patterns frame our interactions with the physical and social world.

The "cognitive" highlights within-person patterns. These are cognitive resources developed over an individual's experiences, continually activated, adapted, and revised to make meaning and guide action in each new situation (Hammer, Elby, Scherr, & Redish, 2005). We blend the particulars of each new unique situation and with the patterns we have developed resources for through our previous experiences, which were themselves structured around LCS patterns. The dynamic interplay of persons developing and acting through within-person resources, in practices organized around cross-person LCS patterns, is the heart of the situative psychological perspective (Gee, 1992; Sperber, 1996).

"Situative" highlights how this "soft assembly" takes place moment by moment as we make our way through the physical and social world. In every action, we activate and blend resources of many kinds and grain sizes, and at different levels. We will see this in the hierarchical structure of the evidence identification process used in the Jackson City challenge. Kintsch and Greeno (1985), for example, described how in solving science problems we blend the specifics of the problem at hand with the abstracted relations of disciplinary models and linguistic structures that relate the models to real-world phenomena. As to the linguistic structures, note that we draw on some more general lexical and grammatical resources, but others that are used in particular ways in science. They have special meanings, not captured in glossary definitions, but in connections to the particular ways we talk, think, and act with particular models and practices in science-related activities (Lemke, 1997). This is true for all learning domains.

Because the terms are not familiar in the assessment literature, it is worth highlighting the distinctions and the relationships between the LCS patterns and resources discussed above, and their relationship to the central assessment concept of constructs:

- *LCS patterns are regularities in between-person interactions among people.* They are not concrete "things." They can appear widely in interactions and artifacts, or they can be quite local. They vary over time and across place. "English" in Sydney in 2017 is not the same as "English" in London in 1600, and in fact is different for every so-called speaker of English, but with enough regularities that meaningful communication is usually possible. In the Python task and SimCityEDU!, LCS patterns of particular interest are the formal, explicit concepts and representations that have been developed to recognize, talk about, and reason through systems. *Practices* are regular, reoccurring, socially-relevant clusters of activities organized around certain LCS patterns for certain purposes, such as ordering food at a restaurant, talking to a friend on the telephone, buying a product from a vendor, and writing a research proposal.
- *Resources are within-person, associations among features of situations, what they mean, and what can be done.* The relationship between LCS patterns and individuals' resources is that we develop resources as we experience the situations throughout our lives that are flexibly structured around LCS patterns. For this is how people learn to interact with the world and others. Everybody's experiences are unique so everybody's resources are unique, but there are similarities when we experience situations structured around LCS patterns in similar ways. It is in this way, for example, that we can communicate with others through our personal strains of English—although we can communicate more or less effectively, about topics and issues where we have more similarities in previous experience. In the Python task and SimCityEDU!, we are interested as assessors in the resources students have developed for interacting with systems in terms of activity structures and knowledge structures associated

with the formal LCS patterns that have been developed for systems thinking.
- *Constructs are organizing concepts we use in assessment to define capabilities for we want to make inferences about students' capabilities.* Through the lens of LCS patterns and practices, we delineate certain kinds of actions that are relevant in situations with certain kinds of features, which can be accomplished by a person who has developed, and can activate, resources for those situations. The Python task and SimCityEDU! both do this, with respect to formal LCS patterns for systems thinking. We then characterize students in terms of their capabilities with such tasks, or their capabilities as viewed through the lens of the construct. The levels in the learning progression for systems thinking used in SimCityEDU!, for example, are broad characterizations of kinds of reasoning students can do in interacting with systems. Individual students' configurations of resources are unique, but commonalities in the systems they study and structured experiences to bring out the formal concepts of systems-thinking LCS patterns made the characterization useful for defining a construct, constructing tasks, and evaluating performances.

One research finding that holds implications for learning and assessment is that initially, resources are closely bound to the conditions of learning. There is not a "systems thinking θ," for example (Mislevy, 2017). Rather, resources begin developing first through life experiences with systems, informal and tacit, in particular situations that involve systems, such as how a certain toy works. Experiences such as discussing a local invasive species with a parent begin to reflect recurring patterns and themes. They develop resources that might be reflected in a student's thinking in the Python task or in SimCityEDU. School learning experiences like SimCityEDU begin to connect these kinds of experiences with more formal language, concepts, tools, and representations. A student might become very good at figuring out and solving problems in SimCityEDU; that is, with SimCityEDU kinds of systems, in the SimCityEDU environment. The same student may not think about a different system such as an invasive species problem in these terms at all. But further experiences with different systems, also explicated as instances of the abstracted systems concepts, can gradually help students develop more generally useful resources.

Some General Implications for Assessment

Educators seek to help students develop, effectively activate, and act through resources for situations built around targeted LCS patterns—specifically, the kinds of disciplinary ideas and practices we learn for school and work. Mathematical models and historical facts and principles are examples, as are scientific practices and concepts such as systems, their elements, and patterns of interacting. We would like students to develop resources to perceive new situations through such a lens, to investigate complex phenomena, to understand how acting on parts of a system can affect other parts in ways both anticipated and unanticipated.

Understanding that these are the kinds of capabilities we want to foster has motivated interest in interactive environments for assessment (and for learning as well). This is because the kinds of moment-by-moment experiences in environments built around targeted LCS patterns provides evidence about the capabilities students are developing. This calls for understanding both the broader and the fine-grained LCS patterns that are involved in the interactions, and for which constellations of effective resources constitute competencies. We might use some of the same high-level words to describe constructs such as systems thinking, but we understand their nature, how they are developed, and how they are used—and how we might assess them—through a sociocognitive lens.

This means that evaluating responses to static tasks, even relevant ones, is not enough. We want to know if students are seeing situations in terms of the elements and relationships in targeted LCS patterns. We want to know if they are acting through effective activity patterns associated with the knowledge structures, and even more importantly, noticing through the same lens how their actions affect the situation. Then we want to see how they re-understand the situation, and re-act, and re-interpret, as working towards a goal. This is where the Python task and SimCityEDU differ critically. Both assessments elicit students' resources for thinking about the system at issue. But SimCityEDU further elicits resources for acting in situations that evolve as the students interact with the system, and captures traces of the ongoing interaction as evidence about resources for acting, not just knowing.

Richness, complexity, and contextualization are valuable for learning, and necessary for obtaining evidence at the level of the resources that together constitute competencies. As the next sections discuss, however, richness, complexity, and contextualization will pose challenges to assessment designers and analysts. A student working through the Jackson City challenge, for example, must incorporate LCS patterns from multiple domains simultaneously:

> A student playing Jackson City draws on LCS patterns of many kinds and at many grain sizes. She must understand something about mayors, cities, jobs, and power plants; maybe not zoning, but enough about the others to learn quickly. She must understand English well enough to make sense of help, scenario descriptions, and simulated citizens' complaints. She must navigate in a SimCity style world, moving from one view to another, and do things like

> zoom, plop, and hover. She must coordinate her play and understanding of Jackson City with all of the activity patterns and knowledge patterns of the classroom... (Mislevy et al., 2014, p. 28)

Although it is not a focus of the present chapter, it should be mentioned that the multiplicity of competencies involved in a rich performance task means there are many ways for something to go wrong (Mislevy, 2017). There are many potential sources of construct irrelevant variance, in Messick's terminology. GlassLab mitigates this problem in SimCityEDU: Pollution Challenge! by recommending the game be used in a classroom or group setting. They provide lesson plans, discussion tools, and practice scenarios so that when students are working through a challenge, they are familiar with the interface, the environment, and the nature of the components that will be interacting. The challenge they face is figuring out how they function as a system, and how to resolve the problem at a level that is necessary for the system to behave as intended.

In other words, to the degree SimCityEDU is an assessment of systems thinking, it is assessment conditional on support for many aspects of the challenge that could otherwise hinder a student. This is true with more familiar task types as well of course, but the more specialized and interactive the environment is and the more deeply the assessment is embedded in context, the more construct-irrelevant capabilities are required. The Python task, for example, poses students with challenges in thinking about the system, but not in understanding where responses are expected, the ways they can respond, and what will be evaluated.

Some Specific Implications for Task Design

As discussed in "Assessment Arguments," the features of a test item are just as important as the features of a student's actions for interpreting the response as evidence about some aspect of their capabilities. Task developers address this need with static tasks in SEMP by working very hard to preconstruct features of tasks that are likely to evoke relevant cognition, which are manifest (imperfectly) in relevant actions. Explicitly or implicitly, good task developers draw upon their knowledge of the domain and the nature of the targeted competencies to address the same kinds of questions that a sociocognitive perspective would suggest as important; for example: What can we put into the situation and ask the student to do that will show she is attending to what is important in the situation? How can we invite the student think through the targeted LCS patterns about what happened to produce a situation we have depicted, and why, or what might be done next? How can we present a situation that requires a student to map its elements into a more abstract knowledge structure, reason through that structure, and indicate they have done so?

The challenge that the designer of a simulation-based, game-based, or other interactive task has two facets, and it mingles issues that would be separated out in evidence identification and task design in SEMP assessment. It arises because the task situation is changing moment by moment as the student(s) interact with the environment (and, in collaborative tasks, with one another). Different students may follow different strategies or take different paths, and at each moment the situation they are addressing depends partly on what the developer has put into the environment and partly on the actions and ensuing consequences of the actions the student has taken thus far.

The first facet of the design challenge is to pre-construct an environment that incorporates overarching features inspired by the targeted LCS patterns, a directive that motivates the student to engage these features, and tools and affordances to act in the environment. In the Jackson City challenge, for example, the underlying SimCity tools, representations, and functioning simulations of citizens, factories, and so on are all in place. Further, the particular interaction patterns of the targeted system put are in place—in this case, the interactions among power sources, pollution, commerce, and jobs. The designers used the systems-thinking learning progression to help determine the features of the system interactions and the problems to be solved that the students would need to explore and rectify in each successive problem.

The second facet of the challenge comes from the fact that each student could take their own path of exploration to try to figure out what was happening and what to do about it. It is here that the designer and the analyst play coordinated, often iterative, roles in task design and evidence identification. The next section explores this facet further.

PROBABILITY-BASED REASONING IN COMPLEX-ASSESSMENTS

Dynamic Arguments, Tasks, and Performances

While the roles of task design and evidence identification are clearly separated in SEMP, they can intermingle in interactive assessments. This is because the features of the situation a student is acting in continually evolve, due to both the players' actions and the functioning of the system itself (e.g., a student shuts down coal power plants; then, as the simulation continues to run, fewer power sources → factories close → fewer jobs).

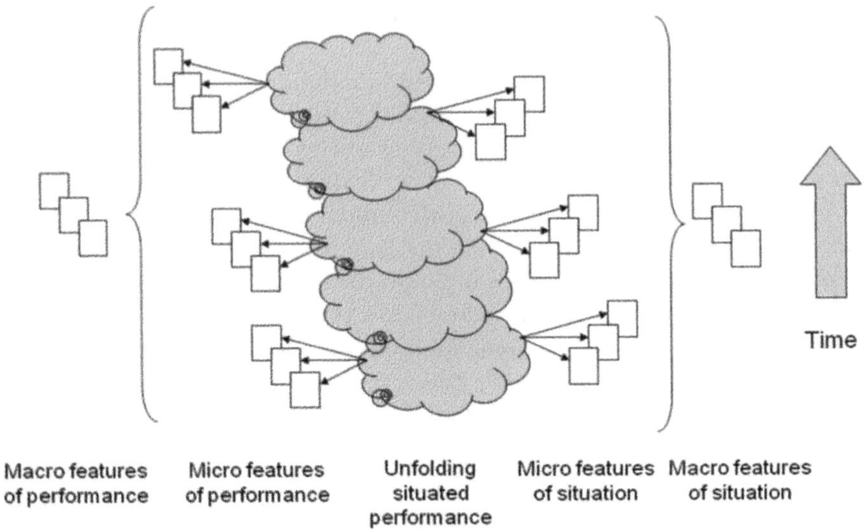

Figure 1.11 Potential points to identify data in interactive assessments. (Adapted with permission from The Regents of the University of California.)

Figure 1.11 depicts the situation. Certain features of an interactive task are preconstructed into the environment, the directives, and the information provided, and the affordances and resources for the student. These are labeled "macro features of the situation." As a student acts, the situation evolves, changing through the student's action and in some cases its own activity (in Jackson City, pollution continues to increase and citizens continue to leave the city if the student does nothing at all). These are labeled "micro features," or emergent contextual features of the evolving situation.

Situation micro features may need to be evaluated in order to make sense of the student's subsequent actions (bulldozing an old high-pollution coal plant reduces pollution, but doing so suggests poor system understanding if it occurs before an alternative energy source has been brought online first; otherwise, the city is underpowered, businesses close, and jobs are lost). Figure 1.12 extends the argument structure to dynamic contexts. At each moment the features of the situation and the student's action in the situation can be evaluated, and this contextualized data provides evidence at that point in the performance about the student's capabilities. Note that the situation at each point in time can be influenced by not only the student's previous actions, but by the simulation's designed-in responses to its evaluations of the previous actions, previous situation states, and the student's capabilities (e.g., give a hint if a student appears to be floundering, or toss in a complication if the challenge is too easy).

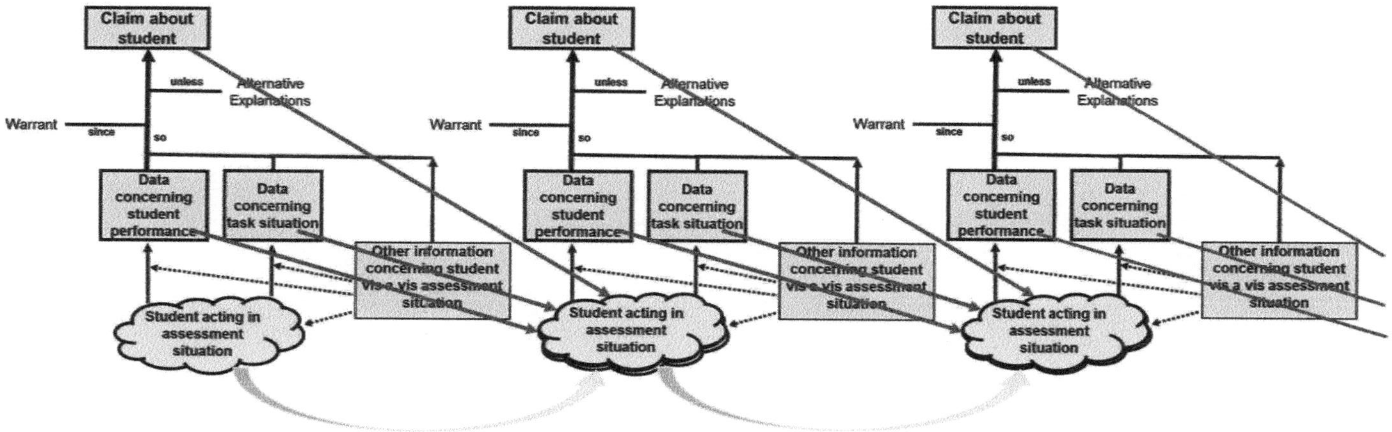

Figure 1.12 Evolving assessment argument structure for an interactive task. (Adapted with permission from The Regents of the University of California.)

Identifying and evaluating contextualized actions produces the analogous "micro features of the performance." Macro features address characteristics of the performance as a whole, and could include final products, overall efficiency of action, and distributions of strategies employed.

Evidence Identification in Interactive Tasks

Hierarchical Evidence Identification

As noted in "Implications of Situative/Sociocognitive Psychology," the situations and activities that constitute our everyday lives are multilayered, combining and tailoring LCS patterns at many levels to give meaning to the activities as a whole. Correspondingly, people develop equally multilayered and re-combinable resources at many levels to understand and act in situations.

Assessment situations are no different. The sparse data and the evidence identification processes in SEMP look simple because they either circumvent the complexity or they hide it. Objectively scored tasks like multiple choice items constrain situations and actions so that it is straightforward to identify and characterize a nugget of evidence. Human scoring deals with the complexity, but encapsulates it within raters as they apply more abstracted rubrics to produce simple scores.

In order to make sense of rich performance data such as log files we must confront the complexity head on. It is in evidence identification that ideas and techniques from "big data," data analytics in particular, play an invaluable role. This section sketches out a hierarchical way of thinking about the problem that is inspired by work in computer vision, which was inspired in turn by research in human vision.

Vision starts with vast numbers of noisy bits of information, in the form of rods and cone nerve cells on the retina each sending a signal when they receive certain light energy. Each by itself carries no meaning, but higher-level nerve cells combine signal from the receptors that indicate areas of dark or light, then lines and edges, then shapes and movements of shapes. This processing is largely bottom up, but top-down expectations formed from previous experience soon also begin to play a role. Reading text, for example, biases expectations and interpretations to letters and words, and even words we expect in the context. In a photograph, we detect edges and perhaps anticipate roundness, which in the presence of other clues we perceive be a bicycle wheel.

Recent advances in the data analytic procedures for computer vision similarly build up in hierarchies. Expectations from higher layers, based on the kinds of objects and activities at those layers, helps resolve the noisiness from lower layers. So-called deep-learning neural-net algorithms work from

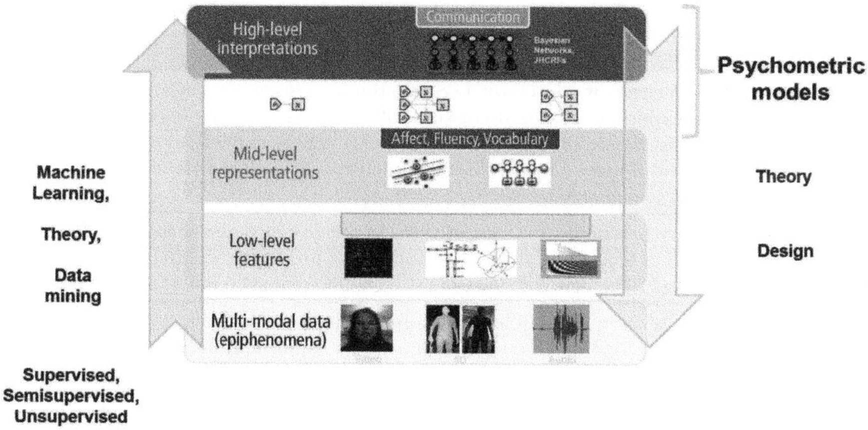

Figure 1.13 Hierarchy of evidentiary reasoning about high-level constructs from low-level data. (Used with permission from Springer-Verlag.)

lower-level features to higher-level features (LeCun, Bengio, & Hinton, 2015). Some theory and expert evaluations can bootstrap the process, as pitons that anchor certain meaningful patterns at various levels. Detection is then automated, tuned, and supplemented by patterns that emerge from the data.

Figure 1.13 schematizes an analogous approach for evidence identification in assessment. The numbers and natures of the layers may vary from one application to another, and the techniques used to work across them can vary as well. A deep-learning neural net might go all the way from the lowest level data to high level descriptors of a work product, or different techniques might be applied in sequence. Rarely, though, would the lowest level features of a performance be input immediately to a psychometric model. Higher-level features, including constructs, are posited to be pertinent across situations, where the details of the lower-level features can be more idiosyncratic.

The schema in this figure addresses *within-task* evidence identification. It culminates at the highest level with the "observable" variables that would be the evidence going into a *cross-task* latent-variable probability model. This schema uses a probability-based articulation between evidence identification and evidence accumulation to attain benefits that latent-variable probability models provide in SEMP, as discussed in the section "On Integrating Psychometric and Learning Analytics."

Evidence Identification in the Jackson City Challenge

Table 1.1 summarizes the layers of evidence identification in the Jackson City challenge in SimCityEDU: Pollution Challenge! Before describing them, however, it should be noted that the development of the overall

TABLE 1.1 Hierarchy of Evidentiary Reasoning in the Jackson City Challenge

The **highest level construct** was levels on a systems-thinking learning progression variable, reflecting kinds of things people can do in kinds of situations. A dynamic Bayesian inference network psychometric model incorporated θ change at the level of challenges. Interpretation is conditional on the student's familiarity with SimCityEDU environment and elements in the system at issue.
Calculating **summary functions of counts of verbs in relation to system-state variables** was the highest level of features of student performance, producing within-challenge "observable variables" to be entered into the cross-challenge psychometric model.
The log file contained a sequence of locations, times, durations and objects of "**verb clauses**"—verbs like "rezone which parcel from X to Y," "bulldoze Building type Z at location W," "query pollution map," along with current values of system-state variables.
The lowest level of data consisted of a **sequence of student actions**—locations, times, and durations of clicks, hovers, drag & drops, etc.—along with current values of system-state variables. These data were interpreted to produce the work product called the logfile, from which assessment activity proceeded.

Note: The "highest level" is most abstract and the lowest level is closest to the data. The table is easiest to read from the bottom up.

design of the tasks and simulation environment and the evidence identification procedures was iterative—much more akin to the design of commercial games than the design of SEMP assessments (Mislevy et al., 2014). DiCerbo et al. (2015) provide additional details about the exploratory data analyses and the data mining techniques that led to the final forms summarized here. They describe how they began with theory-based expectations built into the initial design of the simulation environment and hunches about where evidence would be found, and fed back to improve the design of the environment and challenges and the evidence identification procedures.

One technique that is often available in a rich performance environment is to build in some EBOs. An example in the Jackson City challenge is the systems diagram the students are asked to sketch (Figure 1.3). They can be used to identify evidence-bearing patterns by serving as a target for "feature detectors" from lower-level (interpreted) actions (Gobert, Sao Pedro, Baker, Toto, & Montalvo, 2012).

Returning to Table 1.1, we see that the lowest level of "data" is the sequence of points, clicks, drags, and so on, at certain times and screen locations, and the accompanying values of variables describing the state of the simulation system. These are not meaningful in and of themselves.

It is straightforward in the SimCity environment, however, to characterize sequences of low-level actions as "verbs" that hold meaning to students as they interact with the simulation. They are not thinking "I am positioning the cursor at pixel (xx_1,yy_1), clicking and holding the mouse button, moving the cursor to pixel (xx_2,yy_2), and releasing it." They are thinking, "I am re-zoning the block at Main Street and Fourth Avenue from residential to commercial." There might be many ways of doing this. This layer gives us an idea of what students think their elementary actions *are*, on the way to our understanding what they might *mean*. The work product that assessors began to address is a log file of time-stamped interpreted actions of this kind, along with period dumps of indicators of key status variables of the city as it has evolved to that point, which depend on the student's actions and the actions of the objects that constitute the city (e.g., coal-fired power plants keep generating fuel and producing pollution, and Sim citizens update their happiness levels as functions of employment, pollution, and other variables).

Patterns of verb-level actions in turn are grist for inferring strategies. The key insight in the Jackson City challenge is that old coal-fired power plants produce pollution, but they also create energy that businesses and factories need to produce goods and services and employ citizens. Simply removing them eliminates pollution, but it also eliminates jobs! In order to revise the system to lower pollution and retain jobs, the students must figure out they need to develop new sources of energy and bring them online before they bulldoze the old plants. Further, rezoning parcels of land may be required for population shifts and land-use requirements for the newly configured system.

Patterns of verb-level actions, then, constitute information for higher levels of inference. As mentioned, one more direct source of evidence about a student's level on the systems-thinking construct variable was the quality of the system diagram students completed. It was a preconstructed EBO, as might be used in SEMP.

Another observable variable was a "macro feature" resulting from the performance: the ordered pair of pollution levels and jobs counts at the end of play (Figure 1.14). This feature was arrived at after analyses of think-aloud studies of students' approaches. A fully satisfactory solution had low pollution and employment near or above the beginning level. These results could only be obtained by acting in a manner consistent with Level 4 in the learning progression, in this instance reasoning through the multiple effects in the system from manipulating power sources and zoning. Satisfactory levels of pollution but not jobs or vice versa could be obtained by Level 2 or Level 3 reasoning. Unsatisfactory levels of both is most likely from Level 1 or Level 0 reasoning.

A micro-feature developed the analysis of process data was the identification of a kind of evidence of recognizing multiple effects of a cause, namely that bulldozing a coal plant has the desired effect of reducing pollution but also reduces power generation, which leads to job loss unless anticipated and compensated for. Specifically, whenever a coal plant is bulldozed, check the log to determine whether alternate energy source had been brought online previously to avoid the negative effect on jobs. Counts of instances

Ending States of Pollution and Jobs

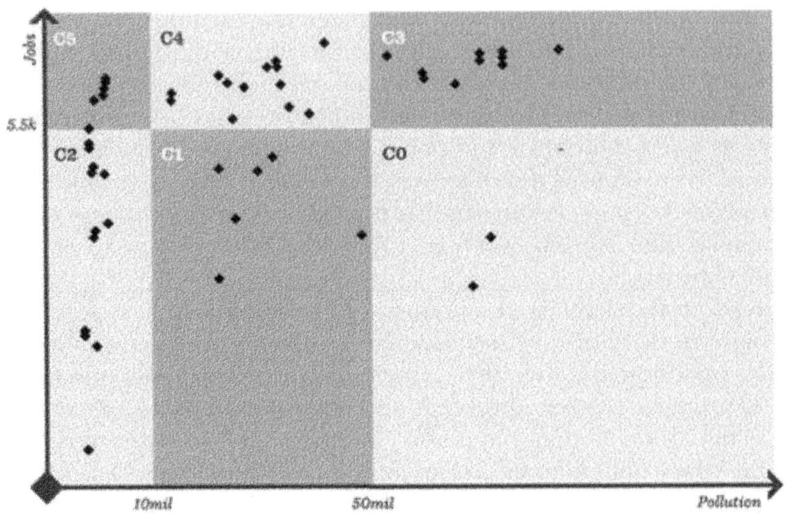

Level	Cell	Evaluation Rule
5	C5	Pollution < 10mil Jobs > 5.5k
4	C4	Pollution > 10mil and < 50mil Jobs > 5.5k
3	C3	Pollution > 50mil Jobs > 5.5k
3	C2	Pollution < 10mil Jobs < 5.5k
2	C1	Pollution > 10mil and < 50mil Jobs < 5.5k
1	C0	Pollution > 50mil Jobs < 5.5k

Figure 1.14 End states of pollution and jobs. (Used with permission from the Institute of Play.)

where this anticipation was and was not observed are the resulting observable variables. Note that it is not the counts of bulldozing coal plants and adding low-pollution plants that matters; it is counts of sequences which can be determined only as they are ordered in the log file.

A Bayesian inference network described in the next section is employed to update belief about a student's level of systems thinking through evidence like this. It may be noted in passing that different forms of observations can be used as evidence—in this case, features of a separate systems diagram, features of the final status of the city pollution and job indicators, and counts of features where it is not actions, but orders of actions, that hold information.

Evidence Accumulation in Interactive Tasks

In SEMP, evidence accumulation affected by a latent-variable model uses information in the form of values of observed variables provided by evidence-identification processes, from test items; that is, preconstructed EBOs. This evidence accumulation may take place at the end of the assessment session, or as assessment proceeds, as in CAT. These modes of updating are also possible with more complex assessments, but they are extended to deal with interactive assessments where evolving contexts determine the evidentiary meaning of actions. This section describes an arrangement that is consistent with the design of game-based and simulation based assessments that are built on finite state machines (FSMs; Moreno-Ger, Burgos, Martínez-Ortiz, Sierra, & Fernández-Manjón, 2008). This approach is suited to identifying EBOs as they arise in the ongoing interaction. (For additional discussion of evidence accumulation processes, see Almond, Steinberg, & Mislevy, 2002, and Chapter 13 of Almond et al., 2015.)

Figure 1.15 presents the schema. In a simulation based on an FSM, there can be a large number of objects that act and interact, but their actions are governed (perhaps deterministically, perhaps stochastically) by rules that operate on a set of variables. These variables in the so-called state vector indicate the current status of the system, and as needed, certain past states or past actions of the student. At each time increment, the objects check the value of the state vector and act (or refrain from acting) accordingly.

To extend the FSM framework to assessment, we augment the state vector if needed with values of *features of the situation* that are relevant to the assessment argument. The figure depicts only two levels, namely, the variables of the state vector, and detectors for higher-level salient features. Intermediate layers may be required to produce variables in the state vector or to synthesize information across them. The dashed lines indicate that certain configurations of the state variables involved indicate that an EBO has been observed. The code objects indicated by the light gray squares detect given EBOs; they can be thought of as agents. They can be constructed by a variety of methods, such as rule-based functions, feature detectors trained on experts' tagging of relevant situations, and Bayes nets. The logic and methods are analogous to those of evidence identification for features of students' performances.

The activation of an EBO agent initiates two event sequences in the system. The first, not shown in the figure, is to activate another agent that will

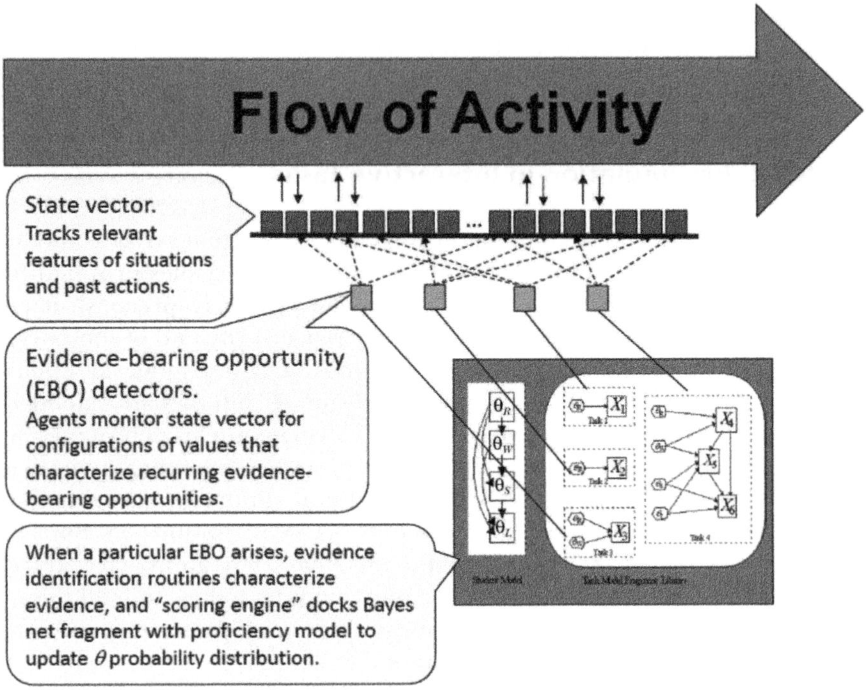

Figure 1.15 Evidence-bearing opportunities in the evidence identification and evidence accumulation in interactive performances. (Used with permission from Educational Testing Service.)

then parse recent and subsequent student actions to detect corresponding *features of the performance* that actually convey the evidence in that class of EBO. In other words, an EBO-detecting agent has spotted an opportunity to obtain evidence—an instance of a class of recurring situations has come about—and the corresponding evidence-identification agent knows what to look for in these kinds of situations and how to characterize it. The result is the value of a (possibly vector valued) observable variable.

The second event sequence is to hook up the corresponding link function to the current distribution for the variables in the latent variable model. Just as in Bayesian updating in IRT CAT ("Adaptive Testing and Modularity"), the evidence is used to update belief about the latent variables that are involved in that class of EBOs. Note that preconstructed EBOs, such as an embedded choice a student must make or a representation they must complete such as the system diagram in Figure 1.3 or a checklist of results in a patient management problem can be expressed as special cases of this scheme. Once the observable variables have been identified, their values ascertained, and appropriate link functions provided, the probability-based updating process is agnostic as to their source.

EBOs that are recognized in ongoing actions are an extension of the LLTM and other psychometric models discussed in "Generalizations." An EBO detector constantly scans certain variables in the state vector for a configuration of values it recognizes—in effect, spotting an instance of a "task situation" described by a particular row in a Q-matrix. An interesting history has led to this technique. Originally item writers wrote tasks based on their knowledge and intuition, and built features into items they thought would elicit evidence about the construct. Work such as Fischer's (1973) formally incorporated such features into the model and was used to study existing items. Subsequent work such as Embretson's (1998) began constructing items around the features, and connecting them with cognitive research in the domain. These developments were carried out for the most part under SEMP. EBO-detecting agents broaden the idea to identifying instances of EBOs as they occur in ongoing interactions.

In most applications of IRT in SEMP assessment, enough examinees are pretested to obtain good estimates of the item parameters β for each item, in known link functions. More recent work, also branching out from research like Fischer's and Embretson's, addresses assessment where one does not have precise information about each item's parameters, but instead has information about the distribution of item parameters in a class of related items, such as items that have the same q vectors. Statistical treatments of this problem in IRT include Glas, van der Linden, and Geerlings (2009), Mislevy, Sheehan, and Wingersky (1993), and Sinharay, Johnson, and Williamson (2003). The idea extends to EBOs. In essence, the inherent uncertainty expressed by the link functions and βs of given instances of a family is overlaid with the uncertainty of not knowing the specific β of the instance at hand.

Additional Observations

A distinction can be made between a latent-variable model in which the values of θs are unknown but constant during the course of observation, and a model in which θs may change over time. These may be called static and dynamic models with respect to θ. SimCityEDU: Pollution Change! used a dynamic Bayesian network psychometric model, because students were pressed to reason about systems requiring increasingly levels of reasoning as played through the challenges. As with the IRT diagram of Figure 1.7, Figure 1.16 overlays a simple psychometric model over the argument form for an interactive assessment. The latent variables θ, the observables X, and the interconnections among them could be more complicated, of course, but the key distinction is whether evidence is updating information about a stationary inferential target or a moving one.

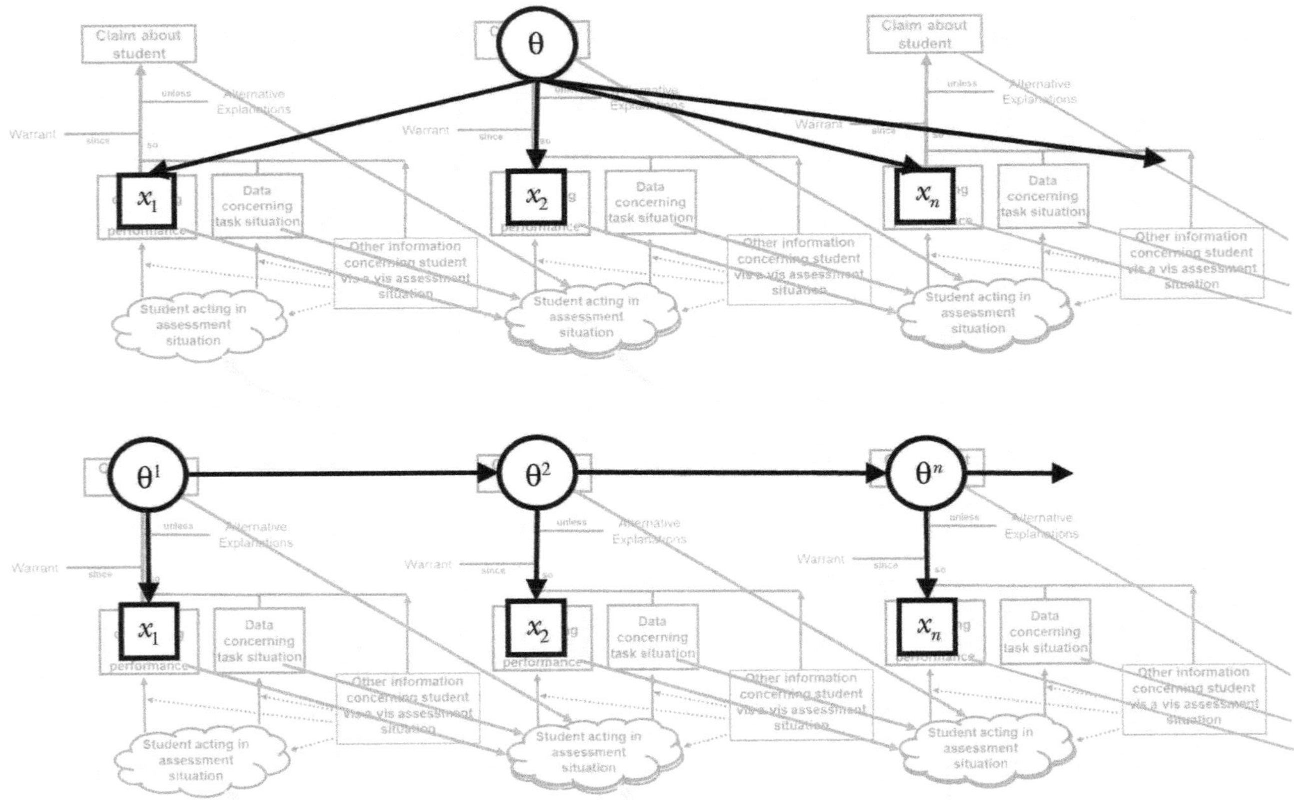

Figure 1.16 Psychometric models overlaying an evolving assessment argument structure, for static and dynamic latent variables. (Adapted with permission from The Regents of the University of California.)

The schema depicted in Figure 1.13 shows a latent-variable probability model crossing tasks only at the highest level. This is the closest analogue to the clear separation of evidence identification and evidence accumulation in SEMP. It is possible, however, to employ latent-variable probability models at multiple levels of the hierarchy of meaning-unit grain sizes in a given application. In larger tasks like the SimCityEDU challenges, one could have a single high-level latent variable model for the systems-thinking construct across tasks, but also have a finer grained latent variable model for of strategy-choice propensities. Multiple sets of θs defined at these levels can be maintained with parallel evidence accumulation processes, either in a single unified model or maintained separately. (Maintaining them separately is simpler, but forgoes exploiting information across them, and does not make explicit the overlap in information). For example, Martin and VanLehn (1995) used a two-tiered model in the OLAE physics tutor. A finer-grained probability model traced students' solution steps within tasks, while a more parsimonious probability model summarized the final within-task information to set prior distributions for the finer-grained model for the next task.

Similarly, small, targeted evidence-accumulation processes and corresponding agents can be maintained for precise targets, such as recognizing known misconceptions and characterizing a student's propensity to make them. Distinct processes can be run to serve different needs, such as ones used by the system to adjust challenges, others to accumulate evidence for reports out of the system, and still others to trigger feedback to the student.

It is possible to add evidence accumulation processes to a system by creating the agents and the psychometric objects needed to implement them, running off a common state vector, without having to modify the interface, the environment, or other identification or accumulation processes. It may be necessary to add variables to the state vector to support the agents needed to obtain the necessary evidence.

It is also possible to add more evidence types and more evidence identification procedures once a system is in operation, and further data-analytic investigations uncover additional evidence-bearing patterns of performance. The first version of a simulation-based assessment can start with only expert-provided identification rules, and continue to add more that dock into the same higher-level latent-variable probability model(s) at high levels. This is an advantage of the θ-to-*X* direction of the model construction and the bi-directional reasoning it then supports.

ON INTEGRATING PSYCHOMETRIC AND LEARNING ANALYTICS

The section "Probability-Based Reasoning in the SEMP" described the way that underlying concepts of assessment argumentation, latent-variable modeling, and probability-based reasoning improved practice in SEMP assessment. In particular, sections "Practical Advantages" and "Measurement Issues Reflect Social Values" described the benefits this approach provided. "Probability-Based Reasoning in Complex-Assessments" described how the same concepts can be extended to complex, interactive assessments, in which evidence identification carried out in in situations that can change moment by moment as the student and the assessment environment interact. This section describes the analogous benefits that obtain.

Practical Advantages Revisited

The foregoing schema for managing evidence and inference is a route for integrating psychometrics and learning analytics in interactive digital assessments (de Klerk et al., 2015; Ifenthaler et al., 2012; Loh et al., 2015; Jaffal & Wloka, 2015). Two factors contribute to this outcome: First, it is made possible by virtue of the properties of latent-variable probability modeling per se. Second, it is accelerated by recognizing, generalizing, and building upon insights gained from insights over the years to solve practical problems under SEMP (e.g., Almond, 2015; Almond & Mislevy, 1999). Benefits accrue analogous to those of using latent-variable probability modeling in SEMP assessment.

1. *A common framework* for synthesizing from different observations for different people. Much innovative work has already taken place for identifying and characterizing evidence in assessment complex performances. Developments in technology, data analytics, and learning sciences promise much more to come, and soon. Less has been done to provide flexible structures for managing information across tasks, such that different students can take different tasks, tasks can be adapted to students' capabilities, tasks can be deleted from assessments and new ones calibrated in, and tasks can be modified and adjustments made for the effects the modifications have on evidence about students. High-level latent-variable probability models support these functions.
2. *A metric for quantifying evidence.* Characterizing students' (possibly vector-valued) θ at a given point in time by probability distributions makes it possible to indicate the weight and direction of evidence

about students' capabilities even as different students take different tasks or follow different paths. This is useful in operational work, to help determine how much information is enough, or to gauge the impact of remaining uncertainty on subsequent score-based decisions. It can be perhaps even more useful in development. The probability framework supports rigorous methods for studying the information contributions of items, or experimental versions of items, or different item-sampling schemes, or different procedures for evaluating performances. Developers of commercial games carry out myriad A/B comparisons (aka, experiments) to improve engagement as measured by play time, surveys, and biophysical markers. Only by characterizing the value of evidence can developers of game- and simulation-based assessments systematically improve their procedures in the same way.

3. *Knowledge-based model construction.* As in SEMP, Points #1 and #2 above provide designers flexibility for assembling assessments flexibly, to suit the characteristics of individuals and populations and the intended use of an assessment. This is important for scaling up economically. The more elements, tools, inferences, and representations that can be used and re-used modularly, the less each new task will cost to develop. Many commercial games that look quite different on the surface run on the same underlying game engine and mechanics. We would like this to be the case for evidence identification procedures, of course. We would also like it to be the case for evidence accumulation procedures. Computational libraries exist with much of the code that would be required for basic probability-based evidence-accumulation frameworks for interactive digital assessments.
4. *Model critiquing tools* are again available to critique model fit at probability-based modeling layers. Misfit of particular individuals and tasks provide valuable insights into unexpected ways students may understand tasks or work through them. An unusually high model misfit index indicates that here is a student or here is a task where things are not happening as we expected, based on the patterns that are more typical for students or tasks. This becomes all the more valuable as task environments become more complex and performances become more open-ended, because we can be sure that some students will do things we don't expect, and some tasks will not function as we intend. The issue is not about whether a model fits. Rather, it is about calling attention to something unexpected so we can improve our schemes for evoking and interpreting evidence.

DiCerbo, Levy, and Mislevy (in press) noted that in low stakes assessments, it may not be necessary to bring out the machinery of latent-variable probability models. The issues of precision, comparability, and flexibility within a system do not matter as much in a one-off assessment task for learning, for example. As noted above in #2 and #4, however, probability models may be used in development to design and tune such an assessment, even if they are not needed in student-by-student operation. Gathering operational data may, in turn however, benefit from application of probability-based methods for further improvement.

Measurement Issues Reflect Social Values Revisited

Reliability

The idea of characterizing the value and direction of evidence remains valuable, particularly "wherever evaluative judgments and decisions are made," as Messick said (1994, p. 13). Latent-variable probability models at higher levels of the hierarchy of evidentiary reasoning (Figure 1.13) can be used to quantify the amount of information obtained about student capabilities. A particular advantage is that probability models provide machinery for doing this with different forms of evidence, different evidence for different people, interactive and continuous observations, and entanglements among aspects of capability and aspects of performance.

Characterizing evidence is obviously important for uses of simulation-based tasks in licensure examinations and accountability tests. It is also useful for guiding decisions inside intelligent tutoring systems and coached practice systems (DiCerbo, Shute, & Kim, 2017). And even for assessments that are designed for low-stakes uses, it is useful to be able to quantify evidence during development, in order to test assumptions about how evidence is working, compare designs, and improve procedures.

Comparability

Comparability on the surface still holds importance in some applications, as when assessments are used for inferences of how people do in situations that are of interest in and of themselves—such as landing a plane to get a pilot's license. Even more useful, however, is being able to synthesize evidence into a common framework of meaning, yet be able to vary surface features to optimize the use of the information for students and purposes.

Validity

Validity remains as important as ever, and increasingly challenging under a more powerful, but more subtle and variegated psychological framework (Mislevy, 2016). More complex evidentiary arguments must be structured, and backed with research and evidence. This is particularly so when evidence identification becomes automated, and is composed of multiple layers.

Concepts and techniques from SEMP are being extended to play useful roles in tackling these problems. The use of process data in validation is relatively new in SEMP, but it is rapidly burgeoning to address validation in increasingly complex forms of assessment (Ercikan & Pellegrino, 2017). Building validity arguments into complex assessments in digital environments from the very start can leverage insights from a history of performance assessment. Messick (1994) remains an excellent source for thinking through the features of simulations to optimize validity.

Fairness

It remains important for fairness to seek out features of tasks that function differently for different students in ways that lead to invalid inferences. But for use with individuals, fairness may be better construed as maximizing opportunities for learning or for demonstrating their capabilities. This can differ for students with different language proficiencies, different instructional histories, and different background knowledge. Latent-variable models and probability-based reasoning are being extended in systems that combine learning and assessment to support this work as well (Shute & Zapata-Rivera, 2012). The real payoff improved psychology and technology is in making instructional experiences and assessment coherent, and tailored, to the capabilities, histories, interests, and goals of individuals.

CONCLUSION

Rapid advancement in digital technology enable us to gather vast data of information about students' capabilities, virtually any time and any place (Behrens & DiCerbo, 2014). Statistical and analytic developments enable us to find, visualize, characterize, and exploit meaningful patterns in large data sets. Psychological research provides insights on how people acquire and use capabilities to understand how to conceptualize learning, and how to design environments to foster learning and reconceive assessment. A fertile area of activity in education has thus become harnessing these capabilities in assessment—rich, complex, performance assessment in digital environments, in particular, such as in games and simulations.

Much of the machinery we need to capitalize on these opportunities did not exist when test theory appeared on the scene. A viable methodology for practical applications of educational testing did however develop over the 20th century. The SEMP is characterized by relatively sparse data gathered from objectively-scored test items or humans' judgments of open-ended performances, and statistical methods focused on these data. Within this paradigm, researchers continually added insights and techniques to the psychometric armamentarium. New types of tasks and models were developed continually. One critical line of development was viewing assessment applications as problems in statistical inference, and another was viewing assessment applications as social practices. This line produced conceptions and practical tools for investigating validity, reliability, comparability, and fairness.

Properly conceived, insights and techniques that improved practice under SEMP can contribute to new forms and new uses of assessment. Statistical methods have always been part of data analytics, but lessons in applying them in SEMP assessment highlight inferential issues in new forms of assessment as well. Social values are, if anything, increasingly important as we seek to use new capabilities effectively and fairly.

The particular approaches for integrating ideas from psychometrics and learning analytics discussed here reach out from the standpoint of psychometrics. They appear to have been useful so far, but more is to be done. We can anticipate a proliferation of approaches and insights will continue to appear as researchers with a variety of different starting points work together to create solutions that draw across domains and experiences.

ACKNOWLEDGMENTS

This chapter is based on presentations given at the Sixteenth Annual Maryland Conference: Test Data Analytics and Psychometrics: Informing Assessment Practices, November 3–4, 2016, at the University of Maryland, College Park, MD, and at the Sixth Annual Learning Analytics and Knowledge (LAK2016) at the University of Edinburgh, Scotland, UK, April 29, 2016. I am grateful for helpful comments from John Behrens, Kristen DiCerbo, Shelby Haberman, Michelle LaMar, Rene Lawless, Roy Levy, Maria Elena Oliveri, and Sandip Sinharay.

NOTES

1. NSF grant DRL-0733172, to SRI International, Geneva Haertel PI; collaborating institutions were the University of Maryland, Pearson Education, and the Minnesota Department of Education. Project web site: http://ecd.sri.com/
2. Or, for tests consisting of multiple parts, approximated from the means, variances, and covariances of the parts.
3. A notable exception is the Spearman-Brown formula for calculating the reliability of a test that is lengthened or shortened—but only if true score expressed as a percentage remains the same. For example, a shortened test form cannot be built to be easier or harder, or better targeted to some group or individual.
4. Actually, an analyst might entertain using an extension of basic IRT model called a testlet model (Wainer, Bradlow, & Wang, 2007), in order to account

for possible dependencies among the item responses that appear on the same screen of the scenario beyond their dependence on the overall level of proficiency in being assessed.

5. This chapter describes a basic version of CAT for illustration. More advanced and efficient versions can include constraints as to item content and format, and look-ahead algorithms for selecting items that can be more efficient than choosing the next best item (van der Linden & Glas, 2000).

REFERENCES

Almond, R. G. (2015). Tips and tricks for building Bayesian networks for scoring game-based assessments. In J. Suzuki & M. Ueno (Eds.), *Workshop on Advanced Methodologies for Bayesian Networks* (pp. 250–263). Basel, Switzerland: Springer International.

Almond, R. G., & Mislevy, R. J. (1999). Graphical models and computerized adaptive testing. *Applied Psychological Measurement, 23*, 223–237.

Almond, R. G., Mislevy, R. J., Steinberg, L. S., Williamson, D. M., & Yan, D. (2015). *Bayesian networks in educational assessment.* New York, NY: Springer-Verlag.

Almond, R. G., Steinberg, L. S., & Mislevy, R. J. (2002). Enhancing the design and delivery of assessment systems: A four-process architecture. *Journal of Technology, Learning, and Assessment, 1*(5). Retrieved from https://ejournals.bc.edu/ojs/index.php/jtla/article/view/1671/1509

Behrens, J. T., & DiCerbo, K. E. (2014). Harnessing the currents of the digital ocean. In J. Larusson & B. White (Eds.), *Learning Analytics* (pp. 39–60). New York, NY: Springer.

Breese, J. S., Goldman, R. P., & Wellman, M. P. (1994). Introduction to the special section on knowledge-based construction of probabilistic and decision models. *IEEE Transactions on Systems, Man, and Cybernetics, 24,* 1577–1579.

Brown, N. J. S. (2005). *The multidimensional measure of conceptual complexity* (Report No. 2005-04-01). Berkeley, CA: University of California, BEAR Center.

De Boeck, P., & Wilson, M. (Eds.). (2004). *Explanatory item response models: A generalized linear and nonlinear approach.* New York, NY: Springer-Verlag.

De Finetti, B. (1974). *Theory of probability* (Vol. 1). London, England: Wiley.

De Klerk, S., Veldkamp, B., & Eggen, T. (2015). Psychometric analysis of the performance data of simulation-based assessment: A systematic review and a Bayesian network example. *Computers & Education, 85,* 23–34.

DiCerbo, K., Bertling, M., Stephenson, S., Jia, Y., Mislevy, R. J., Bauer, M., & Jackson, T. (2015). The role of exploratory data analysis in the development of game-based assessments. In C. Loh, Y. Sheng, & D. Ifenthaler (Eds.), *Serious games analytics: Methodologies for performance measurement, assessment, and improvement* (pp. 319–342). New York, NY: Springer.

DiCerbo, K., Levy, R., & Mislevy, R. J. (in press). The power and flexibility of latent-variable models in simulation-and game-based assessment. *Educational Technology Research and Development.*

DiCerbo, K., Shute, V. J., & Kim, Y. J. (2017). The future of assessment in technology rich environments: Psychometric considerations. In J. Spector, B. Lockee, &

M. Childress (Eds.), *Learning, design, and technology: An international compendium of theory, research, practice, and policy* (pp. 1–21). New York, NY: Springer.

Embretson, S. E. (1998). A cognitive design system approach to generating valid tests: Application to abstract reasoning. *Psychological Methods, 3,* 380–396.

Embretson, S. E. (2017). An integrative framework for construct validity. In A. Rupp & J. Leighton (Eds.), *The handbook of cognition and assessment* (pp. 102–123). Chichester, England: Wiley-Blackwell.

Ercikan, K., & Pellegrino, J. W. (Eds.). (in press). *Validation of score meaning in the next generation of assessments.* Washington, DC: The National Council on Measurement in Educational.

Fischer, G. H. (1973). The linear logistic test model as an instrument in educational research. *Acta Psychologica, 37,* 359–374.

Gee, J. P. (1992). *The social mind: Language, ideology, and social practice.* New York, NY: Bergin & Garvey.

Glas, C. A., van der Linden, W. J., & Geerlings, H. (2009). Estimation of the parameters in an item-cloning model for adaptive testing. In W. van der Linden & C. Glas (Eds.), *Elements of adaptive testing* (pp. 289–314). New York, NY: Springer.

Gobert, J. D., Sao Pedro, M., Baker, R. S. J. D., Toto, E., & Montalvo, O. (2012). Leveraging educational data mining for real time performance assessment of scientific inquiry skills within microworlds. *Journal of Educational Data Mining, 5, 153–185.*

Green, B. (1978). In defense of measurement. *American Psychologist, 33,* 664–670.

Greeno, J. G., Collins, A. M., & Resnick, L. B. (1997). Cognition and learning. In D. Berliner & R. Calfee (Eds.), *Handbook of educational psychology* (pp. 15–47). New York, NY: Simon & Schuster Macmillan.

Gulliksen, H. (1987). *Theory of mental tests.* Hillsdale, NJ: Earlbaum. (Reprinted from *Theory of mental tests,* 1950. New York, NY: Wiley).

Haertel, E. H. (1989). Using restricted latent class models to map the skill structure of achievement test items. *Journal of Educational Measurement, 26,* 301–321.

Hammer, D., Elby, A., Scherr, R. E., & Redish, E. F. (2005). Resources, framing, and transfer. In J. Mestre (Ed.), *Transfer of learning from a modern multidisciplinary perspective* (pp. 89–120). Greenwich, CT: Information Age.

Holland, P. W., & Wainer, H. (Eds.) (1993). *Differential item functioning.* Hillsdale, NJ: Erlbaum.

Ifenthaler, D., Eseryel, D., & Ge, X. (Eds.). (2012). *Assessment in game-based learning: Foundations, innovations, and perspectives.* New York, NY: Springer.

Loh, C. S., Sheng, Y., & Ifenthaler, D. (Eds.). (2015). *Serious games analytics: Methodologies for performance measurement, assessment, and improvement.* New York, NY: Springer.

Jaffal, Y., & Wloka, D. (2015). Employing game analytics techniques in the psychometric measurement of game-based assessments with dynamic content. *Journal of e-Learning and Knowledge Society, 11,* 101–115.

Kintsch, W., & Greeno, J. G. (1985). Understanding and solving word arithmetic problems. *Psychological Review, 92,* 109–129.

LeCun, Y., Bengio, Y., & Hinton, G. (2015). Deep learning. *Nature, 521,* 436–444.

Leighton, J. P., Gierl, M. J., & Hunka, S. M. (2004). The attribute hierarchy model for cognitive assessment: A variation on Tatsuoka's rule-space approach. *Journal of Educational Measurement, 41,* 205–237.

Lemke, J. L. (1997). Cognition, context, and learning: A social semiotic perspective. In D. Kirshner & J. Whitson (Eds.), *Situated cognition: Social, semiotic and psychological perspectives* (pp. 37–55). Mahwah, NJ: Erlbaum.

Lewis, C. (1986). Test theory and psychometrika: The past twenty-five years. *Psychometrika, 51,* 11–22.

Loh, C. S., Sheng, Y., & Ifenthaler, D. (Eds.). (2015). *Serious games analytics: Methodologies for performance measurement, assessment, and improvement.* New York, NY: Springer.

Lord, F. M. (1980). *Applications of item response theory to practical testing problems.* Hillsdale, NJ: Erlbaum.

Martin, J. D., & VanLehn, K. (1995). A Bayesian approach to cognitive assessment. In P. Nichols, S. Chipman, & R. Brennan (Eds.), *Cognitively diagnostic assessment* (pp. 141–165). Hillsdale, NJ: Erlbaum.

Messick, S. (1989). Validity. In R. Linn (Ed.), *Educational measurement* (3rd ed.) (pp. 13–103). New York, NY: American Council on Education/Macmillan.

Messick, S. (1994). The interplay of evidence and consequences in the validation of performance assessments. *Educational Researcher, 23*(2), 13–23.

Mislevy, R. J. (2016). How developments in psychology and technology challenge validity argumentation. *Journal of Educational Measurement, 53,* 265–292.

Mislevy, R. J. (2017). Resolving the paradox of rich performance tasks. In H. Jiao & R. Lissitz (Eds.), *Test fairness in the new generation of large-scale assessment* (pp. 1–46). Charlotte, NC: Information Age.

Mislevy, R. J., Corrigan, S., Oranje, A., DiCerbo, K., John, M., Bauer, M. I., Hoffman, E., von Davier, A. A., Hao, J. (2014). *Psychometric considerations in game-based assessment.* New York, NY: Institute of Play.

Mislevy, R. J., Schank, P., Feng, M., Fried, R., Chang, B., Snow, E., Haertel, G. D., & Colker, A. M. (2013). *A "wizard" for authoring scenario-based tasks, using evidence-centered design principles and structures* (Large-Scale Assessment Technical Report 14). Menlo Park, CA: SRI International. Retrieved April 7, 2016 from http://ecd.sri.com/downloads/ECD_TR14_Wizard_for_Scenario_Based_Tasks.pdf

Mislevy, R. J., Sheehan, K. M., & Wingersky, M. S. (1993). How to equate tests with little or no data. *Journal of Educational Measurement, 30,* 55–78.

Mislevy, R. J., Steinberg, L. S., & Almond, R. A. (2003). On the structure of educational assessments. *Measurement: Interdisciplinary Research and Perspectives, 1,* 3–67.

Moreno-Ger, P., Burgos, D., Martínez-Ortiz, I., Sierra, J. L., & Fernández-Manjón, B. (2008). Educational game design for online education. *Computers in Human Behavior, 24,* 2530–2540.

NGSS Lead States. (2013). *How to read the next generation science standards.* Retrieved from http://www.nextgenscience.org/sites/ngss/files/How%20to%20Read%20NGSS%20-%20Final%204-19-13.pdf

Novick, M. R. (1966). The axioms and principal results of classical test theory. *Journal of Mathematical Psychology, 3,* 1–18.

Novick, M. R., Jackson, P. H., & Thayer, D. T. (1971). Bayesian inference and the classical test theory model: Reliability and true scores. *Psychometrika, 36,* 261–288.

Pearl, J. (1988). *Probabilistic reasoning in intelligent* systems: *Networks of plausible inference.* San Mateo, CA: Kaufmann.

Romero, C. B., Ventura, S. N., Pechenizkiy, M., & Baker, R. S. (Eds.). (2010). *Handbook of educational data mining.* Boca Raton, FL: CRC Press.

Rupp, A. A., Templin, J., & Henson, R. (2010). *Diagnostic measurement: Theory, methods, and applications.* New York, NY: Guilford Press.

Schum, D. A. (1994). The evidential foundations of probabilistic reasoning. New York, NY: Wiley.

Shute, V. J., & Zapata-Rivera, D. (2012). In P. Durlach & A. Lesgold (Eds.), *Adaptive educational systems: Adaptive technologies for training and education* (pp. 7–27). New York, NY: Cambridge University Press.

Sinharay, S., Johnson, M. S., & Williamson, D. M. (2003). Calibrating item families and summarizing the results using family expected response functions. *Journal of Educational and Behavioral Statistics, 28,* 295–313.

Snow, E., Fulkerson, D., Feng, M., & Nichols, P. (2011, April). Design patterns to support storyboards and scenario-based, innovative item types. Presented at the Annual Meeting of the American Educational Research Association, New Orleans, LA. Retrieved from http://ecd.sri.com/downloads/aera/2011/Symp_DsgnPtrnStrybrdInnv.pdf

Spearman, C. (1904). "General intelligence" objectively determined and measured. *American Journal of Psychology, 15,* 201–292.

Sperber, D. (1996). *Explaining culture: A naturalistic approach.* Oxford, England: Blackwell.

Tatsuoka, K. K. (1983). Rule space: An approach for dealing with misconceptions based on item response theory. *Journal of Educational Measurement, 20,* 345–354.

Toulmin, S. E. (1958). *The uses of argument.* Cambridge, England: Cambridge University Press.

Van der Linden, W. J. (2017). *Handbook of item response theory* (Vols. 1–3). Boca Raton, FL: Chapman & Hall/CRC.

Van der Linden, W. J., & Glas, C. A. (Eds.). (2000). *Computerized adaptive testing: Theory and practice.* Dordrecht, Netherlands: Kluwer.

Wainer, H., Bradlow, E. T., & Wang, X. (2007). *Testlet response theory and its applications.* Cambridge, England: Cambridge University Press.

Wainer, H., Dorans, N. J., Flaugher, R., Green, B. F., Mislevy, R. J., Steinberg, L., & Thissen, D. (2000). *Computerized adaptive testing: A primer* (2nd ed.). Hillsdale, NJ: Erlbaum.

Wertsch, J. (1994). The primacy of mediated action in sociocultural studies. *Mind, Culture, and Activity, 1,* 202–208.

Wilbrink, B. (1997). Assessment in historical perspective. *Studies in Educational Evaluation, 23,* 31–48.

CHAPTER 2

EXPLORING PROCESS DATA IN PROBLEM-SOLVING ITEMS IN COMPUTER-BASED LARGE-SCALE ASSESSMENTS

Case Studies in PISA and PIAAC

Qiwei He
Center for Global Assessment

Matthias von Davier
National Board of Medical Examiners

Zhuangzhuang Han
Columbia University Teachers College

ABSTRACT

Technical advances in computer-based testing have made greater efficiency possible and increased the effectiveness of assessment, including the capability to administer dynamic and interactive problems, engage students' interest more fully, and capture more information about the problem-solving pro-

Data Analytics and Psychometrics, pages 53–75

cess. A variety of timing and process data such as sequences of actions can be recorded in log files accompanying test performance data when students respond to items. What we can learn and how we can extract informative features from the process data are essential questions to be answered. This paper draws on process data collected from problem-solving items in technology-rich environment in two large-scale assessments, the Programme for International Assessment of Adult Competencies (PIAAC) and the Programme for International Student Assessment (PISA), to address how sequences of actions are related to task performance. The case study in PIAAC aims to extract and detect robust patterns of sequential actions that are associated with success or failure on a problem-solving item via a data mining approach, while the case study from PISA 2012 focuses on feature generation and selection using process data following a combined strategy of bottom-up (exploring the test takers' behavioral features from the observed process data) and top-down approaches (defining test takers' behavioral features from guiding theories and hypothesis). We conclude that the methods applied in our study hold promise in process data analysis, especially in scenario-based items with similar settings.

Advanced technology offers various opportunities for innovation in educational assessment through rich new assessment tasks and potentially powerful scoring, reporting, and real-time feedback mechanisms online. The growing interest in assessing technology-related skills and knowledge has been facilitated by the move toward delivering assessments via computer and the web, thus, making it more feasible to also assess information and communication technologies (ICT) skills. Several recent large-scale assessments, such as the Programme for International Assessment of Adult Competencies (PIAAC) and the Programme for International Student Assessment (PISA), have sought to assess computer, digital learning, and problem-solving skills, which are essential in the 21st century (Bennett, Persky, Weiss, & Jenkins 2007, 2010; Organisation for Economic Co-operation and Development, 2009, 2012, 2014; Schleicher, 2008).

Computer based assessments (CBAs) are making it possible to include new and innovative item types, such as interactive scenario-based items, and to collect a broader range of information, including timing data and information about the processes that test takers engage in when completing assessment tasks. This capability is, in turn, leading to a broadening of the cognitive constructs being measured. Computers can capture user-computer interactions in log files, enabling the collection of timed navigational actions (e.g., clicking on links while looking for information on a website) and activities related to the usage of computer applications and functions (e.g., using the sort button, creating or copying a text, opening up a window). The analysis of logged data of human-computer interactions became the focus of several research studies during the last few years (e.g., Mislevy, Behrens, Dicerbo, & Levy, 2012; Baker & Yacef, 2009), yet few approaches have emerged to evaluate the efficiency and impact of those processes on learning and assessment results.

PROBLEM SOLVING IN TECHNOLOGY-RICH ENVIRONMENTS (PSTRE)

The theoretical rationale underlying our understanding of problem solving in human-computer interactions goes back to theories rooted in cognitive psychology. The basic argument (Anderson, 1983; Newell, 1980; Tolman, 1932) is that human cognition is always purposeful, directed toward achieving goals and removing obstacles to those goals. Anderson (1985) summarized three essential features for a problem-solving item as *goal directedness, subgoal decomposition,* and *operator selection,* which is consistent with the definition of problem-solving skills in PISA (Organisation for Economic Co-operation and Development, 2013). The problem-solving skill is defined as an individual's "capacity to engage in cognitive processing to understand and resolve problem situations where a method of solution is not immediately obvious. It includes the willingness to engage with such situations in order to achieve one's potential as a constructive and reflective citizen" (Organisation for Economic Co-operation and Development, 2013).

In PIAAC, the PSTRE items are used to assess the skills required to solve problems for personal, work, and civic purposes. The items assess adults' competencies in setting appropriate goals and plans, as well as accessing and making use of information through computers and networks (Organisation for Economic Co-operation and Development, 2009). The construct behind the PSTRE items describes skillful use of ICT as collecting and evaluating information for communicating and performing practical tasks, such as organizing a social activity, deciding between alternative offers, or judging the risks of medical treatments (Organisation for Economic Co-operation and Development, 2009).

This foundational vocabulary of ICT responses can be exploited in analyses of data log files to better understand human problem solving during complex tasks such as those administered in PSTRE. To give a response in the simulated computer environments that form the PSTRE tasks, participants are required to click buttons or links, select from dropdown menus, drag and drop, copy and paste, and so on. These sequences of actions are all recorded in log files in the CBAs, which enable us to trace the problem-solving process of the participants. To better illustrate the interactive environment and "digital" stimulus material used in PSTRE items, we describe one example task from the PSTRE in the PIAAC.

The layout of the first example, which consists of only one item (Figure 2.1), is straightforward. To solve this problem, respondents are required

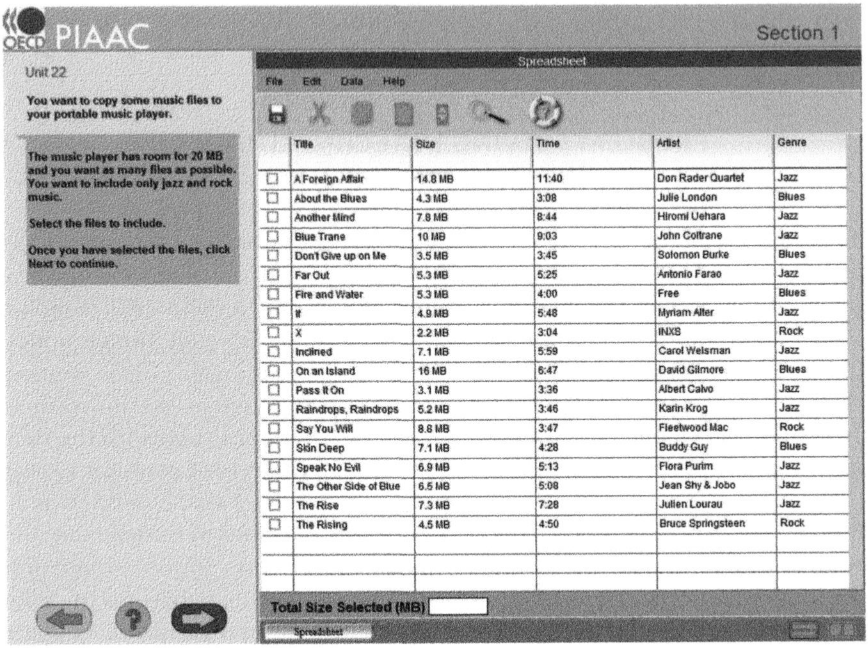

Figure 2.1 An example item with a single environment used in the PIAAC PSTRE test (Organisation for Economic Co-operation and Development, 2012).

to fill in the box by performing calculations based on the table provided. In this item, respondents need to select a set of files to download onto a portable music player. As shown in Figure 2.1, the item requires respondents to select files meeting specified criteria in terms of genre (jazz and rock) and file size (maximum of 20 MB). The software includes an automatic summing functionality ("Total Size Selected") that facilitates the task by updating the total file size as files are selected or deselected. Respondents must monitor progress as they select files, checking against the provided criteria to know when they have satisfied the constraints presented in the problem. It is also possible to sort the spreadsheet by file size and/or genre, a strategy that can increase task efficiency.

PROCESS DATA AND EXPLORATORY METHODS

As a supplementary byproduct of computer-based learning and assessment, process data from log files provide behavioral evidence that may be helpful to gain insights into students' and test takers' problem-solving approaches. This kind of data has been increasingly called upon for use in tracking the path of students' learning in an effort to improve the understanding of factors related to educational gains and gaps. For instance, in a self-regulated learning paradigm, students are encouraged to monitor and adapt their learning processes toward the learning goal.

Technology-rich learning environments not only inspire innovations in educational assessment but also bring challenges in analyzing very large databases (nowadays often referred to as "big data") of process data recorded in log files. Data mining is a useful exploratory tool in education research, especially when examining students' learning behavior in online learning environments. The promise of data mining lies in analyzing and uncovering hidden information in the (process) data, which is difficult and time consuming if done manually (Katz et al., 2013).

Compared to the hypothesis-driven approach that derives a set of features and indicators to describe goal-oriented problem solving, exploratory data mining focuses on searching test takers' observed process data for correlates of achievement without knowing whether the list of features relates to the construct being assessed. For example, data mining may find that rapid clicking on the help button is indicative of poor performance, but it might be unclear whether this relates to the skills and knowledge being assessed or is an expression of frustration. In contrast, if a priori hypotheses were used to describe what features of process data are indicative of "good" experimentation, they can be tested for differences in the distribution of task scores on the task at hand and on the summative assessment of all tasks a test taker received. A feature of "good experimentation" can be, for example, variation of only a single variable at a time in a scientific inquiry task, or the use of a spreadsheet or text field for recording data and observations after each simulated experiment has been run.

On the other hand, exploratory methods such as data mining may help in the early stages to generate hypotheses for additional features that are predictive of successful problem solving. For instance, mini sequences (such as the *n*-grams described in the next section) could be extracted from the sequence data and their distribution compared across performance groups. Such an analysis can help identify other commonly found features that distinguish successful from less successful problem solving. An example is a trigram sequence "next, cancel, next," which means a test taker clicks on the next button, but chooses the cancel option and then next again. This sequence may help identify hesitation in a certain group of test takers, which could possibly be a good predictor of performance (He & von Davier, 2016).

However, data mining alone does not provide information on whether the factors uncovered are meaningful and valid in an instructional context, a determination that has to be provided by content experts who can provide the necessary context. Given concerns in the threat of finding spurious (and hence meaningless) associations in the data, utilizing data mining methods in concert with a construct framework-based approach to define sequence data features would be a new direction in research methodology, especially in big data analysis. Combining these methods will lead to a more hypothesis-driven approach that utilizes both construct framework documents developed by content expert groups and statistical and computational methods to reach the goals of the proposed project. That is, we propose a combined strategy of bottom-up (exploring the test takers' behavioral features from the observed process data) and top-down approaches (defining test takers' behavioral features from guiding theories and hypothesis) in our study. More details will be illustrated in the second case study using the data from a problem-solving item in PISA 2012.

THE PRESENT STUDY

In the current study, we will focus on two research questions: (a) What we can learn from process data?; and (b) What process data can do for us? Specifically, the research addressed questions on what feature can be generated from the process data and what is the most effective way to extract the robust features. Further, we explored whether process data can be used to verify the theory of our top-down, hypothesis driven approach and whether process data as supplementary information can help improve latent trait estimation.

We first used a case study from PIAAC, in which we focused on one example problem-solving item. In this study, we used a completely bottom-up approach, that is, we explored the process data through data mining to find the patterns used by different performance groups. The second case study was conducted using one example problem-solving item from PISA 2012. Besides using the features that we derived from the process data, that is, mini sequences (*n*-grams), we also added the top-down theory-driven approach. In this case study, we combined bottom-up and top-down approaches in order to get better estimation on the latent trait.

Figure 2.2 presented a structure of process data analysis that was used in our case studies. The case study in PIAAC followed the left panel of Figure 2.2, using the bottom-up approach to explore process data and extract from them using the *n*-grams model. The second case study followed the entire flow shown in Figure 2.2. In contrast to the PIAAC case study, we used three sources to prepare for the feature generation process: feature extraction by *n*-grams, theoretical hypotheses, and item development experts' input.

In the next section, we will illustrate the approach in extracting features from process data by using *n*-grams model, which is often used in studies in natural language processing. This approach helps disassemble the long sequences into mini sequences. We will further illustrate our combined

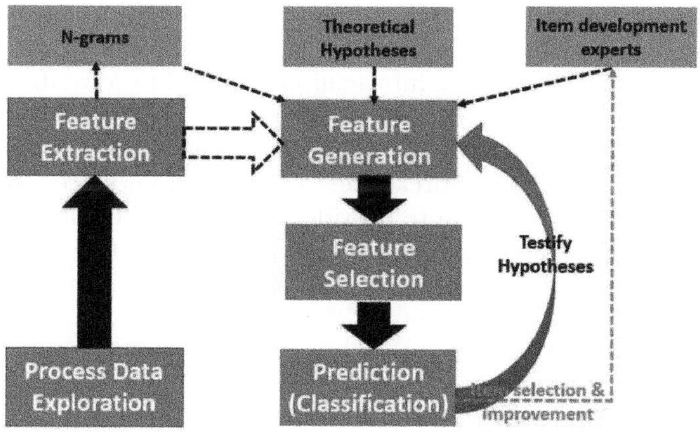

Figure 2.2 Structure of a proposed process data study.

approaches of theory-driven and data-driven approaches in the third section. The paper will be finalized by a discussion and an outlook on the future work in the last section.

FEATURE EXTRACTION FROM ACTION SEQUENCES: A CASE STUDY IN PIAAC

Background

The first case study focuses on addressing how sequences of actions recorded in problem-solving tasks are related to task performance by drawing on process data recorded in PIAAC PSTRE items (He & von Davier, 2016). We investigated the utility of behavioral process data for predicting differences in task performance in the PIAAC PSTRE domain. More specifically, we separated the database into two performance groups (correct and incorrect) for a sample item, extracted sequences of actions, and identified the sequences that were significantly associated with task completion. For our comparative study, we chose the United States, the Netherlands, and Japan as exemplary countries from three continents (North America, Europe, and Asia) among the group of participating countries.

A total of 3,926 test takers who completed the PSTRE items were included in the study. Of these, 1,340 test takers were from the United States, 1,508 from the Netherlands, and 1,078 from Japan. There were 2,025 female test takers (51.6%) and 1,901 male test takers (48.4%). The average age was 39.6 years ($SD = 14.0$). A total of 14 PSTRE items were administered in the PIAAC main study. We focused on the sequence data resulting from the task requirements of one item. This item consisted of two environments: a spreadsheet environment (which served as the stimulus) that contained a database with the information required to solve the task, and an email environment to provide the response. The task was to identify the ID number of a specified club member (e.g., "David Smith")[1] and email it to a correspondent. On the spreadsheet (SS) page, four pieces of information for each club member were provided by columns: ID number, name, number of activities this year, and years as a member. On the email (E) page, test takers were required to enter the ID number into an email to a correspondent.

N-grams and Term Weights

The data analysis was undertaken in two phases. First, we explored the relationship between sequence patterns and binary classification (i.e., correct and incorrect groups) by decomposing the complete sequences into smaller units (*n*-grams) and extracting the most robust units to distinguish the two groups. Secondly, we conducted a comparative study among the three countries to examine whether the patterns of action sequences differed across countries. Motivated by the methodologies and applications in natural language processing (NLP) and text mining (e.g., He, Veldkamp, & de Vries, 2012; He, Glas, Kosinski, Stillwell, & Veldkamp, 2014), we used the *n*-gram representation model and chi-square feature selection algorithm (Oakes, Gaizauskas, Fowkes, Jonsson, & Beaulieu, 2001) in analyzing the process data in this study, and used the weighted log likelihood ratio (WLLR) test to validate the selected features.

N-grams

In NLP, textual data is usually encoded via a data representation model. Namely, each document is often represented as a vector of (possibly weighted) word counts (Manning & Schütze, 1999). The simplest and most commonly used data representation model is the "bag of words" (BOW), where each word in a document collection acts as a distinct feature. As an extension of BOW, *n*-grams that consider the interaction effect of two, three, or more consecutive words are proposed as a way to expand the standard unigram representation model (e.g., Bekkerman & Allan, 2003; Tan, Wang, & Lee, 2002).

Analogous to textual data, action sequences collected in computer-based performance tasks can be decomposed into n-grams. That is, the unigrams are defined as "bags of actions," where each single action in a sequence collection represents a distinct feature. Moving away from unigrams, which are not informative about transitions between actions, we looked at *n*-grams.

Specifically, we considered bigrams and trigrams, which are defined as action vectors that contain either two or three ordered adjacent actions, respectively. Here is a concrete example. A typical action sequence "START, SP, SP_Type_FN, E, E_S, Next, Next_OK, END" in this task could be disassembled into eight unigrams (e.g., "START"), seven bigrams (e.g., "START, SP"), and six trigrams (e.g., "START, SP, SP_TYPE"). It can be interpreted as: A test taker started this item ("START") by clicking on the spreadsheet page ("SP") and then typed in the full name of the specified person to execute the search ("SP_Type_FN"). Afterward, the person switched to the email environment ("E") to fill in the answer and then send the email out ("E_S"). Finally, the test taker clicked on the arrow button to continue to the next item ("Next"), confirmed readiness to move to the next item ("Next_OK"), and finalized the current item ("END"). For a more efficient coding system, we subsequently combined the actions that always concurrently appeared in the same order into one code. For instance, the action "END" was always preceded by "Next_OK", hence, we re-coded "Next_OK, END" into one code "FINALENDING."

Term Weight

To scale the weight to each action, we denoted the total number of sequences in the collection by N and defined the inverse sequence frequency (ISF) of an action i as $\mathrm{ISF}_i = \log(N / \mathrm{sf}_i) \geq 0$. sf_i is the number of sequences where the action i appears. The ISF is a term revised from "inverse document frequency" (IDF; Spärck Jones, 1972), which was borrowed from NLP as a weighting mechanism in text mining. It was applied for attenuating the effect of actions or action vectors that almost always occurred, meaning they happened too often in the collection to be meaningful. The ISF of a rare action is high, whereas the ISF of a frequent action is low. The ISF of an action that occurs in all the sequences, namely, used by all the test takers, is zero. Therefore, the low-informative actions such as START or FINALENDING were eliminated from further analyses. This can be compared to the removal of frequent words (i.e., stop words) in textual responses such as "an," "a," and "the" (Manning & Schütze, 1999).

Another concern about term frequency is about clustering at the individual level. The importance of an action that is taken multiple times by one individual should be different from when the action is taken once each by multiple individuals. NLP provides a commonly used solution to the problem by dampening the term frequency by a function $f(\mathrm{tf}) = 1 + \log(\mathrm{tf})$, $\mathrm{tf} > 0$, because more occurrences of a word in the same document indicate higher importance, but not as much relatively as the undampened count would suggest (Manning & Schütze, 1999). We applied rescaling of frequencies in the current study. For example, we used $1 + \log 3$ to slightly dampen the importance of an action with three occurrences in a single respondent sequence. Such a sequence is somewhat more important than a sequence with one occurrence under the rescaling, but not three times as important.

Analogous to the weighting scheme in NLP, an action's term frequency $\mathrm{tf}_{i,j}$ (action i in sequence j) and its ISF was further combined into a single weight as follows:

$$\mathrm{weight}(i,j)=\begin{cases}\left[1+\log(\mathrm{tf}_{i,j})\right]\log(N/\mathrm{sf}_i) & \text{if } \mathrm{tf}_{ij}\geq 1\\ 0 & \text{if } \mathrm{tf}_{ij}=0\end{cases} \tag{2.1}$$

where N is the total number of sequences. The first clause applies to actions occurring in the same sequence, whereas for actions that do not appear ($\mathrm{tf}_{i,j} = 0$), we use $\mathrm{weight}(i,j) = 0$.

Feature Selection Models

Chi-square feature selection takes the basic premise of the traditional chi-square test by comparing the frequencies of events in a 2-by-2 contingency table as shown in Table 2.1. The (weighted) number of action occurrences in two groups C_1 (i.e., correct group) and C_2 (i.e., incorrect group) is indicated by n_i and m_i, respectively by each item. The sum of the weighted action occurrences in each group is defined as the group length $\mathrm{len}(C)$. The idea behind this method is to test whether occurrence and nonoccurrence of actions and correctness are independent. Thus, the method compares two groups to determine how far C_1 deviates from C_2 in terms of action frequencies.

Under the null hypothesis the two collections are randomly equivalent, so their distribution of actions is proportional to each other. A chi-square value is computed to evaluate the departure from this null hypothesis. For a 2-by-2 contingency table, the chi-square value is computed as

TABLE 2.1 2-by-2 Contingency Table for Action in Chi-Square Score Calculation

	C_1	C_2
action i	n_i	m_i
¬ action i	$\mathrm{len}(C_1) - n_i$	$\mathrm{len}(C_2) - m_i$

Note: C_1 and C_2 represent the two study groups (e.g., correct and incorrect). and n_i and m_i indicate the weighted frequency of the action i occurs in C_1 and C_2, respectively. $\mathrm{len}(C)$ indicates the sum of the weighted action occurrences in each group.

$$\chi^2 = \frac{M(O_{11}O_{22} - O_{12}O_{21})^2}{(O_{11}+O_{12})(O_{11}+O_{21})(O_{12}+O_{22})(O_{21}+O_{22})}, \tag{2.2}$$

where M is the total number of actions in the collection, and O_{ij} represents the weighted counts in each cell in the matrix (see more in Bishop, Fienberg, & Holland, 1975; Agresti, 1990). Actions with higher χ^2 scores are more discriminative in classification (Manning & Schütze, 1999). Therefore, we ranked the χ^2 score of each action in descending order. The actions ranked at the top were defined as robust classifiers.

The features extracted by the χ^2 model in a certain problem-solving item were further validated by WLLR in He & von Davier (2015). The WLLR is defined as the product of the probability of each action sequence and the logarithm of the ratio between the conditional probabilities of the sequence in different performance groups. Analogous to the WLLR being applied in feature selection for text categorization (Nigam, McCallum, Thurn, & Mitchell, 2000), the WLLR of each action sequence for the purpose of binary classification (i.e., correct group and incorrect group at the item level) can be defined as follows:

$$\text{WLLR}(a, C_i) = p(a|C_i)\log\frac{p(a|C_i)}{p(a|\bar{C}_i)}, \tag{2.3}$$

where $p(a|C_i)$ is the conditional probability of action a given in group C_i and $p(a|\bar{C}_i)$ is the conditional probability of action *a not* in group C_i. The validation study not only supported our findings from the previous study but also proved that the mini sequences (e.g., bigrams and trigrams) were more useful than single actions (i.e., unigrams) in interpreting test takers' behaviors in the process data analysis.

Results

It was found that actions related to using tools such as sorting and searching (e.g., "SS_Type_SN", "SS_So_OK", "SS_So_1B", "SS_Se", "SS_So") occurred significantly more often in the group of respondents that produced a correct response, while actions suggesting hesitative behaviors such as repeatedly clicking the cancel button (e.g., "Next_C," "SS_So_C") were found more often in the incorrect group. Further, among these robust indicators we noticed that the correct group had a better understanding of the subgoals of different environments and were more likely to recover from initial errors in the problem-solving process. Conversely, respondents in the incorrect group appeared to have only a relatively vague idea about what was expected in the item and were more likely to use the help function. Table 2.2 presents

TABLE 2.2 Example Sets of Five Robust Features (Actions and Action Sequences) Distinguishing Between Correct and Incorrect Groups

	Unigrams		Bigrams		Trigrams	
	Actions	χ^2	**Actions**	χ^2	**Actions**	χ^2
Correct	SS	70.72	E, SS	229.99	E, SS, E	272.49
	SS_Type_SN	68.04	SS, E	191.18	START, E, SS	226.42
	SS_So_OK	64.58	SS_So_OK, E	153.90	SS, E, E_S	211.37
	SS_So_1B	59.66	SS_So_1B, SS_So_OK	122.49	SS_So_OK, E, SS	150.25
	SS_Se	22.53	SS_Type_SN, E	120.56	SS_So_1B, SS_So_OK, E	137.53
Incorrect	Next_C	892.80	START, Next	2416.20	START, Next, FINALENDING	2420.26
	SS_Save	98.90	Next, Next_C	521.74	Next, Next_C, Next	478.16
	SS_Type_PGN	33.19	Next_C, Next	504.22	START, E, Next	399.02
	SS_H	15.75	E_S, E_S	492.26	Next_C, Next, FINALENDING	392.59
	SS_So_3D	14.56	E_S, E	364.66	E_S, Next, Next_C	374.83

Source: He & von Davier (2016).

the "best" five features (actions and action sequences) that distinguished the correct and incorrect group based on an aggregated sample. The top eight classifiers of *n*-grams that typically represent each performance group are listed in a descending order according to their chi-square scores. These observed result patterns based on the aggregate level were subsequently also found in performance groups analyzed by country.

In addition, we noticed that the process data of action sequences could also be used as indicators of missing data. For instance, the most robust trigram in the incorrect group, "START, Next, FINALENDING," was found 321 times in the dataset, which implied that these 321 participants (which corresponded to 8.18% in the whole sample) simply skipped this item. For better precision, they should be labeled as missing rather than as incorrect responses.

In the study aimed at country comparisons, it was clear that the U.S. test takers were more likely to multiply click on the email page (e.g., "E, E" and "E, E, E") from the robust bigrams and trigrams. The test takers in the Netherlands group were more likely to identify information in the spreadsheet by typing in full names ("SS_Type_FN") or given names ("SS_Type_GN") of the specified person in a searching strategy. An issue with spelling variations in search patterns was identified in the Japanese version because of the strange robust pattern of spelling mistakes shown by participants using the search function. However, this did not significantly alter the results. In fact, this spelling variation, which can be remedied in future versions of the assessment, demonstrated how process data can inform our interpretation of respondent behaviors.

The action features extracted from the chi-square selection method were further validated in a recent study by using a second feature selection approach, WLLR, which has been extensively applied in NLP as well (He & von Davier, 2015). The validation study not only supported our findings from the previous study but also proved that the mini sequences (e.g., bigrams and trigrams) were more useful than single actions (i.e., unigrams) in interpreting test takers' behaviors in the process data analysis. The methodology presented in this study shows promise in analyzing process data and extracting robust information about how performance groups differ in terms of their interaction with a complex task.

This case study is a typical example showing how to use the big data in hand to acquire information in deeper understanding about the test takers' problem-solving behavior. However, the mere *n*-grams may not be sufficient to make accurate classification prediction. More features from an aggregate level and derived from the process data would be helpful additions. We will further discuss this aspect from the second case study.

FEATURE GENERATION AND SELECTION: A CASE STUDY IN PISA

The second case study was conducted on a problem-solving item, "Climate Control," in PISA 2012 to address how to generate features from process data and select the ones that best predict the performance group (Han, He, & von Davier, 2016). A total of 30,224 observations from 42 countries with process information and binary response were used in this study. As shown in the screenshot in Figure 2.3, in this item, examinees were required to figure out how a new air conditioner functions by adjusting controls on temperature and humidity. They were instructed to manipulate input variables (i.e., move the top control, central control, and bottom control sliders) and plot how the input variables are related to the output variables (i.e., temperature, humidity). The initial position of each control slider was indicated by a triangle. Dragging the sliders or clicking on the numbers on the scale resulted in a change of either temperature or humidity. To gain credit, examinees were required to plot the lines from the control bars to the levels to be controlled (the top bar controlled temperature while the middle and bottom bars controlled humidity).

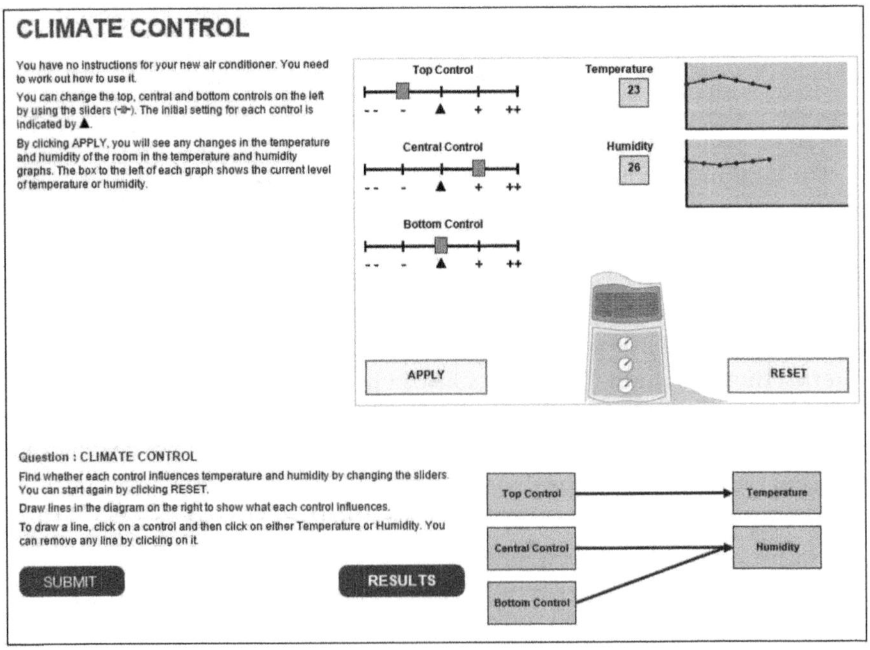

Figure 2.3 A snapshot problem-solving item (Climate Control) in PISA 2012.

To get meaningful codes for process data, we recoded each action into a 4-letter string (XXXX). The coding was as follows:

The first letter indicates the type of action, standing for the following:

"S": "START" the item
"E" : "END"
"R": clicking on the "RESET" button
"A": clicking on "APPLY"
"D": plotting the "DIAGRAM"

Other parts of the string are as follows:

If the first letter of the string is "A," the subsequent three letters indicate the position of each slider (–2, –1, 0, 1, 2). For the sake of this study, we recode those positions as:

–2 = A
–1 = B
0 = C
1 = D
2 = E

Note: "NULL" is assigned as "N."

For example, "ABCD" means APPLY, and then that the top slider means "–1," the central slider "0," and the bottom "1."

If the first letter of the string is "D," the subsequent three letters indicate each state of the diagram. The process data set provides the binary coding for the diagram state. "00" indicates "no link from left connecting to either two of right diagrams," "01" indicates "diagram from left side connecting to the temperature diagram," "10" indicates "diagram from left side connecting to the humidity diagram," and "11" indicates "the diagram from left side connecting to both two right diagrams." We recode those states as "F, G, H, I," respectively (see Table 2.3).

TABLE 2.3 Recoding of the Diagram States

Original Code	New Code	Code Definition
00	F	no link from left connecting to either two of right diagrams
01	G	diagram from left side connecting to the "temperature" diagram
10	H	diagram from left side connecting to the "humidity" diagram
11	I	the diagram from left side connecting to both two right diagrams

For example, “DGHH” means DIAGRAM, and then that the first diagram is left connecting to “temperature” and the second and third diagram in left connecting to “humidity,” which is also the correct solution to the problem shown in Figure 2.3.

There could also be strings “SNNN” and “ENNN” indicating the state associated with the “START” and “END,” respectively, followed by nulls.

The code “RCCC” is defined as the slider being reset to “0” after clicking “RESET.”

Multiple Sources for Feature Generation

The principle of feature generation is to gather as much information as possible based solely on the timing and process data. This information may give us insight into respondents’ reading and problem-solving processes, which are associated with the digital literacy and problem-solving skills performed in the assessments. The features collected in log files can be roughly categorized into three groups: (a) behavioral indicators that represent respondents’ problem-solving strategies or interactions with computer; (b) actions and mini action sequences that are directly extracted from test takers’ process data; and (c) timing data, such as duration of the test, time spent in the simulation environment, and time taken for the first actions when solving a digital task. We generated features via these three sources in the case study.

First, we extracted information about participants’ solving strategies or behaviors on an aggregate level. For instance, the vary-one-thing-at-a-time (VOTAT) strategy, which was explored by Greiff, Wüstenberg, and Avvisati (2015), turned out to be strongly related to performance on this item, thus, was included as a strategy indicator in our study. Another indicator extracted in our study was labeled “AD (Apply/Diagram) Predictor” because it captured the student behavior of applying the simulation and linking the diagrams. This predictor recorded the order used by students to solve the simulation and diagrams. The sequence of switching between the environments (i.e., following the simulation first, doing the diagrams first, or doing both together) may indicate the strategy of respondents solving this task and thus may impact their performance.

The second category of features are mainly contributed by *n*-grams that decomposed the long action sequences into mini sequences to simplify the analysis. Similar to the *n*-gram feature selection in the first case study, we extracted the first letter in each 4-letter code as the action sequence. Consider, for example, a participant with an action sequence of “SNNN, ACCD, RCCC, ACDC, RCCC, ABCC, DHGG, ENNN.” The sequence action type was “SARARADE” after extracting the first letter. Then we created mini action sequences consisting of *n*-grams (unigrams, bigrams, and trigrams) and their frequencies as predictors. For this example, the unigrams and frequencies are "S(1), A(3), R(2), D(1), E(1)," the bigrams and frequencies are "SA(1), AR(2), RA(2), AD(1), DE(1)," and the trigrams and frequencies are "SAR(1), ARA(2), RAR(1), RAD(1), ADE(1)." Thus, each *n*-gram can be taken as a feature, that is, a predictor variable for the binary response. It's easy to see that "S(1)" and "E(1)" are trivial for prediction. Obviously, the higher-order *n*-grams are highly correlated with lower-order ones, but it is not safe to replace one with the other in terms of the information they carry.

The third category focuses on the time features gathered from the process data. "A time" indicates the total time spent on applying simulations and "D time" on linking the diagrams; "R time" records the time between applying "RESET" and the last action before the "RESET"; "E time" gives the time between the "END" and the last action before "END"; "time_bf_action" represents the time between "Start" and the first action (which can be considered as "reading time"; see Table 2.4).

Feature Selection

We used random forest (RF) to step backward to find the most distinguishing features. RF, introduced by Breiman (2001), is one of the most commonly used ensemble learning methods; they increasingly adjust themselves by combining simpler learning algorithms via particular mechanisms to improve overall prediction accuracy (Dietterich, 2000). RF provides accurate predictions on various types of applications (RF can cope with complex interaction structures as well as highly correlated variables). It measures the importance of each feature (predictor) with model training. In addition, trained model offers pairwise sample proximity that can be used

TABLE 2.4 A Total of 77 Features Generated From Process Data to Predict Student's Performance

Unigram (3)	D, R, A
Bigram (16)	DD, AA, RA, AR, AD, DA, AE, SD, SA, DR, DE, RD, RE, RR, SR, SE
Trigram (48)	ADD, AAR, SRD, DDR, AAE, DRE, AAA, ARD, SDR, ADE, RAA, RRE, DDD, DAR, ARR, DAA, RDA, RRA, DAD, SDA, RRR, AAD, RAD, RRD, ADR, ARE, DRR, RDE, DRR, SRA, ADA, SAR, SRE, ARA, RAR, SDE, DRA, RDD, RDR, SDD, DAE, SAR, DDA, DRD, SRR, SAA, SAD, RAE
Timing Features (6)	D time, A time, R time, E time, total time, time_bf_action.
Strategy Indicators (4)	AD predictor, VOTAT group, VOTAT num (number of times VOTAT is used), n_actions (number of actions).

in a proximity-based clustering or multidimensional scaling procedure to give insight about the data structure. There are two advantages in the RF application to select features: First, the RF can comprehensively conduct the feature selection without losing the information from the complex variable structure, that is, highly correlated features and multiple interactions; and second, RF has computational advantages compared to others, such as log-linear and log-nonlinear models, in the case of dealing with large-size categorical feature pool.

Results

The 77 extracted features consist of action sequences at the aggregate level (e.g., the order of using simulation settings) and the action level (*n*-grams or mini sequences of respondent actions), strategy indicators (e.g., VOTAT), and timing features (e.g., problem solving total time). Using the RF by 3-time-repeat 10-fold cross-validation, a total of 15 features

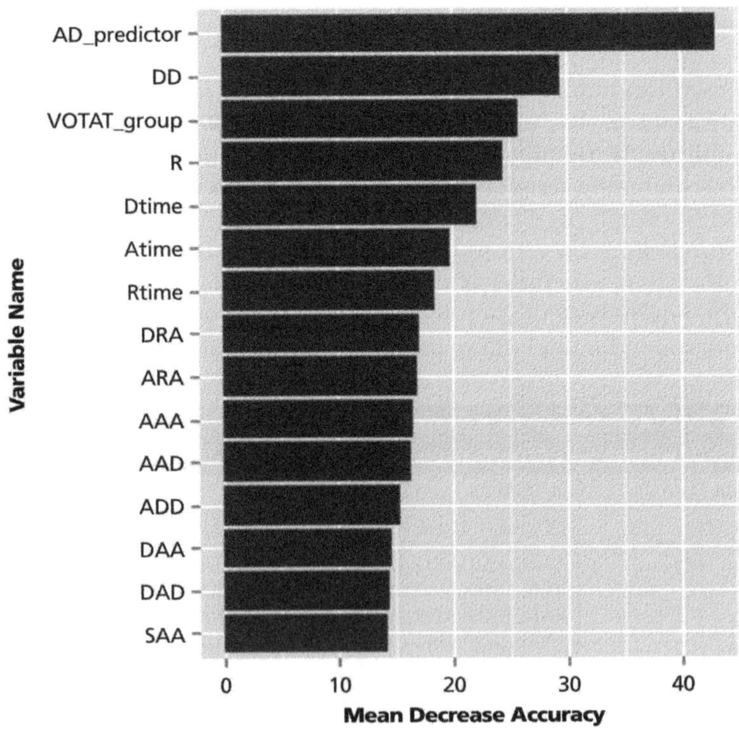

Figure 2.4 Permutation variable importance for model with 15 features.

TABLE 2.5 Averaged Predictive Performance of Full Model Versus Simple Model Over 10-fold Cross Validation

	77-Feature Model	15-Feature Model
Accuracy	.892 (.006)	.857 (.006)
Cohen's Unweighted Kappa	.784 (.012)	.714 (.012)

Note: Indices in parentheses are standard errors caused by resampling.

remained in the model. These 15 selected features appear to be sufficient to describe student strategies as they allow for prediction of task performance at a level of accuracy that is very close to the level reached when using all features. As shown in Table 2.5, the average predictive accuracy over resampling data for the simple model is only .035 less than the full model after excluding 62 features. That is, the extracted 15 predictors yield 85.7% accuracy in classifying features into the correct and incorrect response groups, which is only marginally lower than using the total of 77 features (which yields 89.2% accuracy).The prediction agreement indicated by Cohen's Kappa also holds well for the simple model.

Moreover, some of the 15 important features were also proved to exist in other studies using the same sample data. For example, "VOTAT group," "R," and "R time" cover the same information as Greiff et al.'s study (2015), which claimed that applying the strategy of "experiment control" and utilizing the RESET option helped test takers perform better. "AD predictor" became one of the most important predictive features, as expected, since it covered most of the information related to student's problem-solving behaviors. The importance of "AD predictor" also indicates that the derivation of levels applied in the previous section performed well. Trigrams such as "AAA," "DRA," "ARA," and "ADA" offer more specific information than "AD predictor" and "VOTAT group" do. For instance, the student, who had a large number of "AAA" mini action sequences, drew diagrams immediately after applying experiments (the level "AD only" in "AD predictor"), and then conducted VOTAT on all of three controls might intend to observe the consistency of the slope for temperature or humidity simulated by repeatedly changing one control.

In summary, we used a combination of top-down and bottom-up approaches to generate features from process data in the second case study. In the previous study, the features were mainly extracted by only one approach, either top-down or bottom-up, with the combination explored to a lesser degree. This study filled the gap and proved the efficiency of the combination. Using this approach, more information can be used in the prediction process than from using one approach alone.

DISCUSSIONS AND CONCLUSION

With the rapid growth of computer-based testing, process data play an increasingly important role in tracking test takers' thinking and action sequences, which is especially helpful in analyzing problem-solving items. The two pilot studies presented what we think is a promising method to analyze process data and extract robust sequence features that are informative for differentiating between performance groups.

Future studies may focus on adapting existing methods for sequence data mining and developing a generalized toolkit for process data analysis. Background variables are also recommended to be taken into consideration as a supplementary source for validation.

The processing power of modern-day information technology far surpasses the power needed to process the data stream coming from the keystrokes and mouse clicks of the test taker. Therefore, it is important to use cross-validation methods to rule out correlations that are spurious or not meaningful. To validate findings of exploratory analyses, we need to check whether the features derived from the data mining approach are also valid predictors of success with respect to the overall performance of test takers. That is, we need to test whether the features identified as predictive of task-based success generalize to cognitive skill measures aggregated over a number of tasks. Other variables such as response latency as well as student background data may also be used for the purpose of validation. For instance, test takers' familiarity with common daily computer applications were measured in the background questionnaires in PIAAC and PISA. These measures could be used as evidence of whether the features generated in a data mining approach are valid reflections of meaningful differences between test takers. Any features found not to be sufficiently meaningful could be removed them from further analysis. In other instances, aggregated features that describe behavior at a higher level and that integrate multiple, more finely grained features could be more directly related to problem-solving behaviors and hence more predictive of test outcomes. For example, repetitive clicking on one button (e.g., reset) hundreds of times might cause a mini sequence (e.g., a bigram "reset, reset") that is highly frequent but meaningless. We would aggregate such sequences into "multiple resets" as an indicator for the repetitive behavior. Weighting is another alternative to minimize correlations that are spurious.

Dynamic records of actions generated during the item-response process form a distinct sequence derived from test-taker input. Following and analyzing these sequences using expert-guided and hypothesis-driven analyses can facilitate the understanding of how individuals plan, evaluate, and select operations to achieve the problem-solving goal. With the help of these results based on process data from CBAs, new problem-solving items may be developed that are better designed for collecting valuable information about student learning and skills.

NOTE

1. The name of the specified club member differed by language version.

REFERENCES

Agresti, A. (1990). *Categorical data analysis.* New York, NY: Wiley.

Anderson, J. R. (1983). *The architecture of cognition.* Cambridge, MA: Harvard University Press.

Anderson, J. R. (1985). *Cognitive psychology and its implications.* New York, NY: W. H. Freeman.

Baker, R., & Yacef, K. (2009). The state of educational data mining in 2009: A review and future visions. *Journal of Educational Data Mining, 1*(1), 3–16.

Bekkerman, R., & Allan, J. (2003). *Using bigrams in text categorization* (Report No. IR-408). Retrieved from http://maroo.cs.umass.edu/getpdf.php?id=552

Bennett, R. E., Persky, H., Weiss, A. R., & Jenkins, F. (2007). *Problem solving in technology-rich environments: A report from the NAEP technology-based assessment project* (NCES 2007–466). U.S. Department of Education. Washington, DC: National Center for Education Statistics.

Bennett, R. E., Persky, H., Weiss, A. R., & Jenkins, F. (2010). Measuring problem solving with technology: A demonstration study for NAEP. *Journal of Technology, Learning, and Assessment, 8*(8), 1–43.

Bishop, Y. M. M., Fienberg, S. E., & Holland, P. W. (1975). Discrete multivariate analysis: Theory and practice. Cambridge, MA: MIT Press.

Breiman, L. (2001). Random forests. *Machine Learning, 45*(1), 5–32.

Dietterich, T. (2000). Ensemble methods in machine learning. *Proceedings of multiple classifier system,* 1857, 1–15.

Greiff, S., Wüstenberg, S., & Avvisati, F. (2015). Computer-generated log-file analyses as a window into students' minds? A showcase study based on the PISA 2012 assessment of problem solving. *Computers & Education, 91,* 92–105.

Han, Z., He, Q., & von Davier, M. (2016, April). *Predictive feature generation and selection from process data in simulation-based environment: An implementation of random forest.* Paper presented at the 78th National Council on Measurement in Education (NCME) Conference, Washington DC.

He, Q., Glas, C. A. W., Kosinski, M., Stillwell, D. J., & Veldkamp, B. P. (2014). Predicting self-monitoring skills using textual posts on Facebook. *Computers in Human Behavior,* 33, 69–78.

He, Q., Veldkamp, B. P., & de Vries T. (2012). Screening for posttraumatic stress disorder using verbal features in self narratives: A text mining approach. *Psychiatry Research, 198*(3), 441–447.

He, Q., & von Davier, M. (2015). Identifying feature sequences from process data in problem-solving items with n-grams. In A. van der Ark, D. Bolt, S. Chow, J. Douglas, & W. Wang (Eds.), *Quantitative psychology research: Proceedings of the 79th annual meeting of the psychometric society* (pp. 173–190). New York, NY: Springer.

He, Q., & von Davier, M. (2016). Analyzing process data from problem-solving items with n-grams: Insights from a computer-based large-scale assessment. In Y. Rosen, S. Ferrara, & M. Mosharraf (Eds.), *Handbook of research on technology tools for real-world skill development* (pp. 749–776). Hershey, PA: Information Science Reference.

Katz, S., Albacete, P., Ford, F., Jordan, P., Lipschultz, M., Litman, D., & Wilson, C. (2013). Pilot test of a natural-language tutoring system for physics that simulates the highly interactive nature of human tutoring. In *Proceedings of the 16th International Conference on Artificial Intelligence in Education* (pp. 636–639), Memphis, TN.

Manning, C. D., & Schütze, H. (1999). *Foundations of statistical natural language processing.* Cambridge, MA: MIT Press.

Mislevy, R. J., Behrens, J. T., Dicerbo, K. E., & Levy, R. (2012). Design and discovery in educational assessment: Evidence-centered design, psychometrics, and educational data mining. *Journal of Educational Data Mining, 4*(1), 11–48.

Newell, A. (1980). Reasoning, problem-solving, and decision processes: The problem space as a fundamental category. In R. Nickerson (Ed.), *Attention and Performance* (Vol. 8). Hillsdale, NJ: Erlbaum.

Nigam, K., McCallum, A. K., Thurn, S., Mitchell, T. (2000). Text classification from labeled and unlabeled documents using EM. *Machine Learning, 39*(2–3), 103–134.

Oakes, M., Gaizauskas, R., Fowkes, H., Jonsson, W. A. V., & Beaulieu, M. (2001). A method based on chi-square test for document classification. *Proceedings of the 24th Annual International ACM SIGIR Conference on Research and Development in Information Retrieval* (pp. 440–441). New York, NY: ACM.

Organisation for Economic Co-operation and Development. (2009). *PIAAC problem solving in technology-rich environments: A conceptual framework* (OECD Education Working Paper No. 36). Paris, France: Author.

Organisation for Economic Co-operation and Development. (2012). *Literacy, numeracy and problem solving in technology-rich environments: Framework for the OECD Survey of Adult Skills.* Paris, France: Author. doi:10.1787/9789264128859-en

Organisation for Economic Co-operation and Development. (2013). *Time for the U.S. to reskill?* Retrieved from https://www.oecd-ilibrary.org/docserver/9789264204904-en.pdf?expires=1541743388&id=id&accname=guest&checksum=F5F58196E3F91D57B2A2F70A356135D2

Organisation for Economic Co-operation and Development. (2014). *PISA 2012 Results: Creative Problem Solving: Students' Skills in Tackling Real-Life Problems (Volume V).* PISA, OECD. doi:10.1787/9789264208070-en

Schleicher, A. (2008). PIAAC: A new strategy for assessing adult competencies. *International Review of Education, 54,* 627–650.

Spärck Jones, K. (1972). A statistical interpretation of term specificity and its application in retrieval. *Journal of Documentation,* 28, 11–21.

Tan, C. M., Wang, Y. F., & Lee, C. D. (2002). The use of bigrams to enhance text categorization. *Information Processing & Management, 38*(4), 529–546.

Tolman, E. C. (1932). *Purposive behavior in animals and men.* New York, NY: Appleton Century Crofts.

CHAPTER 3

THE USE OF DATA MINING TECHNIQUES TO DETECT CHEATING

Sarah L. Toton
Caveon Test Security

Dennis D. Maynes
Caveon Test Security

Imagine that you have been studying for years to enter a profession, and that the only thing standing between you and applying for your dream job is a standardized certification exam. As the testing date approaches, you spend copious amounts of time studying and taking practice quizzes to make sure you know the material. The day of the test arrives and you feel a pit of anxiety in your stomach, but as you begin to take the test, you begin to feel more and more confident. As you leave the testing center, you hear someone bragging about finding the answers to the test online, just 2 days before. When the results come in, you find that you did not perform as well as you wanted to, but that the person you overheard bragging about finding the answers to the test online received an almost perfect score. It just isn't

Data Analytics and Psychometrics, pages 77–108

fair! To make matters worse, that person may go on to get a better job or a higher salary because of their impressive score and all that it implies.

Cizek (2003) has defined cheating as:

> any action that violates the established rules governing the administration of a test or the completion of an assignment; any behavior that gives one student an unfair advantage over other students on a test or assignment; or any action that decreases the accuracy of the intended inferences arising from a student's performance on a test or assignment. (pp. 3–4)

Although there are many types of cheating, this chapter addresses examinee pre-knowledge. Examinees gain pre-knowledge when they access and memorize proprietary test content that has been stolen and disclosed (McLeod, Lewis, & Thissen, 2003). Data forensics, which is the use of statistical analysis to identify potential threats to exam security and validity, are particularly important in cases of examinee pre-knowledge, as compared to other types of test fraud, because there are few external signs that an exam proctor might detect (Bliss, 2012). This is because the retrieval of memorized content occurs internally, rather than externally.

In this chapter, we discuss research methodologies for studying pre-knowledge, the basics of data mining techniques, and how data mining can uniquely contribute to the study of pre-knowledge. We then present two case studies where data mining techniques were used to investigate various aspects of pre-knowledge. The point of these case studies is not to present the research in minute detail, but to provide a general overview of the research project and its findings. The final part of the chapter is a discussion on the future of using data mining to advance the detection of cheating.

METHODOLOGIES FOR INVESTIGATING PRE-KNOWLEDGE

There are several methodologies available for conducting research on pre-knowledge, including simulations, experiments, and using measures that provide information about pre-knowledge in real data. One benefit of simulations is that data can be generated to represent examinees with pre-knowledge and honest examinees, which provides the researcher with known categories of examinees. This is necessary for testing the accuracy of new methodologies, as there must be a "ground truth" with which to compare the results. For example, if data for 100 examinees in a simulation were generated in the "pre-knowledge" condition and data for 100 examinees were generated in the "honest" condition, one could assess how well a method performed in separating those two categories of examinees. Simulations are also great for assessing the performance of methodologies across a variety of conditions. A major weakness of simulations, however, is that they produce data which do not represent the full variability of human behaviors, which limits their practical use and generalizability. As an example of the variability of test-taking behaviors, let us consider which option on a test item is most likely to be chosen for a particular examinee. If an examinee is knowledgeable and prepared, we might assume the correct option is the most likely to be selected (depending on item difficulty, see Guttman, 1950). However, research by Attali and Bar-Hillel (2003) has shown that both test takers and test makers are known to have a bias against edge options (e.g., A and D on a 4-point multiple choice item). This means that edge options are less likely to be chosen in general. Now, on top of these premises, consider the test-taking strategies an examinee might employ. For example, the examinee might decide to choose C each time they do not know the answer to an item. Taking these things into account, which option is an examinee most likely to choose? This simple example shows that individuals are able to vary test-taking behaviors in a way that simulated data does not always capture. Additionally, a methodology that performs well on simulated data may not perform well on real data. Are simulated data truly representative of the underlying behavior? As an example of how simulations may not accurately represent behaviors, van der Linden (2016) postulated that examinees with pre-knowledge would answer disclosed items correctly with a probability of one even though evidence suggests that answer keys of disclosed items may contain errors (Scott, Cooper, & Maynes, 2015). In the case of examinee pre-knowledge, I would argue that we do not know enough about the underlying behaviors, both test taking in general and responding to test items with pre-knowledge, in the real world to simulate it accurately.

Like simulations, experiments can also produce known categories of examinees. In experimental research, this is achieved through the random assignment of participants to conditions. However, unlike simulations, experiments capture more of the variability in real data that is due to test-taking strategies, idiosyncratic testing habits, or other types of noise introduced by human behavior and error. Thus, experiments engender the benefits of simulation work with the additional benefit of producing more realistic data. In addition to providing realistic testing data for testing the accuracy of new methods, experimental data can be used to determine clear cause and effect. For example, the effect of disclosing a specific amount of proprietary content (e.g., disclosing half of the test items for 30 minutes before taking the test) on the test score can be determined. In this way, we can advance the study of cheating behaviors. Because experiments produce more realistic data than simulations, they may produce more generalizable results than simulations. But, it is important to keep in mind that participants in empirical studies who are assigned to "pre-knowledge" conditions may not represent examinees with pre-knowledge in the real world. Participants in lab studies often have less motivation and fewer resources (e.g., time, money, etc.) invested in the outcome than examinees with pre-knowledge in the real world. Experimental studies are also time-consuming and costly to conduct. Additionally, there is no guarantee that an experiment will produce quality data.

In one experimental study of pre-knowledge, twenty participants were asked after taking a 40-item test to write down any test content they remembered for the next participant to use while taking the test (Tiemann, Miller, Kingston, & Foster, 2014). This part of the study was designed to assess how well participants could recall test content after taking the exam. Some participants were aware that they would be asked to recall the content after taking the exam and some were not. The results indicated that many participants recalled vague or nonspecific information about the content of the exam. The results also showed that the participants who knew they would be asked to recall the content after the test ($N = 10$) demonstrated fairly poor recall of content specifics with only two specific answers and seven specific items being recalled correctly. Ironically, participants who did not know they would be asked to recall the content after the test ($N = 10$) demonstrated somewhat better recall of content specifics than those who knew, with 11 specific answers and nine specific items being recalled correctly. The second part of the study assessed whether or not access to test content before taking the exam boosted scores. Cheat sheets were created from the recalled test content in the first part of the study, one for the content recalled by participants who did not know they would be asked to do so and one for the participants who did know. These cheat sheets were then given to 97 and 84 students, respectively, who studied them and then took the test. The results showed no statistically significant difference between the conditions in terms of scores for either of the two item types on the exam. It is likely these results would have been very different if the participants were being paid to steal as many items as possible (e.g., item harvesters employed by coaching schools). Thomas, Maynes, Schmidt, and Nabhani (2017) also used an experimental design to study pre-knowledge of test content. This study contained three randomly assigned conditions, a control condition and two experimental pre-knowledge conditions (Item and Item + Answer). In the control condition, participants took a quantitative reasoning test and were not exposed to any test items in advance. In the experimental conditions, half of the test items were disclosed to the participants to study before the test. In the Item condition, only the items were disclosed to the participants, and in the Item + Answer condition, both the items and the correct answers were disclosed to the participants. To increase motivation, participants were told that if they scored above a certain score on the test, they would be entered into a drawing for a gift card. As expected due to random assignment, the results showed there was no difference in test scores for the items that were not disclosed across the three conditions. However, there was a statistically significant difference in the test scores on the disclosed items for the three conditions. The group with disclosed items and answers had the highest scores, the group with disclosed items had the next highest scores, and the control group had the lowest scores on the disclosed items. The results showed that access to test content before the exam resulted in higher scores on disclosed items, higher test scores, and equivalent scores on undisclosed items. Thus, this experiment yielded data that can be used to assess the accuracy of methods in detecting examinees with pre-knowledge and can be used to identify potentially important distinguishing characteristics of examinees with pre-knowledge and disclosed items.

A third methodology for studying examinee pre-knowledge is the use of measures that provide information about cheating behaviors in real data. Real data captures the full variability of test-taking behaviors, but understandably does not contain known categories of examinees in regards to pre-knowledge. Information on cheating in real data is fairly difficult to obtain; imagine walking into a test session and asking, "Will all of the cheaters please stand up?" Such a tactic is unlikely to yield the desired results. Methods that provide information about pre-knowledge in real data include using confirmed cases, Trojan Horse (TH) item scores, score differences, and similarity statistics, each of which will be discussed below. The first way to create examinee classifications in real data is to separate confirmed cases of cheating from the remainder of the data. However, confirmed cases of cheating only represent a small number of examinees who might be cheating and potentially only the most extreme cheaters. Additionally, the accuracy of such an outcome variable is unclear, as it depends at what level a case of cheating is "confirmed" in each dataset. Another way to obtain information about pre-knowledge in real data is the use of TH items. TH items are easy, unscored items that are leaked with an erroneous answer key (Radwin, 2008). They are designed to detect when an answer key has been stolen and disclosed (for more information see the section "Measure of Pre-knowledge" in Case Study #2). Another way to create examinee classifications in real data is to look at score differences. For example, if an examinee shows dramatic score differences between disclosed and undisclosed test items, especially if their performance on disclosed items is significantly better than their performance on undisclosed items, that is an indicator that they may have pre-knowledge (this is the condition that was studied in the experiment by Thomas et al., 2017). If information on the status of items' potential disclosure is unknown, other item groups which are postulated to be associated with pre-knowledge can be used such as older versus newer items. Yet another way to obtain information about pre-knowledge is to examine the similarity of response patterns. Large groups of examinees with very similar response patterns may indicate that an answer key has been disclosed. Answer keys with errors create similarity patterns that often include identical incorrect answers, which are relatively rare under normal test taking conditions, providing strong evidence for the existence of a disclosed answer key (Frary, 1993). These methodologies are just a few of those that can be used to obtain information about cheating in real data.

Ultimately, using a combination of methodologies will probably yield the best research results, as weaknesses and strengths of different methodologies can be compared and studied. Additionally, this provides an opportunity to evaluate and make recommendations for using multiple data sources. Stable results across varying contexts and participant samples create a stronger case for confirming that cheating behaviors have actually occurred than when a single methodology is used. The combination of simulations, experiments, and real data can provide a strong basis of internal validity and external validity, building a solid foundation for new research to expand upon.

AN INTRODUCTION TO DATA MINING TECHNIQUES

Data mining techniques are mostly automated methods for discovering patterns in large datasets. Data mining techniques are an increasingly popular methodology today, but should be selected and used with care. Such techniques are often used for exploratory research with a large number of variables. When selecting a data mining technique to use, it is important to choose a technique which is appropriate for the type of data and the research questions of the project. Data mining techniques vary widely in terms of the situations in which the use of a given technique is appropriate, the availability and flexibility of functions in current software, and the quality and clarity of the documentation. Perhaps the first step is to decide between supervised and unsupervised techniques. Supervised techniques are used when data with known outcomes are available as training data. For example, the iris dataset (Anderson, 1936; Fisher, 1936) is used in a famous demonstration of training Support Vector Machines (SVM) to be able to distinguish between three known species of irises. The training data consists of features of the flowers (e.g., petal width, petal length, sepal width, and sepal height) and the species to which the flower belongs (i.e., the outcome variable). Once the SVM has been trained on this data, it is applied to a test set of data, in which the species of the flowers are not included. Then the predictions of the flower species for the test set are compared to the actual species of the flowers to assess the performance of the SVM. A few examples of supervised data mining techniques are support vector machines, regression, and random forests. If no outcome variables are obtainable from the data, one cannot use supervised techniques. Unsupervised techniques, on the other hand, do not require training data and are used to identify patterns of underlying structures within data. For example, suppose that in the iris dataset, there were no information on the species of the flowers. One could use unsupervised techniques to identify groups of flowers and then make inferences about why those groups exist. A few examples of unsupervised data mining techniques are cluster analysis, factor analysis, and neural networks. Once the decision between supervised or unsupervised techniques has been made, one should determine the research questions to be addressed.

The research questions of a project are important to consider when choosing an appropriate data mining technique, because they describe the desired information that should be gained from the results of the analyses. If a specific technique does not allow the research questions to be addressed, analysis with that technique would be inappropriate for the project. For example, if the research questions of a project were: "What are the best predictors of an outcome?" and "In what directions are those predictions?"; using SVM would be problematic, as the first research question could only be answered in relative terms (e.g., comparing the strength of the predictors to each other) and the second research question could not be addressed. Perhaps a better analysis in this case would be regression as it would allow both research questions to be addressed.

One weakness of exploratory research in general, which is also true of data mining techniques, is that Type I errors (i.e., false positives) become more likely as the number of statistical hypothesis tests increases. The benefit of using data mining techniques is that a vast quantity of information can be analyzed, but the downside is that more spurious findings will emerge from the analyses. To address Type I errors, the alpha level can be adjusted (e.g., rather than $\alpha = .05$, $\alpha = .01$) using corrections such as the Bonferroni correction (Bonferroni, 1935). However, false positive and true positive rates are positively correlated. In other words, decreasing alpha in order to reduce Type I errors decreases ability to find effects that exist. Thus, reducing the alpha level controls Type I errors at the cost of decreased statistical power. The appropriateness of alpha adjustment depends on the context of the data and the goals of the analysis. Another way to address Type I errors, which we would argue is preferable to alpha-adjustment, is to use cross-validation. Cross-validation is the use of hold-out samples to verify that measured effects are consistent across datasets. Thus, the power of the study is not decreased, but the findings must be consistent across the results in order to be considered valid.

It is important to consider the relative performance of data mining techniques. Performance of data mining techniques is directly related to the underlying statistical and data-fitting models that are implicitly or explicitly embedded within the technique. If the models do not provide adequate approximations to the data, the techniques will suffer in performance. Thus, data mining techniques will have better performance on some datasets than others. Despite modeling differences, most data mining techniques are adaptable to many types of problems and data. As an example, some research has found differences in the performance of data mining techniques in the context of predicting death in breast cancer patients (Edeki & Pandya, 2012). However, the magnitudes of these differences are relatively small and performance may differ based on the size, dimensionality, and cleanliness of the data. Research on data mining techniques has exploded in recent years and there is no doubt that this trend will contribute improved methods to the field of data mining. It is important to consider the limitations of the current available methodologies when selecting a data mining technique.

Data Mining Outcomes

The goal of supervised data mining is often to develop a system of equations for predicting a specific outcome. The performance of the data mining technique in the data is assessed by comparing predicted outcomes to actual outcomes. In Table 3.1, we present an example of these outcomes for a situation in which there are two possible outcomes. The true condition represents the actual class membership of a data point and the predicted result represents the predicted class membership of that data point. The upper left and lower right cells represent accurate predictions, but the lower left and upper right cells represent prediction errors. The false positive category represents cases which were classified as positives, but are actually negatives. The false negative category represents cases which were classified as negatives, but are actually positives. From these four categories, a multitude of performance variables can be calculated, including overall accuracy, balanced accuracy, sensitivity, specificity, negative predictive value, positive predictive value, and ROC curves (see Appendix A for the calculation of performance variables used in this chapter).

TABLE 3.1 Outcomes for a Two Category Situation

	True Condition: Positive	True Condition: Negative
Predicted Result: Positive	True Positive	False Positive
Predicted Result: Negative	False Negative	True Negative

Note: This table shows classification outcomes for a situation with two categories where predictions are made of a true condition.

WHY USE DATA MINING FOR INVESTIGATING PRE-KNOWLEDGE?

The field of cheating detection, especially the area of pre-knowledge, is a prime candidate for data mining. Many previous investigations into the detection of pre-knowledge have focused largely on comparisons of person-fit indices (Clark et al., 2014; Karabatsos, 2003; Marianti, Fox, Avetisyan, Veldkamp, & Tijmstra, 2014; Sinharay, 2015). However, person-fit indices capture many types of aberrant behavior; for example, Karabatsos (2003) used person-fit statistics to capture patterns of careless responding, random responding, lucky guessing, creative responses, and cheating. Person-fit statistics tend to perform poorly as indicators of pre-knowledge in real data and, even if they performed well, it would be difficult to justify and defend conclusions of pre-knowledge based on such statistics. Much of the current research on the detection of pre-knowledge is exploratory and information about the best predictors of pre-knowledge and the accuracy of prediction that can be achieved is sparse. A major benefit of data mining is that it allows a wide variety of variables that might be important to be assessed and compared in an exploratory manner. Many techniques assess not only the raw variables, but map the raw variables into higher dimensional space, which allows nonlinear effects to be automatically assessed. Thus, the exploratory nature of current research in detecting pre-knowledge provides an opportunity to utilize data mining techniques.

Testing data are generally large and often complex. Some datasets even contain more information than a data analyst could potentially analyze in a lifetime. There is often a wealth of variables available for testing data which might be helpful for detecting pre-knowledge including: item response data, response time data, classical test theory statistics, and item response theory statistics. However, the very abundance of variables becomes problematic when the most useful predictors of pre-knowledge are not known. Traditional data analysis techniques would typically require specifying linear or log-linear models and evaluating them, which can result in a very large number of possible models for analysis. The danger with fitting, exploring, and evaluating so many models is the great likelihood of fitting the idiosyncrasies of the data, without discovering a generalizable model (cross validation protects against this problem). Data mining is very flexible because a large number of variables and their interactions can be evaluated simultaneously. However, these techniques often provide predictive power without the ability to understand the structure of the model that was eventually selected. Because of this, data mining seems especially well-suited to exploratory analyses which can be followed up with traditional data analyses in order to learn and understand the models that have been found with the greatest predictive power. The findings of a data mining analysis on a large-scale data set can help guide and direct future research for determining effective predictors of pre-knowledge.

Many data mining techniques, when used in a supervisory mode, can optimally predict pre-knowledge, which is extremely helpful for guiding real life decisions. The goal of the study of pre-knowledge is to understand how examinees with pre-knowledge differ from honest examinees *and* to make predictions about examinees who might have pre-knowledge in real data. These predictions will allow actions to be taken (i.e., prompting an investigation or the invalidation of scores) that will increase the security and fairness of exams. In the future, data forensics may be calculated in real time, making it possible to identify examinees with pre-knowledge of exam content while they are taking the test. Such advances would greatly help to combat cheating associated with standardized testing. Currently, however, information on the characteristics of examinees with pre-knowledge or disclosed items is limited. In this chapter, two case studies are presented demonstrating how data mining has allowed us to investigate pre-knowledge: One that focuses on the detection of items that may have been disclosed and one that focuses on the detection of examinees with pre-knowledge.

CASE STUDY #1 OVERVIEW

This study sought to build a system that would be able to detect items that have been disclosed or leaked. To this end, we used SVM (Vapnik, 1998), a supervised data mining technique that learns to classify an outcome from a set of training data and then can be used to predict the same outcome in a test set of data, and a combination of Rasch and Item Response Theory model estimates, along with other item properties. We used this combination of methods to detect items on an international healthcare certification exam ($N = 13{,}584$) for which the test publisher found evidence of disclosure; In this case, screenshots or notes containing the items were found. Thus, the items were grouped into two categories, suspected disclosed items, which were found in illicit screenshots or notes, and suspected undisclosed items, which were not found in any materials. In addition to assessing how accurate the SVMs were at classifying the items, we also wanted to know which variables were important in this classification. The predictive variables, called item features in the SVM literature, were Rasch item difficulty (an estimate of how difficult the item was; Rasch, 1960), standard error (the precision of the item difficulty estimate; Rasch, 1960), item infit (indicating the extent to which an examinee's responses deviate from their expected responses when the item difficulty and the examinee's estimated trait level are similar; Wright, 1980; Wright & Masters, 1982), item outfit (indicating the extent to which an examinee's responses deviate from their expected responses when the item difficulty and the examinee's estimated trait level are dissimilar; Wright, 1980; Wright & Masters, 1982), 3PL item difficulty (an estimate of item difficulty that incorporates discrimination and lower limit; Birnbaum, 1968), discrimination (how well the item distinguishes between low and high ability test-takers; Birnbaum, 1968), lower limit (an estimate of how much guessing occurs on an item; Birnbaum, 1968), average item response time (across participants), and the range of *Q3* estimates for each item (an estimate of local dependence between items; Yen, 1984).

The performance of the SVM models classifying suspected disclosed and suspected undisclosed items was assessed under several conditions, varying the kernel, sample size, and item split. A kernel is the function that is used in SVMs to map the data into higher dimensional space (Vapnik, 1998). A separation is then drawn between the classes in the higher dimensional space. Two kernels were utilized in the current study, the radial basis function (RBF) kernel, which maps the data into higher dimensional space and then uses a linear or nonlinear function to separate the groups, and the polynomial (POLY) kernel, which maps the data into polynomial space and then uses a linear function to separate the groups. Sample size (N) was varied over five values; starting from the original sample size of 13,584 down to a sample size of 200. Random selection of participants continued until the desired sample size was reached for each sample size. The split of uncompromised to compromised items was varied to assess the effect of class sizes on the SVMs performance. The original data had 61 suspected uncompromised items and 86 suspected compromised items, yielding a split of .41 to .59. However, we also wanted to investigate cases in which each class of items was much more prevalent than the other, so datasets were created with suspected uncompromised to suspected compromised item splits of .25/.75 and .75/.25. The splits were labeled Split 1, Split 2, and Split 3, as shown in Table 3.2. All model variants were crossed with the others leading to a total of 30 models ($2 \times 5 \times 3$; see Table 3.2). For additional information, see Thomas (2016a).

All of the SVMs were run under two additional conditions, one with class weights, representing the relative proportion of suspected compromised

TABLE 3.2 SVM Model Variants

Kernels (2)	*N* (5)	Uncompromised to Compromised Split (3)
RBF POLY	200 500 1,000 5,000 13,584	Split 1: .25/.75 Split 2: .41/.59 Split 3: .75/.25

Note: This table shows all the SVM model variants investigated in the study.

and suspected uncompromised items in the data, and one without class weights. The class weights were passed to the parameter tuning function and to the SVM function. The results presented below were obtained from the SVMs without class weights, as there appeared to be minimal differences (an average of about 6% difference for outcome measures) between the SVMs with and without class weights. All SVMs were fitted using C-classification, which is also called C-SVM or Classification SVM Type 1.

CASE STUDY #1 METHOD

Participants

The participants were 13,584 examinees from 423 schools who took an international healthcare certification exam. The participants were degree holders of five different degrees. There were 13,508 examinees who took the exam once, 74 examinees who took the exam twice, and two examinees who took the exam three times, resulting in a total of 13,662 exams. Data from exam retakes were excluded to meet the assumption of local independence, leaving only data from examinees' first exam sittings (N = 13,584 exams).

Data

Minimal information on the data was provided by the test sponsor because of the proprietary nature of the test. Item level data consisted of scored item responses, item order, and item response times in seconds. Although there were 160 items of various types, we only retained multiple-choice single-answer items, leaving 147 items for analysis. The remaining 13 items (i.e., non-multiple choice or multiple correct answers) were excluded to eliminate noise in the item features. For example, the average item response time might be different for multiple choice, multiple answer items than it would be for multiple choice, single answer items, which could cause the results to be influenced by unimportant differences in item types rather than showing meaningful differences in items reflecting their suspected compromised or suspected uncompromised status. Person level data (N = 13,584) consisted of a participant ID, testing session ID, school ID, and degree type.

CASE STUDY #1 RESULTS

Descriptive Statistics

Presented in Table 3.3 are the descriptive statistics for the item features split by suspected category. The separation of these distributions for most

TABLE 3.3 Item Features for Suspected Item Categories

	Suspected Uncompromised				Suspected Compromised			
	M	*SD*	Min	Max	*M*	*SD*	Min	Max
R Diff	–.19	.86	–2.45	2.85	.14	.86	–1.83	1.80
R SE	.02	.01	.02	.05	.02	.00	.02	.03
R Infit	.23	2.79	–7.41	8.81	.46	4.11	–9.90	9.90
R Outfit	.20	3.62	–9.28	8.87	.18	4.53	–9.90	9.90
3PL Diff	–.77	2.70	–8.00	8.00	.55	2.47	–4.22	8.00
3PL Discr	.50	.24	.16	1.31	.52	.21	.05	1.05
3PL Lower	.10	.14	.00	.48	.13	.15	.00	.52
Q_3 Range	.10	.03	.06	.16	.10	.05	.05	.38
Avg Time	56.31	22.88	24.12	169.50	54.49	10.92	26.68	79.82

Note: Descriptive statistics for the item features separated by suspected item category.

of these features appeared to be minimal, as the means were generally similar and the standard deviations were usually wide enough to encompass both means. However, a benefit of SVM is that they can find separations in data that appear to be non-separable because they map the data into higher dimensional space.

Support Vector Machine Analyses

The SVMs were assessed in terms of overall accuracy, balanced accuracy, sensitivity, and specificity. In general, the model variants with the RBF kernel slightly outperformed those with the POLY kernel in terms of overall accuracy, collapsing across sample size and suspected uncompromised to suspected compromised item splits (see Table 3.4). However, the variability of overall and balanced accuracy for models with POLY kernels was smaller than the variability of overall and balanced accuracy for models with RBF kernels.

TABLE 3.4 SVM Outcomes by Kernel Type

	RBF	POLY
Overall Accuracy	.77 (.12)	.72 (.07)
Balanced Accuracy	.64 (.16)	.54 (.02)
Sensitivity	.76 (.39)	.68 (.47)
Specificity	.51 (.45)	.40 (.44)

Note: The average outcomes are shown by kernel, with standard deviations of those outcomes in parentheses.

TABLE 3.5 SVM Outcomes by Item Split

	Split 1	Split 2	Split 3
Overall Accuracy	0.81 (.08)	0.63 (.04)	0.79 (.07)
Balanced Accuracy	0.63 (.16)	0.56 (.06)	0.58 (.14)
Sensitivity	1.00 (.00)	1.00 (.01)	0.16 (.28)
Specificity	0.25 (.32)	0.12 (.12)	1.00 (.00)

Note: The average outcomes are shown by item split, with standard deviations of those outcomes in parentheses.

There were differences in the accuracy outcomes based on item split (see Table 3.5), as overall and balanced accuracy were higher for Split 1 and Split 3 than for Split 2. This suggests that these SVMs may be more accurate when the classes are more imbalanced in the data, which will be investigated further in the sections below.

The results of the SVMs indicate that in Split 1 and Split 2 models, which were those with a majority of suspected compromised items (75% and 59%, respectively), sensitivity was generally much higher than specificity (see Table 3.5). This indicates that the SVMs on Split 1 and Split 2 were classifying a large proportion of the suspected compromised items as predicted compromised, but a very small proportion of the suspected uncompromised items were being classified as predicted uncompromised. Thus, these SVMs seemed to be biased towards classifying items as predicted compromised.

The results of the SVMs for Split 3 models, which were those with a majority of suspected uncompromised items (75%), show the opposite results, indicating that specificity was much higher than sensitivity (see Figures 3.1–3.4). Thus, these SVMs appeared to be biased as well, but in the opposite direction of the Split 1 and Split 2 models. The Split 3 models showed apparent bias towards classifying items as predicted uncompromised. These results seem to indicate that the classifications of the SVMs were biased by the relative size of the classes.

Important Item Features

Our data analysis plan included assessing not only the overall performance of the SVMs, but also which psychometric characteristics of the items were the most important for the classifications. However, the classifications made by the models in the current study showed apparent bias depending on the relative class sizes and were often inaccurate. Feature weights (i.e., coefficients for the features in the SVMs) show the relative importance of the features in separating the classes, based on the current system of classification. Because of this, the weights appear to be influenced by

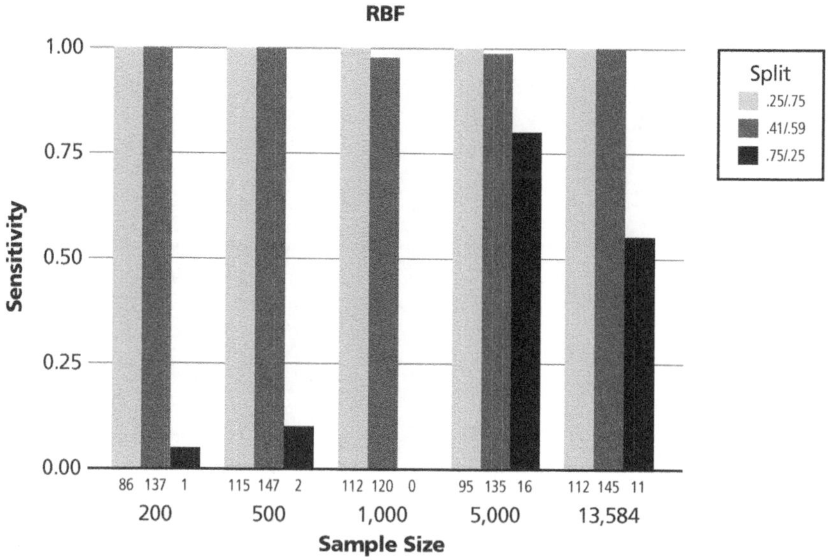

Figure 3.1 Sensitivity of SVM models for the RBF kernel. Missing bars indicate a value of zero. The numbers under each bar represent the number of items in each model variant that were predicted compromised.

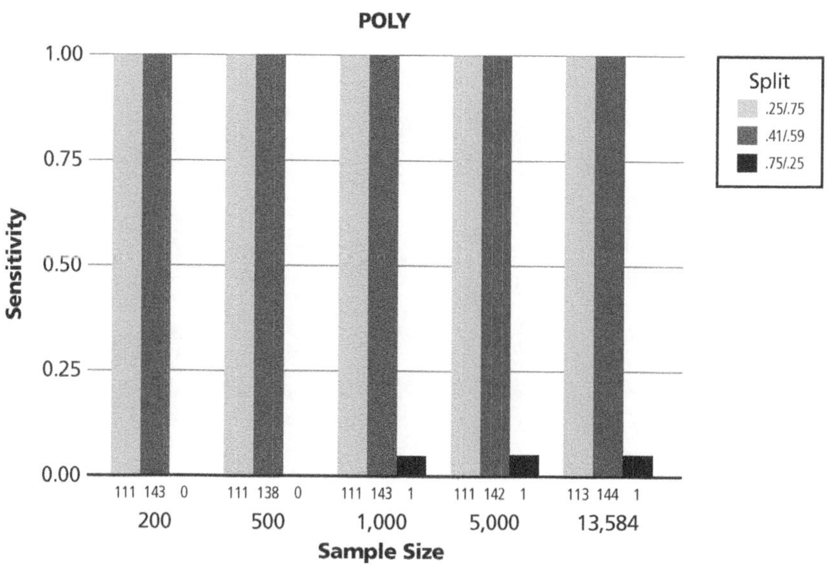

Figure 3.2 Sensitivity of SVM models for the POLY kernel. Missing bars indicate a value of zero. The numbers under each bar represent the number of items in each model variant that were predicted compromised.

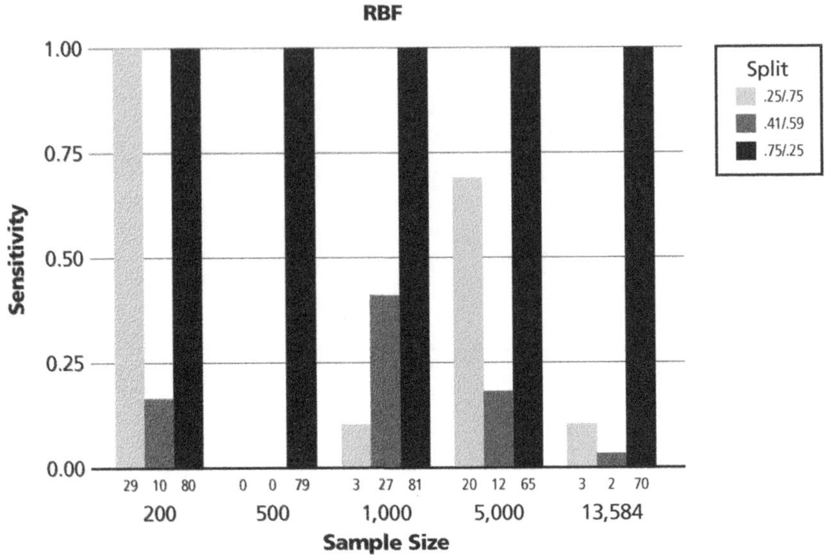

Figure 3.3 Specificity of SVM models for the RBF kernel. Missing bars indicate a value of zero. The numbers under each bar represent the number of items in each model variant that were predicted uncompromised.

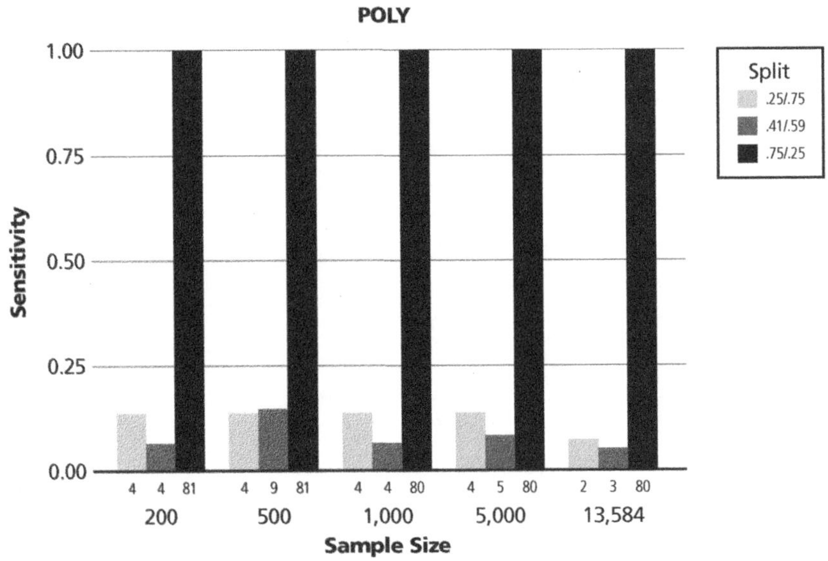

Figure 3.4 Specificity of SVM models for the POLY kernel. The numbers under each bar represent the number of items in each model variant that were predicted uncompromised.

the posterior distributions of the disclosed and non-disclosed items. They do not appear to help us understand the item properties that discriminate between suspected uncompromised and suspected compromised items.

CASE STUDY #1 DISCUSSION

This study combined Rasch and Item Response Theory estimates, along with other item features such as average response times and local dependence estimates, with SVMs to classify and predict suspected compromised and suspected uncompromised items.

The overall accuracy seemed to show that the models were somewhat accurate at classifying suspected compromised and suspected uncompromised items, but the relative size of the classes was strongly related to the classifications of the models. Specifically, the results indicated that models with a majority of suspected compromised items (Split 1 and Split 2) showed apparent strong bias towards classifying items as predicted compromised and that models with a majority of suspected uncompromised items (Split 3) showed apparent strong bias towards classifying items as predicted uncompromised. Thus, the imbalance of the classes appeared to be strongly related to the classifications of the models and the accuracy of the SVMs, balanced for class size, was much lower than desired. Note that explicitly providing the SVMs with the class sizes did not overcome this bias.

A limitation of the study is that the quality of the suspected item categories from the testing company cannot be verified by the researchers. It is possible that the suspected item categories do not reflect actual compromised and uncompromised items. For example, suppose that screenshots of an item were found but the item was never shared or posted online. Or the items could have been posted online but viewed by few examinees. The unknown extent of the item compromise was a confounding factor in the results of this study, caused by the use of real testing data. Thus, it is possible that this combination of methods was performing as best as it could, given the errors and inadequacies in labeling of the suspected item categories. If the suspected item categories do not represent actual differences in the level of item compromise, the feature weights would not be valid estimates of the importance of the features in predicting compromise. They would instead represent the importance of the item features in distinguishing between items that the testing company deemed suspected compromised and suspected uncompromised, which is not particularly useful in detecting item compromise.

This study attempted to use SVMs to learn more about characteristics of compromised items. However, the overall performance of the predictions was poor and heavily biased by sample size. Further analysis should investigate the performance of SVMs that are designed to compensate for unbalanced classes or SVMs that use other error functions. These adjustments may allow us to build a system of equations that can predict which items may be compromised. Such a system would allow actions to be taken to minimize the damage to test validity that is associated with compromised items.

CASE STUDY #2 OVERVIEW

This study sought to develop and utilize a predictive equation to identify examinees with pre-knowledge. The predictive variables we used were item response latency statistics and test performance. Several authors (e.g., van der Linden, 2006) have proposed using item response latencies, the time taken to answer test questions, to detect cheating, but this research has been hampered by a lack of credible information about which examinees are suspected cheaters. In the current study, we identified examinees who were suspected to have pre-knowledge based on their responses to TH items. Scores on the TH items were predicted by latency statistics representing the general amount of time taken on the exam, variability in response times, skewness of response times, and the mismatch between actual and expected item response times. The specific predictors were examinees' total time (TT), median latency (MED), working rate (WR), standard deviation in response times (SD), wild swings in latencies (WILD), skewness in response times (SKEW), the correlations between examinees' item response latencies and the expected item response latencies (TAU), test performance or proportion correct (SCORE), and combinations of these predictors. We ran multiple regression models to assess the strength of these predictors and logistic regression models to predict pre-knowledge in a subset of the sample. For more information see Thomas (2016b).

Measure of Pre-knowledge

TH items are easy, unscored items that are disclosed with an erroneous answer key in order to detect when an answer key has been stolen and disclosed (Radwin, 2008). For example, suppose that the following item was disclosed with the following answer options. Option B, which appears in bold face font, is indicated as the correct answer.

Who was the first president of the United States?
A. John Adams
B. Abraham Lincoln
C. George Washington
D. Thomas Jefferson

The disclosed answer key wrongly indicates that B is the correct answer, but C is, in fact, the correct answer. However, a person who is trying to quickly memorize the answer key might simply associate the item stem with option B, which is marked as correct, but is actually incorrect. Thus, examinees who have accessed a disclosed answer key may respond to this item with option B, which is incorrect, but an honest test taker may respond to this item with option C, which is the correct answer. Answering this item with option B indicates a lack of content knowledge, because the item is easy but the examinee is unable to answer correctly, and also indicates that the examinee is more likely to have accessed a disclosed key for the exam, because they selected option B over the other answer options. This particular example item is incredibly easy and would only be content valid for a low-level test on American history or government, but the concept of TH items can be applied in a variety of contexts. Currently, TH items are used most commonly in the IT industry (D. Maynes, personal communication, October 18, 2016). A single TH item does not provide sufficient evidence to make strong inferences concerning answer key pre-knowledge, but the ability to draw inferences increases with more TH items on a test. For example, suppose that an exam contains six TH items. The probability of an examinee answering all six TH items in accordance with the disclosed key without pre-knowledge is very small (e.g., less than one chance in 1,000,000 if the probability of a truly competent person would give the incorrect key was .10). Thus, we conclude that examinees who answer large numbers of TH items in accordance with the disclosed key are likely to have pre-knowledge of the exam content. TH items provide us with a credible means to make inferences about use or pre-knowledge of disclosed exam content in real data.

Latency Statistics

In the current study, we aim to expand upon previous work that uses item response latency statistics to detect examinees with pre-knowledge by directly comparing the performance of a variety of latency statistics. Scores on the TH items were predicted by latency statistics representing the general amount of time taken on the exam (three predictors), variability in response times (two predictors), skewness of response times (one predictor), and the mismatch between actual and expected item response times (one predictor). The specific predictors were examinees' TT, MED, WR, SD, WILD, SKEW, TAU (Kendall, 1938), SCORE, and combinations of these predictors. For more information on how these predictors were computed, see Thomas (2016b).

CASE STUDY #2 METHOD

Participants

The participants were 3,757 examinees who took certification exams given through a testing company between October 1, 2015 and March 31, 2016. The exams were administered at 1,291 testing sites around the world. Since this is live data, randomization was not used. Instead the study used the complete population of all tests administered during the testing window.

Data

Due to confidentiality agreements with the test sponsor, minimal information on the data is presented in this paper. The data represent two quarters (i.e., 3 month windows) of data from six exams for a single testing program. The number of TH items per exam ranged from six to nine; three of the six exams tests included seven TH items. Because two quarters of data were provided, the data were treated as 12 separate datasets for the regression analyses to assess the consistency of the variables' predictive power.

CASE STUDY #2 RESULTS

Descriptive Statistics

The examinees, on average, answered 69% of test items correctly ($SD = .16$). The range of scores across all tests was large ($Min = 6\%$; $Max = 94\%$). Descriptive statistics on TH scores, total times, and performance for each dataset can be seen in Table 3.6.

Correlations Between Variables

The correlations between variables of interest were calculated across all of the data (see Table 3.7). All of the correlations in Table 3.7 were significant at the $p < .05$ level, with two exceptions. The strongest correlation was between median latency and working rate, r (4974) = 0.84, $p < .001$. This correlation was sufficiently strong to indicate that multicollinearity should be monitored and addressed in the analyses of these data. Additionally, it is important to note that because the presented correlations were computed using all of the data, the correlations between predictors in a single data set

TABLE 3.6 Descriptive Statistics for Each Dataset

Data Set	*N*	TH Items	TH Score			Total Time			Test Score		
			Mean	(SD)	Med	Mean	(SD)	Med	Mean	(SD)	Med
1	1,020	7	2.57	(2.47)	2	6123.30	(2128.03)	5762.50	.61	(.15)	.62
2	263	9	3.66	(3.05)	4	2033.87	(955.46)	1841.00	.75	(.11)	.78
3	395	7	2.94	(2.45)	3	5990.14	(2052.36)	5615.00	.73	(.12)	.74
4	349	7	4.26	(2.66)	5	2619.05	(1455.59)	2247.00	.76	(.16)	.83
5	146	7	3.87	(2.47)	4	2856.90	(1314.39)	2718.50	.66	(.20)	.74
6	230	6	1.56	(2.05)	0	4312.53	(1561.15)	4167.00	.62	(.13)	.62
7	1,195	7	2.67	(2.43)	2	4632.41	(2456.22)	4207.00	.69	(.17)	.73
8	236	9	4.01	(3.11)	4	2096.66	(975.14)	1935.00	.76	(.10)	.78
9	473	7	3.74	(2.50)	4	3931.36	(2620.50)	3329.00	.77	(.12)	.81
10	372	7	4.88	(2.41)	6	2622.87	(1329.41)	2349.00	.77	(.14)	.83
11	95	7	2.80	(2.22)	2	3414.34	(1579.91)	3209.00	.61	(.19)	.58
12	202	6	0.81	(1.69)	0	5013.26	(1769.09)	5063.50	.56	(.14)	.57

Note: The mean, standard deviation, and median TH score, response latency, and proportion correct are presented for each of the 12 datasets.

TABLE 3.7 Correlations Between Variables of Interest

	TT	MED	SD	WILD	SKEW	WR	TAU	SCORE
TT								
MED	0.46***							
SD	0.51***	0.59***						
WILD	–0.03*	–0.04**	0.16***					
SKEW	0.40***	–0.44***	–0.16***	0.12***				
WR	0.52***	0.84***	0.41***	–0.14***	–0.29***			
TAU	0.11***	0.00	0.10***	–0.05**	0.10***	–0.08***		
SCORE	–0.39***	–0.32***	–0.27***	–0.02	–0.09***	–0.10***	–0.17***	
TH Score	–0.24***	–0.38***	–0.27***	0.03*	0.06***	–0.22***	–0.25***	0.35***

Note: † = $.05 \leq p \leq .10$
* $p < .05$, ** $p < .01$, *** $p < .001$

may be different. For example, the correlation between median latency and working rate could be higher in individual datasets.

Multicollinearity

Multicollinearity, which consists of strong relationships between predictive variables, is known to cause unreliable estimates of the unique contribution of each variable (Field, Miles, & Field, 2013). Multicollinearity does not influence the overall amount of variance explained or the accuracy of predictions obtained from the model. A common method for reducing multicollinearity is to remove all but one of the highly related predictors (Field, Miles, & Field, 2013). To further investigate how the latency variables related to one another, we investigated the regression for each dataset individually. To investigate multicollinearity, we computed the variance inflation factors (VIF) and tolerances for the twelve regressions (i.e., one for each data set) with all main effects. The VIF and tolerances were problematic for total time (8 of 12), median latency (10 of 12), and working rate (12 of 12). Thus, the variables total time, median latency, and working rate were deemed highly multicollinear, indicating these predictors were somewhat redundant. To select which variables to remove, we ran multiple regression models including each highly multicollinear variable one at a time.

The average absolute change in R^2 between the full main effects models and the models with MED, but not TT or WR, was $M = .04$ ($SD = .03$). The average absolute change in R^2 between the full main effects models and the models with WR, but not TT or MED, was $M = .06$ ($SD = .06$). The average absolute change in R^2 between the full main effects models and the models with

TT, but not MED or WR, was $M = .07$ ($SD = .06$). Retention of median latency resulted in equal or greater values of R^2 than retaining working rate or total time for all 12 datasets. Thus, we retained median latency in our final main effects model, and excluded working rate and total time from further analyses.

Main Effects Multiple Regression Models

The data for each of the 12 datasets were kept separate, and not merged, in the regression analyses. This separation was maintained because each dataset represents a unique context and set of circumstances. The strongest predictors in one dataset may not be the strongest in another and merging the data would prevent the assessment of these nuances. A predictive equation that is true in general, but not true for any single dataset, is relatively useless. Thus, the regression for each dataset was assessed individually. Aggregates of the regression coefficients were calculated as a way to assess general predictive strength across the datasets.

Multiple regression analyses were conducted to predict examinees' TH scores from the MED, SD, SKEW, TAU, and WILD, and their SCORE. The R^2s for this model ranged from .11 to .70, $ps < .001$. To assess the relative strengths of predictors, the average absolute standardized regression weight (beta) was calculated across all 12 datasets. Higher values for this analysis represent stronger predictive power. However, it is also possible that large beta weights in a few models could have artificially inflated the average absolute regression weights. To account for this, the ranks of the absolute beta weights were also computed (ranging from one to six for each model with one representing the largest weight), and then an average of the ranks across all 12 models was calculated. Generally, median latency, performance, and tau were the strongest predictors of pre-knowledge (see Table 3.8).

TABLE 3.8 Average Absolute Betas and Average Absolute Beta Ranks for Main Effects Models

Predictor	Average Absolute Beta (SD)	Average Rank
SCORE	.27 (.23)	3.00
MED	.25 (.15)	2.17
TAU	.18 (.09)	2.75
SKEW	.11 (.13)	4.08
SD	.08 (.06)	4.25
WILD	.07 (.08)	4.75

Note: The average absolute standardized regression weights (betas) and average rank are presented for the six predictors in the model. The numbers in parentheses are the standard deviations of the betas for the 12 datasets.

Individual regressions for each dataset are provided in Appendix B. These results allow us to assess the direction in which the latency statistics predicted TH scores. Investigating only statistically significant main effects indicated that median latency negatively predicted TH score, standard deviation positively predicted TH score, wild time was inconsistent in the direction of prediction, skew positively predicted TH score, tau negatively predicted TH score, and performance positively predicted TH score.

Higher Order Effects Models

In addition to investigating the main effects of latency statistics and performance, we wanted to investigate higher order effects, or interactions, that might predict TH scores. To identify such interactions, we assessed fully saturated models and conducted effect selection using stepwise regression.

Fully Saturated Models

Multiple regression analyses were conducted to predict examinees' TH scores from fully saturated models including all possible higher order effects between the MED, SD, SKEW, TAU, and WILD, and their SCORE. These models include all main effects and interactions (e.g., TH ~ MED*SD*SKEW*TAU*WILD*SCORE). The fully saturated models had 63 total predictors: 6 main effects, 15 two-way interactions, 26 three-way interactions, 9 four-way interactions, 6 five-way interactions, and 1 six-way interaction. Multiple regression analyses were conducted to predict examinees' TH scores from these 63 effects. To assess the relative importance of the effects, we calculated the sum of the significant standardized regression values ($p < .05$) for each effect across all 12 datasets. Higher values represent increased importance. The number of significant results for each effect across the 12 datasets ranged from zero to two. The effects with two significant results were: WILD, MED, SCORE, WILD:MED, and MED:SCORE. Thus, WILD:MED and MED:SCORE were potential higher order effects, but they were present in only a small minority of the datasets.

Stepwise Regression Models

To further investigate potential higher order effects, stepwise regressions were conducted on the fully saturated models. Stepwise regression is an automated variable/effect selection procedure. Backwards selection is used to assess the extent to which the deletion of each effect contributes to model fit (Field, Miles, & Field, 2013). The effect that most improves model fit when it is deleted is removed from the model. This process is repeated until the model fit does not improve through the deletion of additional variables. Forwards selection is used to assess the extent to which the addition of each effect contributes to model fit. Forwards selection begins with a null model and the effect that most improves model fit when it is added is included in the model. This process is repeated until the model fit does not improve through the addition of additional variables. Bidirectional selection is the combination of backwards and forwards selection at each step.

All three modes of selection were employed in the current study and the counts of retention for each effect in the models were calculated. The results showed that MED:SCORE was the most retained higher order effect. Thus, we investigated whether including this higher order effect in addition to the main effects (e.g., TH ~ MED + SD + SKEW + TAU + WILD + SCORE + MED:SCORE) significantly increased the amount of variance explained. We also tested TAU:SCORE, SD: SCORE, SKEW:SCORE, and SKEW:WILD as they were the other top higher order effects identified by the stepwise regressions. Additionally, we tested WILD:MED because the results of the comparison of the fully saturated models suggested that it might also be an important higher order effect. The results show that these effects significantly improved the amount of variance explained in four or fewer of the 12 datasets. Thus, no higher order effects will be included in further analyses.

Logistic Regression Models

Previously, we assessed the efficacy of latency statistics in predicting TH scores. Now, we aim to assess those same predictors in relation to dichotomized TH scores. This was completed in order to gauge the usefulness of the current research for guiding decision-making in the real world. We wanted to assess the degree to which our findings could be used to predict the dichotomized TH scores of unknown examinees. As such, we randomly divided the 12 datasets into nine datasets that were used to build the predictive equations (called the training set) and three datasets that were used to test the performance of the predictive equations (called the test sets: Data 3, Data 6, and Data 11). It is important to note that we merged the data for all nine datasets to create the predictive equations due to the difficulty of combining nine individual regression equations.

A logistic regression analysis was conducted to predict examinees' dichotomized TH scores from the MED, SD, SKEW, TAU, and WILD, respectively, and their SCORE on the merged data from the nine training sets. The amount of variance explained by this model was about 16% of the variance in the dichotomized TH scores, McFadden's R^2 (7) = .16. The results of this analysis were not directly comparable to the multiple regression analyses as the amount of variance explained in the logistic analysis was calculated as McFadden's (1974) pseudo-R^2, which is calculated as the log likelihood difference between an intercept only model and the full model.

TABLE 3.9 Logistic Predictive Equation Outcomes

	Overall Accuracy	Sensitivity	Specificity	Balanced Accuracy
Data 3	.49	.30	.81	.56
Data 6	.52	.01	.98	.49
Data 11	.84	.63	.98	.81

Note: The outcomes for the predictive analyses are presented above.

Similar to the results of the multiple regressions, proportion correct, median latency, and tau were the strongest predictors of pre-knowledge in the logistic regression.

The results showed that the predictive equation performed poorly for two of the three test sets. In the cases of Data 3 and Data 6, it appears that low accuracy was due to low sensitivity, indicating low ability to detect positive cases (i.e., dichotomized TH scores of one; see Table 3.9). The specificity of the model for these datasets was better, indicating good ability to detect negative cases. In the third case, Data 11, performance was good with high sensitivity and high specificity. Overall, the results of the predictive equation were about 55% accurate, with higher specificity than sensitivity.

CASE STUDY #2 DISCUSSION

The purpose of this study was to assess the efficacy of item latency statistics in predicting examinee pre-knowledge, as measured by responses to TH items. Twelve datasets of certification exam data from six exams given by a technology company were used in the analyses. Overall, the results showed that the strongest predictors of TH item scores (raw and dichotomized) across 12 datasets were the proportion correct, median latency, and the correlation between each examinee's item response latencies with the median item latencies of the sample (TAU). Proportion correct was a positive predictor of TH score, indicating that individuals with higher test scores were more likely to have higher TH scores. Median latency negatively predicted TH score, such that faster examinees were associated with higher TH scores. However strong the predictive power of proportion correct and median latency in the current study, it is important to keep in mind that with only those predictors of pre-knowledge, one must simply search for faster examinees with higher scores. How does one decide that one examinee is likely to have pre-knowledge while another is likely to be a person of high ability? Tau, the third best predictor, has a clear logic behind why it predicts pre-knowledge as it represents the misfit between expected item response latencies and an individual's latencies, which could occur if an individual had prior exposure to proprietary test content. As expected, tau was a negative predictor, such that lower correlations between examinees' response latencies and the expected latencies were associated with higher TH scores. Predictors that were less important were measures of the variability (e.g., standard deviation or wild time, a measurement of wild swings in response times) of the response latencies or a measure of outliers (e.g., skew).

This case study shows an application of data mining to cheating research that expanded on the knowledge gained from the project. The multiple regression analyses provided estimates of how well the models fit in the context of this data and which predictors were the strongest, but the predictive logistic regression analyses allowed us to assess how well those models performed when predicting outcomes used to make decisions (e.g., yes, investigate this person for cheating or no, do not investigate this person for cheating). The results indicated that the current models yielded poor prediction accuracy.

The Future of Using Data Mining to Detect Cheating

The two case studies presented in this chapter represent applications of data mining techniques to real data containing instances of suspected cheating. The first case study used SVM and psychometric characteristics of items to attempt to build a classifier to distinguish between items that were suspected to be compromised and items that were suspected to be uncompromised. The second case study used logistic regression analyses and latency (i.e., timing) statistics to attempt to predict whether or not examinees had pre-knowledge of the material. In both cases, the final predictions were poor, indicating that we have much to learn about how disclosed items can be detected and how pre-knowledge of disclosed exam content can be predicted. In the first case study, adjustments to the statistical methodology may greatly improve the prediction accuracy, which would allow testing companies to respond quickly when items have been compromised in order to minimize the loss of test integrity. Once these statistical adjustments have been made, the study should be replicated in additional real data or in experimental data to ensure that the predictive characteristics of compromised items generalize to other contexts and situations. For the second case study, looking at additional predictors or looking at item-level predictors may be beneficial. Ultimately, the goal is to identify a set of reliable predictors of item compromise and examinee pre-knowledge. These predictors should be investigated in different contexts, as predictors may vary by the type of testing, nature and extent of the test compromise, or other factors of the testing process. Then, these predictions may be used to identify potential targets for investigation. The two case studies presented here furthered the goal of identifying such a set of predictors, but show much potential for improvement.

When items have been compromised, testing programs face serious questions: Can the scores be trusted? Should the items be completely rewritten? What steps should be taken to minimize losses to the testing program's integrity? Data forensics, while being a relatively new field, has the potential to answer these and other critical questions. There are many effects of item compromise and pre-knowledge of disclosed items which are not fully understood by measurement professionals. Because of this, data mining has a huge potential to advance research in this field. Because the complexity and size of testing data makes it difficult to thoroughly explore all variable combinations, data mining techniques offer the promise that critical knowledge may be gained at a broad level, by investigating the predictive power of many variables, and sometimes non-linear combinations of variables. The combination of data mining techniques with large scale testing data provides a powerful direction for future research.

APPENDIX A

The overall accuracy was calculated as:

$$\textit{Overall Accuracy} = \frac{\textit{True Positives} + \textit{True Negatives}}{N}.$$

Balanced accuracy was calculated as:

$$\textit{Balanced Accuracy} = \frac{\textit{Sensitivity} + \textit{Specificity}}{2}.$$

Sensitivity was calculated as:

$$\textit{Sensitivity} = \frac{\textit{True Positives}}{\textit{True Positives} + \textit{False Negatives}}.$$

Specificity was calculated as:

$$\textit{Specificity} = \frac{\textit{True Negatives}}{\textit{True Negatives} + \textit{False Positives}}.$$

APPENDIX B

Multiple regression models including effects of median latency, standard deviation, skew, tau, and performance, for each dataset. $^{\dagger} = .05 \leq p \leq .10$, $^{*}p < .05$, $^{**}p < .01$, $^{***}p < .001$

DATA 1

	β	SE_B	*t*	*p*
MED	–.29	0.19	–6.79	<.001
SD	.15	0.00	2.88	.004**
WILD	.05	0.83	1.70	.090†
SKEW	.09	0.21	1.86	.064†
TAU	–.20	0.79	–6.72	<.001***
SCORE	.04	0.50	1.43	.154

Note: $R^2 = .11$, $F(6, 1013) = 20.90$, $p < .001$.

DATA 2

	β	SE_B	*t*	*p*
MED	–.04	0.64	–0.38	.703
SD	.05	0.02	0.60	.548
WILD	.02	2.80	0.29	.773
SKEW	.12	0.54	1.48	.139
TAU	–.14	1.73	–2.41	.017*
SCORE	.35	1.74	5.77	<.001***

Note: $R^2 = .21$, $F(6, 256) = 11.06$, $p < .001$.

DATA 3

	β	SE_B	*t*	*p*
MED	–.17	0.26	–2.68	.008**
SD	.21	0.00	2.57	.010*
WILD	.07	1.29	1.50	.134
SKEW	.50	0.43	6.79	<.001***
TAU	–.20	1.31	–4.36	<.001***
SCORE	–.05	0.94	–1.02	.308

Note: $R^2 = .25$, $F(6, 388) = 21.83$, $p < .001$.

DATA 4

	β	SE_B	*t*	*p*
MED	–.21	0.35	–3.00	.003**
SD	–.06	0.01	–0.96	.335
WILD	.02	1.06	0.53	.594
SKEW	–.07	0.31	–1.29	.197
TAU	–.27	0.93	–7.28	<.001***
SCORE	.52	0.69	12.62	<.001***

Note: $R^2 = .58$, $F(6, 342) = 78.68$, $p < .001$.

DATA 5

	β	SE_B	*t*	*p*
MED	–.18	0.44	–2.07	.040*
SD	–.12	0.01	–1.66	.099†
WILD	.11	1.84	1.82	.071†
SKEW	.03	0.36	0.49	.628
TAU	–.03	1.42	–0.62	.538
SCORE	.61	0.71	10.69	<.001***

Note: $R^2 = .70$, $F(6, 139) = 54.93$, $p < .001$.

DATA 6

	β	SE_B	*t*	*p*
MED	–.38	0.33	–4.41	<.001***
SD	.01	0.00	0.11	.916
WILD	–.29	0.78	–4.12	<.001***
SKEW	.15	0.41	1.66	.099
TAU	–.23	1.41	–3.73	<.001***
SCORE	–.11	0.95	–1.81	.072†

Note: $R^2 = .26$, $F(6, 223) = 12.90$, $p < .001$.

DATA 7

	β	SE_B	*t*	*p*
MED	–.30	0.16	–8.94	<.001***
SD	.08	0.00	2.41	.016*
WILD	.07	0.63	2.57	.010*
SKEW	.06	0.10	1.89	.059†
TAU	–.20	0.63	–6.85	<.001***
SCORE	.13	0.42	4.45	<.001**

Note: $R^2 = .17$, $F(6, 1188) = 41.05$, $p < .001$.

DATA 8

	β	SE_B	*t*	*p*
MED	–.13	0.55	–1.58	.115
SD	–.09	0.02	–1.10	.271
WILD	.01	2.81	0.10	.919
SKEW	.05	0.57	0.63	.527
TAU	–.11	1.83	–1.73	.086†
SCORE	.36	2.02	5.60	<.001***

Note: $R^2 = .25$, $F(6, 229) = 12.48$, $p < .001$.

DATA 9

	β	SE_B	*t*	*p*
MED	–.29	0.24	–5.29	<.001***
SD	–.01	0.00	–0.21	.833
WILD	.01	1.19	0.13	.901
SKEW	.14	0.17	2.80	.005**
TAU	–.35	0.96	–7.73	<.001***
SCORE	.02	0.98	0.49	.624

Note: $R^2 = .22$, $F(6, 466) = 21.81$, $p < .001$.

DATA 10

	β	SE_B	*t*	*p*
MED	–.05	0.27	–0.93	.351
SD	–.04	0.01	–0.79	.431
WILD	–.05	1.44	–1.15	.251
SKEW	.01	0.30	0.23	.818
TAU	–.25	0.82	–6.55	<.001***
SCORE	.57	0.71	13.32	<.001***

Note: $R^2 = .54$, $F(6, 365) = 71.23$, $p < .001$.

DATA 11

	β	SE_B	*t*	*p*
MED	–.48	0.49	–3.97	<.001***
SD	.13	0.01	1.32	.192
WILD	.08	2.00	1.15	.253
SKEW	–.09	0.49	–0.99	.323
TAU	–.18	2.00	–2.32	.023*
SCORE	.44	1.09	4.80	<.001***

Note: $R^2 = .59$, $F(6, 88) = 20.88$, $p < .001$.

DATA 12

	β	SE_B	*t*	*p*
MED	–.52	0.24	–7.32	<.001***
SD	–.01	0.00	–0.12	.908
WILD	–.09	0.67	–1.31	.193
SKEW	.06	0.23	0.83	.407
TAU	.05	1.22	0.89	.374
SCORE	.02	0.74	0.29	.775

Note: $R^2 = .32$, $F(6, 195) = 15.17$, $p < .001$

REFERENCES

Anderson, E. (1936). The irises of the Gaspe Peninsula. *Bulletin of the American Iris Society, 59,* 2–5.

Attali, Y., & Bar-Hillel, M. (2003). Guess where: The position of correct answers in multiple-choice test items as a psychometric variable. *Journal of Educational Measurement, 40,* 109–128. Retrieved from http://www.jstor.org/stable/1435341

Birnbaum, A. (1968). Some latent trait models and their uses in inferring an examinee's ability. In F. M. Lord & M. R. Novick (Eds.), *Statistical theories of mental test scores* (pp. 395–479). Reading, MA: Addison-Wesley.

Bliss, T. J. (2012). *Statistical methods to detect cheating on tests: A review of the literature* (Unpublished doctoral dissertation). Brigham Young University, Provo, UT.

Bonferroni, C. E. (1935). Il calcolo delle assicurazioni su gruppi di teste [The calculation of significance with multiple tests]. In *Studi in Onore del Professore Salvatore Ortu Carboni* [Studies in Honor of Professor Salvatore Ortu Carboni], pp. 13–60. Rome, Italy: Bardi.

Cizek, G. J. (2003). *Detecting and preventing classroom cheating: Promoting integrity in schools.* Thousand Oaks, CA: Corwin Press.

Clark, M., Skorupski, W., Jirka, S., McBride, M., Wang, C., & Murphy, S. (2014). *An investigation into statistical methods to identify aberrant response patterns.* Retrieved from https://www.pearson.com/content/dam/one-dot-com/one-dot-com/global/Files/efficacy-and-research/schools/021_Data-Forensics-RD-Research-Report-Person-Fit.pdf

Edeki, C., & Pandya, S. (2012). Comparison of data mining techniques used to predict cancer survivability. *International Journal of Computer Science and Information Security, 10,* 1–6.

Field, A., Miles, J., & Field, Z. (2012). *Discovering statistics using R.* London, England: SAGE.

Fisher, R. A. (1936). The use of multiple measurements in taxonomic problems. *Annals of Eugenics, 7,* 179–188.

Frary, R. B. (1993). Statistical detection of multiple choice answer copying: Review and commentary. *Applied Measurement in Education, 6,* 153–165.

Guttman, L. (1950). The basis for scalogram analysis. In S. A. Stouffer et al. (Eds.), *Measurement and prediction* (pp. 60–90). Princeton, NJ: Princeton University Press.

Karabatsos, G. (2003). Comparing the aberrant response detection performance of thirty-six person-fit statistics. *Applied Measurement in Education, 16,* 277–298.

Kendall, M. G. (1938). A new measure of rank correlation. *Biometrika, 30,* 81.

Marianti, S., Fox, J., Avetisyan, M., Veldkamp, B. P., & Tijmstra, J. (2014). Testing for aberrant behavior in response time modeling. *Journal of Educational and Behavioral Statistics, 39,* 426–451.

McFadden, D. (1974). Conditional logit analysis of qualitative choice behavior. In P. Zarembka (Ed.), *Frontiers in econometrics* (pp. 104–142). New York, NY: Academic Press.

McLeod, L., Lewis, C., & Thissen, D. (2003). A Bayesian method for the detection of item preknowledge in computerized adaptive testing. *Applied Psychological Measurement, 27,* 121–137.

Radwin, G. (2008). Fingerprinting certification cheaters. In N. Kingston & A. Clark (Eds.), *Test fraud.* Retrieved from http://www.testpublishers.org/assets/documents/TP%20Fall%202008.pdf

Rasch, G. (1960). *Probabilistic models for some intelligence and attainment tests.* Copenhagen, Denmark: Danish Institute for Educational Research. (Expanded ed., 1980 Chicago: University of Chicago Press).

Scott, M., Cooper, C., & Maynes, D. (2015, November). *Analysis of flawed answer keys to detect braindump usage.* Annual Conference on Test Security, Lawrence, KS.

Sinharay, S. (2015). Assessment of person fit for mixed-format tests. *Journal of Educational and Behavioral Statistics, 40,* 343–365.

Thomas, S. L., Maynes, D. D., Schmidt, K. M., & Nabhani, Y. H. (2017, September). *Is time on our side? An item-level latency analysis to detect pre-knowledge.* Presented at the Conference on Test Security. September 6–8, Madison, WI.

Thomas, S. L. (2016a). *So happy together? Combining rasch and item response theory model estimates with support vector machines to detect test fraud* (Unpublished doctoral dissertation). University of Virginia, Charlottesville, VA.

Thomas, S. L. (2016b, October). *The efficacy of using item response latency statistics to detect pre-knowledge.* Paper presented at the meeting of the Conference on Test Security, Cedar Rapids, IA.

Tiemann, G. C., Miller, H. L., Kingston, N. M., & Foster, D. (2014, September). *Protecting item content via the discrete-option multiple-choice item type.* Presented at the 2014 Conference on Test Security, Iowa City, IA.

van der Linden, W. J. (2006). A lognormal model for response times on test items. *Journal of Educational and Behavioral Statistics, 31,* 181–204.

van der Linden, W. (2016). Bayesian detection of cheating on tests. Annual Conference of Test Security. October 18–20. Cedar Rapids, IA.

Vapnik, V. (1998). *Statistical learning theory.* New York, NY: Wiley.

Wright, B. D. (1980). [Afterword]. In G. Rasch (reprint), *Probabilistic models for some intelligence and attainment tests.* Chicago, IL: University of Chicago Press.

Wright B. D., & Masters G. N. (1982). *Rating scale analysis.* Chicago, IL: MESA Press.

Yen, W. M. (1984). Effects of local item dependence on the fit and equating performance of the three-parameter logistic model. *Applied Psychological Measurement, 8,* 125–145.

CHAPTER 4

SELECTED APPLICATIONS OF DATA SCIENCE IN CYBER SECURITY

Yue (Richard) Xie
RSA

The high-profile data breaches of recent years paint a grim picture of our cybersecurity reality. It is well recognized (Lancope, 2015) that conventional Security Information and Event Management (SIEM) solutions and other legacy security products can't keep up with today's quickly evolving offensive technologies, creating the need for a new generation of cybersecurity. Big data is not new to the cybersphere, but it remains misunderstood by many. Big data is a reality when it comes to securing cyberspace, but not a solution unto itself. The Google search results for "cybersecurity big data" are mostly misleading because many of the authors of the articles confused data science with big data. Consider that billions of users are on the Internet every day browsing social media websites, conducting business transactions, transferring pictures and files, or searching information. Big data focuses on collecting and managing large amounts of data both in quantity and variety, while data science aims to extract the underlying knowledge and insights from the data.

Data Analytics and Psychometrics, pages 109–128

USING PASSIVE DNS DATA TO ANALYZE MALWARE

Most of the time, DNS services—which produce the human-friendly, easy-to-remember domain names that map to numerical IP addresses—are used for legitimate purposes. But they are also heavily used by hackers to route malicious software (or malware) to victim computers and build botnets to attack targets. In this section, I will demonstrate how data science techniques can be applied to passive DNS query data in order to identify and analyze malware.

A botnet is a network of hosts affected by malware to conduct nefarious activities, usually without the awareness of their owners. A command-and-control host hidden in the network communicates with the affected computers to give instructions and receive results. In such a botnet topology, the command-and-control becomes the single point of failure. Once its IP address is identified, it could be easily blocked and the whole communication with the botnet would be lost. Therefore, hackers are more likely to use a domain name to identify the command-and-control, and employ techniques like fast flux to switch IP addresses mapped to a single domain name.

We leverage data sets in large variety and volume to tackle botnets. While the data we analyze daily is often proprietary and confidential, there is a publicly available data set provided by Georgia Tech (Antonakakis, Perdisci, Lee, Vasiloglou, & Dagon, 2011) that documents DNS queries issued by malware across the years 2011–2014. The malware were contained in a controlled environment and had limited Internet access. Each and every domain name query was recorded, and if a domain name could be resolved, the corresponding IP address was also recorded.

This malware passive DNS data alone would not provide sufficient information to conduct a full-fledged botnet analysis, but it does possess rich and valuable insights about malware behaviors in terms of DNS queries. I'll explain how to identify malware based on this data set, using some of the methods the Endgame data science team employs daily.

Graphical Representation of DNS Queries

Here is the data set I will examine. Each row is a record of DNS query, including date, MD5 of the malware file, the domain name being queried, and the IP address if the query finds a result.

```
2011-01-01,0003b97144cf06801627fdd07a917f51,mozilla.com,63.245.209.106
2011-01-01,0003b97144cf06801627fdd07a917f51,rapidshare.com,195.122.131.12
2011-01-01,0003b97144cf06801627fdd07a917f51,tagshare.in,69.10.39.21
2011-01-01,00134ecf2477c1f477a8767c87572107,mozilla.com,63.245.209.106
2011-01-01,00134ecf2477c1f477a8767c87572107,rapidshare.com,195.122.131.5
2011-01-01,00134ecf2477c1f477a8767c87572107,tagshare.in,69.10.39.21
2011-01-01,002c6d8f0732bc7d833a6b4fb48ed50f,ns1.player1253.com,195.3.145.196
2011-01-01,0032c28aea706ffcc396fd7fc5652f7b,defedd.zapto.org,188.53.18.247
2011-01-01,003ae43f441eebef7386467fa740a1c8,ns1.player1253.com,195.3.145.196
2011-01-01,0065df8bfdc9e1435637b627535922f0,mozilla.com,63.245.209.106
2011-01-01,0065df8bfdc9e1435637b627535922f0,rapidshare.com,195.122.131.5
```

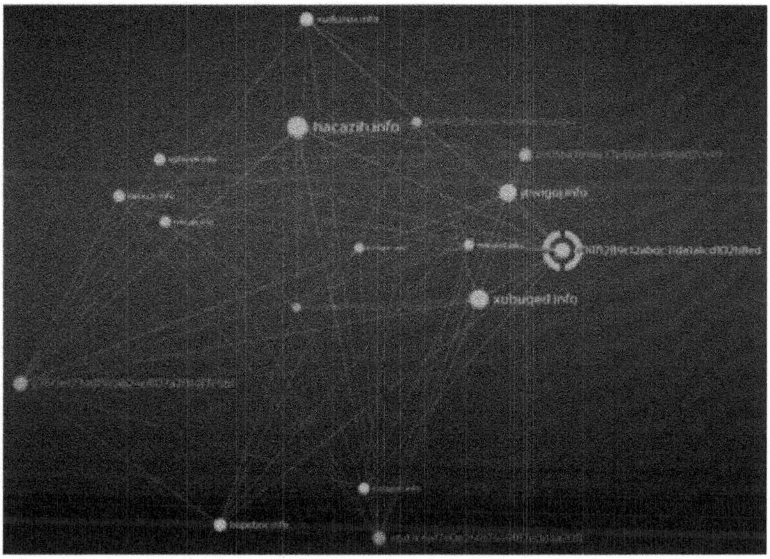

Figure 4.1 A small DNS query network.

What approach might enable the grouping of malware or suspicious programs based on specific domain names? As we have no information about the malware, the conventional static analysis of malware focusing on investigating binary files would not be helpful here. Clustering using machine learning may work only if each domain name is treated as a feature, but the feature space will be very sparse. That would result in expensive computation.

Instead, we can represent the DNS queries using a graphic network showing what domain names a malware is interested in, as displayed in Figure 4.1. Each malware program is labeled by an MD5 string. While Figure 4.1 only demonstrates a very small part of the network, the entire data set could actually be transferred into a huge network.

There are numerous advantages to expressing the queries in the format of a graph. First, this expedites querying complex relationships. A modern graph database, such as Neo4j, Orientdb, or Titandb, can efficiently store a large graphic network and conduct joint queries that normally are computationally expensive for relational databases, such as MS SQL Server, Oracle, or MySql. Second, network analytic methods from a diverse range of scientific fields can be employed to analyze the data set to gain additional insights.

GRAPH ANALYSIS ON THE MALWARE NETWORK

The entire passive DNS data set covers several years, so I randomly picked a day during the data collection period and will present the analysis on the reduced data set. A graph was created out of a day's worth of data, and the nodes include both domain names and malware MD5 strings. In other words, a node in the graph can either be an MD5 string, or a domain name, and an edge (or a connection) links an MD5 and a domain if the MD5 queries that domain name. The total number of nodes is 17,629, and the number of edges is 54,939. The average number of connections per node is about three.

In my graph representation of DNS queries, there are two distinct sets of nodes: domain names and malware. A node in one set only connects with a node in the other set, and not one in its own set. Graph theory defines such a network as a bipartite graph, as shown in Figure 4.2. I wanted to split the graph into two graphs, one containing all the nodes of domain names, and the other containing only malware programs. This can be done by projecting the large graph onto the two sets of nodes, which creates two graphs. In each graph, two nodes are connected by an edge if they have connections to the same node of the other type. For example, domains xudunux.info and rylicap.info would be connected in the domain graph because both of them have connections with the same malware in the larger graph.

Let's look at the graph of malware first. For the day September 29, 2012 alone, there are 9,876 unique malware recorded in the data set. First, I would like to know the topological layout of these malware and find out how many connected components exist in the malware graph.

A connected component is a subset of nodes where any two nodes are connected to each other by one or multiple paths. We can view connected components (or just components) as islands that have no bridge connecting each other.

Python programming language has an excellent network analysis package called networkx. It has a function to compute the number of connected components of a graph. The result of running that function, named number_connected_components, shows there are 2,114 components in the

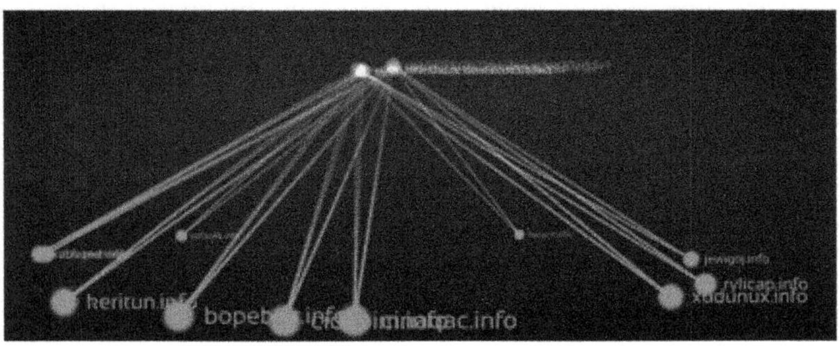

Figure 4.2 Bipartite graph showing two distinct types of nodes.

9,876-node graph, 1,619 of which are one-node component. There are still 11 components that have more than 100 nodes within them. I will analyze those large components because the malware inside may be variants of the same program.

Figure 4.3 shows four components of the malware graph. The nodes in each component are densely connected to each other but not to any other components. That means the malware assigned to a component clearly possess some similar characteristics that are not shared by the malware from other components.

Component 1 contains 201 nodes. I computed the betweenness centrality of the nodes in the graph, which are all zeros, while the closeness centrality values of the nodes are all ones. This indicates that each node has a direct connection with each other node in the component, meaning that each malware queried exactly the same domain names as the other malware programs. This is a strong indication that all 201 malware are variants of a certain type of malicious executable.

Let's return to the large DNS query graph to find out what domains the malware targeted. Using a graph database like Neo4j or OrientDB, or a graph analytic tool like networkx, the search is easy. The result shows that the malware in Component 1 were only interested in three domain names: ns1.musicmixa.net, ns1.musicmixa.org, and ns1.musiczipz.com.

I queried VirusTotal for each of the 201 malware in Component 1. VirusTotal submits the MD5 to a list of scanning engines and return the

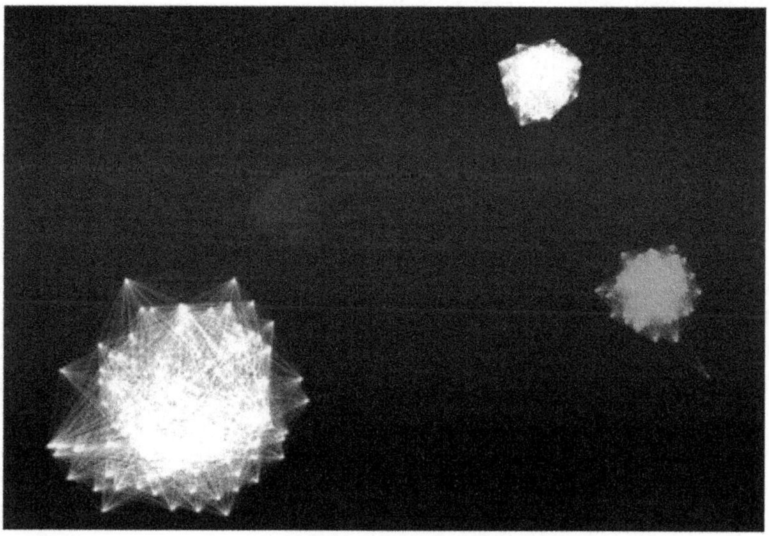

Figure 4.3 Four out of eleven components in the malware graph.

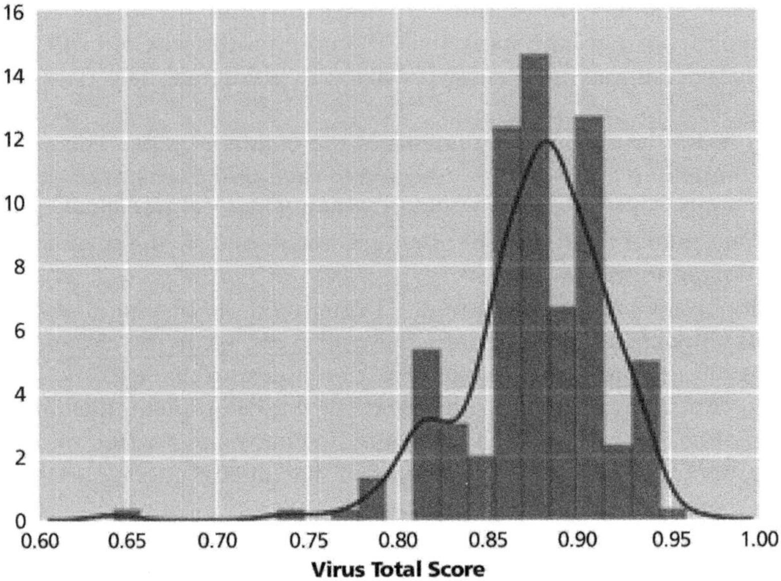

Figure 4.4 Histogram of VirusTotal score of malware in Component 1.

reports from those engines. A report includes its determination of the MD5 to be either positive or negative. If it's positive, the report would provide more information about what kind of malware the MD5 is, based on the signature that the scanning engine uses.

I assigned a score to each malware by computing the ratio of the number of positive results to the total number of results. The distribution of the scores is shown in Figure 4.4. The scanning reports imply that the malware is a Wind32 Trojan.

Using Social Network Analytics to Understand Unknowns

When I look at each of the components, not all of them have such high level of homophily as Component 1 does. A different component has 2,722 malware nodes, and 681,060 edges. 309 of the 2,722 malware in this component were not known to VirusTotal, while the rest, 2,413 malware, had reports on the website. We need a way to analyze those unknown malware.

Social network analytic (SNA) methods provide insights into unknown malware by identifying known malware that are similar to the unknowns. The first step is to try to break the large component into communities. The concept of community is easy to understand in the context of a social network. Connections within a community are usually much denser than those outside a community. Members of a community tend to share some common trait, such as mission, geolocation, or profession. In this analysis, malware were connected if they queried the same domain that could be interpreted as two malware exhibiting a common interest in a domain name. Therefore, we can expect that malware programs that have queried similar domains represent a community. Communities exist inside a connected component and differ from the concept of components in that communities still have connections between each other.

Community detection is a particular kind of data clustering within the domain of machine learning. There are a wide variety of methods for community detection in a graphic network. The Louvain method (De Meo, Ferrara, Fiumara, & Provetti, 2011) is a well-known and well-performed one, and tries to optimize the measure of modularity by partitioning a graph into groups of densely connected nodes. By applying the Louvain method to the big component with 2,722 nodes, I can identify 15 communities and the number of nodes within each community as shown in Figure 4.5.

Let's take a specific malware as an example. The MD5 of this malware is 0398eff0ced2fe28d93daeec484feea6, and the search of it on VirusTotal found no result.

I want to know what malware programs have the most similar behavior in terms of DNS queries to this unknown malware. By looking into the similar malware that we do have knowledge about, we could gain insights into the unknown one.

I found malware 0398eff0ced2fe28d93daeec484feea6 in Community 4, which has 256 malware within it. To find the most similar malware programs, we need a quantitative definition of similarity. I chose to use Jaccard index to compute just how similar two sets of queried domains are.

Suppose malware M1 queried a set of domains D1, and malware M2 queried another set of domains D2. The Jaccard index goes from 0 to 1, with 1 indicating an exact match.

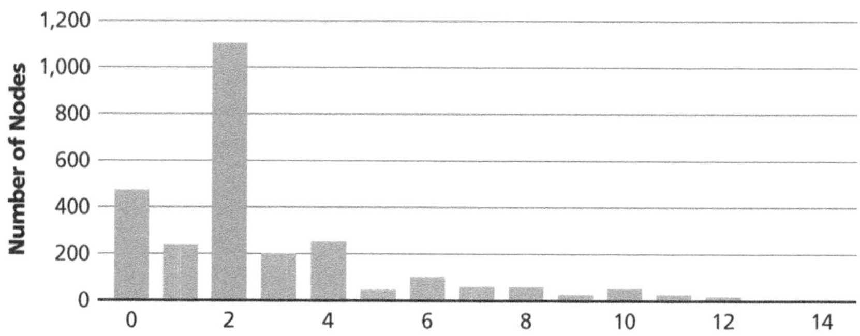

Figure 4.5 Number of nodes in each community.

Out of the total 2,722 nodes in Component 1, 100 malware programs have exactly the same domain queries as malware 0398eff. That means their Jaccard indices against malware 0398eff are 1. However, only nine malware are known to VirusTotal. The nine malware are shown in Table 4.1.

Each of the 100 malware programs, including the nine known ones that have the same domain queries as malware 0398eff appear in Community 4. The histogram of Jaccard index is shown in Figure 4.6.

We can tell from the histogram that the malware programs in Community 4 could be generally split into two sets. One set contains 100 malware that have exactly the same domain queries as malware 0398eff, and the other set has nodes that are much less similar to it. The graph visualization in Figure 4.7 demonstrates the split. *By this analysis, we have found those previously unknown 91 malware behaving similarly to some known malware.*

Given the vast quantities of data those of us in the security world handle daily, data science techniques are an increasingly efficient and informative way to identify malware and targeted domains. While machine learning and clustering tend to dominate these kinds of analyses, social network based graphic methods should increasingly become another tool in the data science toolbox for malware detection. Through the identification of communities, betweenness, and similarity scores, network analysis helps show not only connectivity, but also logical groupings and outliers within the network. Viewing malware and domains as a network provides another more intuitive approach for wrangling the big data security environment. Given the limited features available in the DNS passive query data, graph analytic approaches supplement traditional static and dynamic approaches and elevate capabilities in malware analytics.

HUNTING FOR HONEYPOT ATTACKERS

Hardly a day goes by without news of cyber intrusions. As an example, according to databreachtoday.com, just in recent months PNI Digital Media and many retailers such as Wal-Mart and Rite-Aid had their photo services compromised, UCLA Health's network was breached, and information of 4.5 million people may have been exposed. Criminals and nation-state actors break into systems for many reasons with catastrophic and often irremediable consequences for the victims.

Traditionally, security experts are the main force for investigating cyber threats and breaches. Their expertise in computers and network communication provides them with an advantage in identifying suspicious activities. However, with more data being collected, not only in quantity but also in variety, data scientists are beginning to play a more significant role in the adventure of hunting malicious attackers. In this section, I'll explain

TABLE 4.1 VirusTotal Details of Scanned MD5's

MDS	Detection ratio (VirusTotal)	TriO (VirusTotal)
020fcdecc4cd852cb8ef979e3fd6fc49	50/55	Win32 Executable MS Visual C++ (generic) (42.1 %) Win64 Executable (generic) (37.3%) Win32 Dynamic Link Library (generic) (8.8%) Win32 Executable (generic) (6.0%) Generic Win/DOS Executable (2.7%)
03cfa5158eeb57e66d25e75ed8312702	37/42	Generic Win/DOS Executable (49.9%) DOS Executable Generic (49.8%) Autodesk FLIC Image File (extensions: fic, fli, cel) (0.1%)
030c63c3bd8c6f75218d147953dd8119	35/43	Win64 Executable Generic (59.6%) Win32 Executable MS Visual C++ (generic) (26.2%) Win32 Executable Generic (5.9%) Win32 Dynamic Link Library (generic) (5.2%) Generic Win/DOS Executable (1.3%)
e0d7a9e9eb3c468984bb60e90e8915b1	39/42	Windows Screen Saver (39.4%) Win32 Executable Generic (25.6%) Win32 Dynamic Link Library (generic) (22.8%) Generic Win/DOS Executable (6.0%) DOS Executable Generic (6.0%)
01527da2370c16f176099b4ff46bee7f	35/43	Generic Win/DOS Executable (49.9%) DOS Executable Generic (49.8%) Autodesk FLIC Image File (extensions: fic, fli, cel) (0.1%)
02c842bde2711fe9c81e43ae4dae04e0	52/55	Win32 Executable MS Visual C++ (generic) (42.1%) Win64 Executable (generic) (37.3%) Win32 Dynamic Link Library (generic) (8.8%) Win32 Executable (generic) (6.0%) Generic Win/DOS Executable (2.7%)
210921877f761629a41d9bc3c69dc2e6	35/41	Win64 Executable Generic (59.6%) Win32 Executable MS Visual C++ (generic) (26.2%) Win32 Executable Generic (5.9%) Win32 Dynamic Link Library (generic) (5.2%) Generic Win/DOS Executable (1.3%)
0392cbb8c4c52b0191ebc64473a7fce6	36/41	Generic Win/DOS Executable (49.9%) DOS Executable Generic (49.8%) Autodesk FLIC Image File (extensions: fic, fli, cel) (0.1%)
263eca1e7954e48a0e804189fe93c218	41/46	Win32 Executable MS Visual C++ (generic) (65.2%) Win32 Executable Generic (14.7%) Win32 Dynamic Link Library (generic) (13.1%) Generic Win/DOS Executable (3.4%) DOS Executable Generic (3.4%)

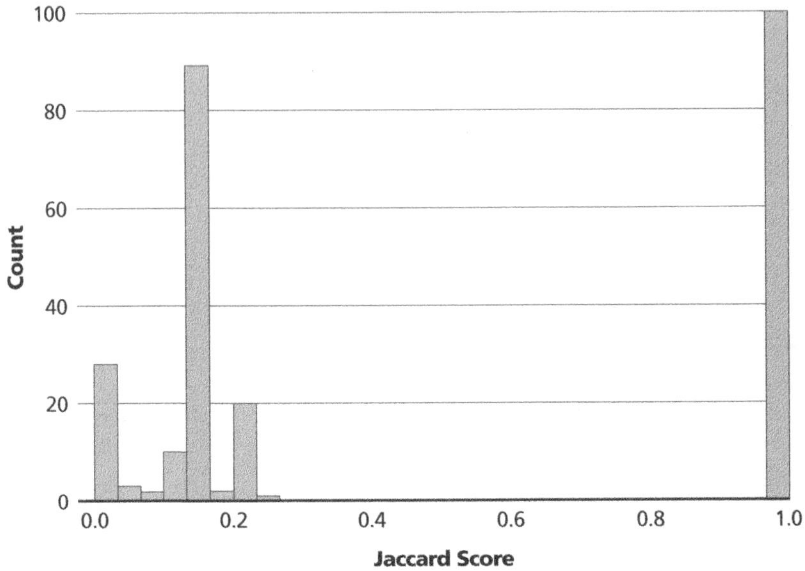

Figure 4.6 Histogram of Jaccard index for nodes in community 4.

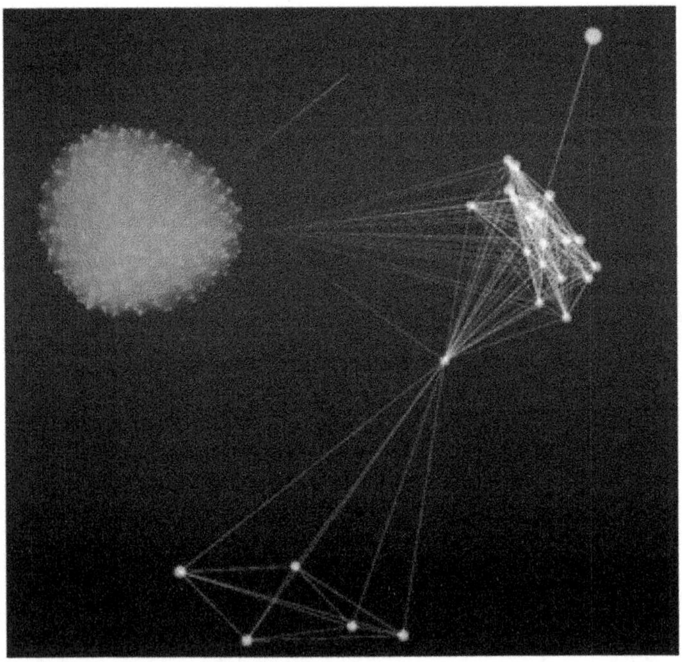

Figure 4.7 Two dense sets in community 4.

how we analyze attack data collected from a honeypot network, which provides insight into the locations of attackers behind those activities. The analysis captures those organized attacks from a vast amount of seemingly separated attempts.

This section is divided into three parts. The first part describes the context of the analysis and provides an overview of the hacking activities. The second part focuses on investigating the files that the attackers implanted into the breached systems. Finally, the third part demonstrates how I identified similar attacks through uncovering behavioral characteristics. All of this demonstrates one way that data science can be applied to the security domain.

Background

Cyber attackers are constantly looking for targets on the Internet. Much like a lion pursuing its prey, an attacker usually conducts a sequence of actions, known as the cyber kill chain, including identifying the footprints of a victim system, scanning the open ports of the system, and probing the holes trying to find an entrance into the system. Professional attackers might be doing this all day long until they find a weak system.

All of this would be bad news for any weak system the attacker finds—unless that weak system is a honeypot. A honeypot is a trap set up on the Internet with minimum security settings so an attacker may easily break into it, without knowing his/her activities are being monitored and tracked. Though honeypots have been used widely by researchers to study the methods of attackers, they can also be very useful to defenders. Compared to sophisticated anomaly detection techniques, honeypots provide intrusion alerts with low false positive rates because no legitimate user should be accessing them. Honeypots set up by a company might also be used to confuse attackers and slow down the attacks against their networks. New techniques (Meer & Slaviero, 2015) are on the way to make setting up and managing honeypots easier and more efficient, and may play an increasingly prominent role in future cyber defense.

A network of honeypots is called a honeynet. The particular honeynet for which I have data logged activities showing that an attacker enumerated pairs of common usernames and passwords to enter the system, downloaded malicious files from his/her own hosting servers, changed the privilege over the files and then executed them. During the period from March 2015 through the end of June 2015, there were more than 21,000 attacker IP addresses being detected, and about 36 million SSH attempts being logged. Attackers have tried 34,000 unique usernames and almost 1 million unique passwords to break into those honeypots. That's a lot of effort by the attackers to break into the system. Over time, the honeynet has identified about 500 malicious domains and more than 1000 unique malware samples.

The IP addresses that were owned by the attackers and used to host malware are geographically dispersed. Figure 4.8 shows that the recorded attacks mostly came from China, the United States, the Middle East, and Europe. While geographic origination doesn't tell us everything, it still gives us a general idea of potential attacker locations.

The frequency of attacks varies daily, as shown in Figure 4.9, but the trend shows that more attacks were observed during work days than weekends, and peaks often appear on Wednesday or Thursday. This seems to support the suspicion that humans (other than bots) were behind the scenes, and professionals instead of amateur hobbyists conducted the attacks.

Now that we understand where and when those attacks were orchestrated, we want to understand if any of the attacks were organized. In other words, were they carried out by the same person or same group of people over and over again?

Attackers change IP addresses from attack to attack, so looking at the IP addresses alone won't provide us with much information. To find the answer to the question above, we need to use the knowledge about the files left by the attackers.

Figure 4.8 Attacks came from all around the world, color coded on counts of attack. The darker the color, the greater the number of attacks originating from that country.

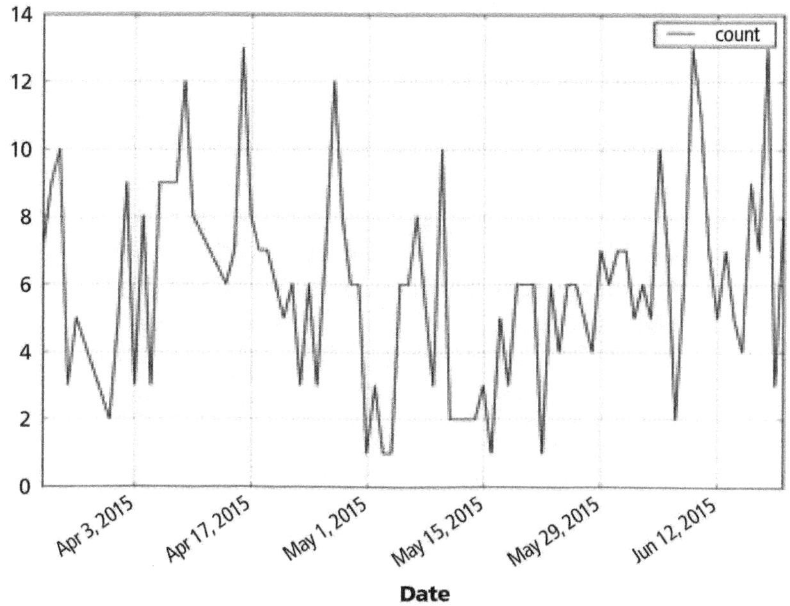

Figure 4.9 Daily attack counts.

FILE SIMILARITY

Malware to an attacker is like a hammer and level to a carpenter. We expect that an attacker would use his/her set of malware repeatedly in different attacks, even though the files might have appeared in different names or variants. Therefore, the similarity across the downloaded malware files may provide informative links to associated attacks.

One extreme case is a group of 17 different IPs (shown in Figure 4.10) used on a variety of days containing exactly the same files and folders organized in exactly the same structure. That finding immediately portrayed a lazy hacker who used the same folder time and time again. However, we would imagine that most attackers might be more diligent. For example, file structures in the hosting server may be different, folders could be rearranged, and the content of a malicious binary file may be tweaked. Therefore, a more robust method is needed to calculate the level of similarity across the files, and then use that information to associate similar attacks.

How can we quantitatively and algorithmically do this?

The first step is to find similar files to each of the files in which we are interested. The collected files include different types, such as images, HTML pages, text files, compressed tar balls, and binary files, but we are probably

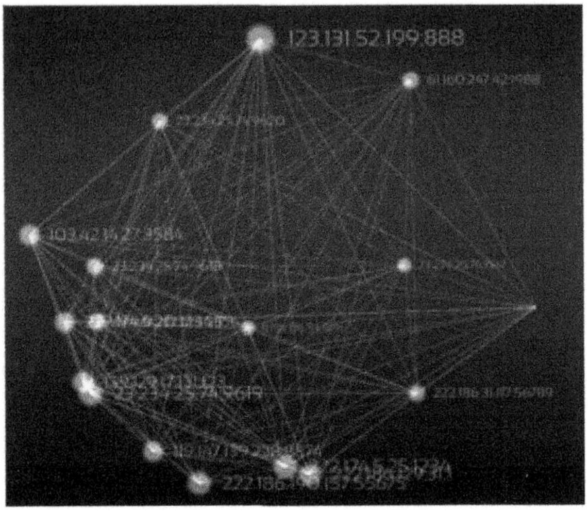

Figure 4.10 17 IPs have exactly the same file structure.

only interested in binary files and tar balls, which are riskier. This reduces the number of files to work on, but the same approach can be applied to all file types.

File similarity computation has been researched extensively in the past two decades but still remains a rich field for new methods. Some mature algorithms to compute file similarities include block-based hashing (Xiang & Yang, 2012), Context-Triggered Piecewise (CTP) hashing (also known as fuzzy hashing; Kornblum, 2006), and Bloom filter hashing (Kirsch & Mitzenmacher, 2008). For this investigation I used fuzzy hashing to compute file similarities for simplicity and since open source code is widely available.

I took each of the unique files based on its fuzzy hashing string and computed the similarity to all the other files. The result is a large symmetric similarity matrix for all files, which we can visualize to check if there are any apparent structures in the similarity data. The way I visualize the matrix is to connect two similar files with a line, and here I would choose an arbitrary threshold of 80, which means that if two files are more than 80% similar, they will be connected. The visualization of the file similarity matrix is shown in Figure 4.11.

It is visually clear that the files are indeed partitioned into a number of groups. Let's zoom into one group and see the details in Figure 4.12. The five files, represented by their fuzzy hash strings, are connected to each other, having mutual similarity of over 90%. If we look at them very carefully, they only differ in one or two letters in the strings, even they have totally different file names and MD5 hashes. VirusTotal (www.virustotal.com)

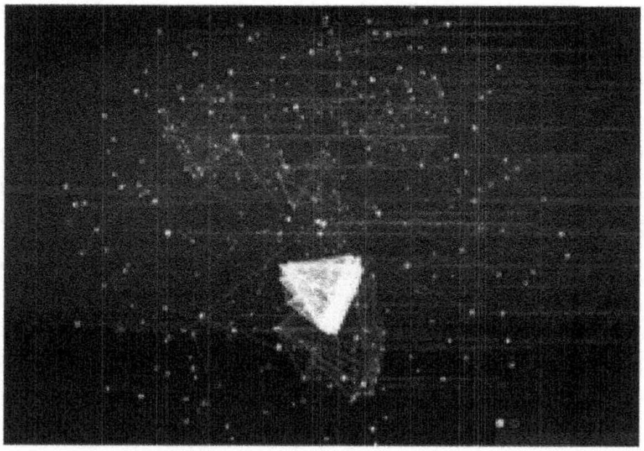

Figure 4.11 Graph of files based on similarity.

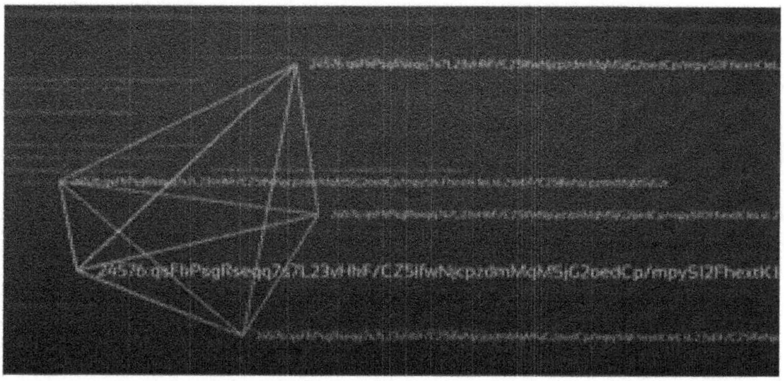

Figure 4.12 One group of similar files.

recognizes four out of the five malware, and the scan reports indicate that these malware are Linux Trojan.

IDENTIFYING SIMILAR ATTACKS

Now that we have identified the groups of similar files, it's time to identify the attacks that used similar malware. If I treat each attack as a document, and the malware used in an attack as words, I can construct a document-term matrix to encapsulate all the attack information. To incorporate the malware similarity information into the matrix, I tweaked the matrix a bit. For malware that were not used in a specific attack, but that still share a certain amount of similarity with the malware being used, the malware will assume the value of the similarity level for that attack. For example, if malware M1 was not used in attack A1, but M1 is most similar to malware M2 which was used in attack A1, and the similarity level is 90%, then the element at cell (A1, M1) will be 0.9, while (A1, M2) be 1.0.

For readers who are familiar with NLP (Natural Language Processing) and text mining, the matrix I've described above is similar to a document-term matrix, except the values are not computed from TF-IDFs (Term Frequency-Inverse Document Frequency). The essence of such a matrix is to reflect the relationship between data records and features. In this case, data records are attacks and features are malware, while for NLP they are documents and words. The resulting matrix is an attack-malware matrix, which has more than 400 columns representing malware hashes. To get a quick idea of how the attacks (the rows) are dispersed in such a high dimensional space, I plotted the data using the T-SNE (*t*-Distributed Stochastic Neighbor Embedding; van der Maaten & Hinton, 2008) technique and colored the points according to the results from *K*-means ($K = 10$) clustering. I chose $K = 10$ arbitrarily to illustrate the spatial segmentation of the attacks. The T-SNE graph is shown in Figure 4.6, and each color represents a cluster labeled by the *K*-means clustering. T-SNE tries to preserve the topology when projecting data points from a high dimensional space to a much lower dimensional space, and it is widely used for visualizing the clusters within a data set.

Figure 4.13 shows that *K*-Means did a decent job of spatially grouping close data points into clusters, but it fell short of providing a quantitative measurement of similarity between any two data points. It is also quite difficult to choose the optimum value for *K*, the number of clusters. To

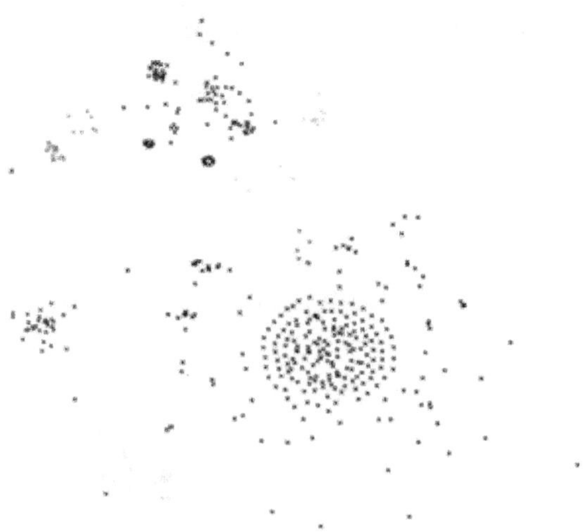

Figure 4.13 T-SNE projection of Attack-Malware matrix to 2-D space.

overcome the challenges that *K*-Means faces, I will use Latent Semantics Indexing (LSI; Rosario, 2000) to compute the similarity level for the attack pairs, and build a graph to connect similar attacks, and eventually apply SNAs to determine the clusters of similar attacks.

LSI is the application of a particular mathematical technique, called Single Value Decomposition or SVD, to a document-term matrix. SVD projects the original n-dimensional space (with n words in columns) onto a k-dimensional space, where k is much smaller than n. The projection then transforms a document's vector in n-dimensional space into a vector in the reduced k-dimensional space under the requirement that the Euclidean distance between the original matrix and the resulting matrix after transformation is minimized.

SVD decomposes the attack-malware matrix into three matrices, one of which defines the new dimensions in the order of significance. We call the new dimensions principal components. The components are ordered by the amount of explained variance in the original data. Let's call this matrix attack-component matrix. With the risk of losing some information, we can plot the attack data points on the 2-D space using the first and the second components just to illustrate the differences between data points, as shown in Figure 4.14. The vectors pointing to perpendicular directions are most different from each other.

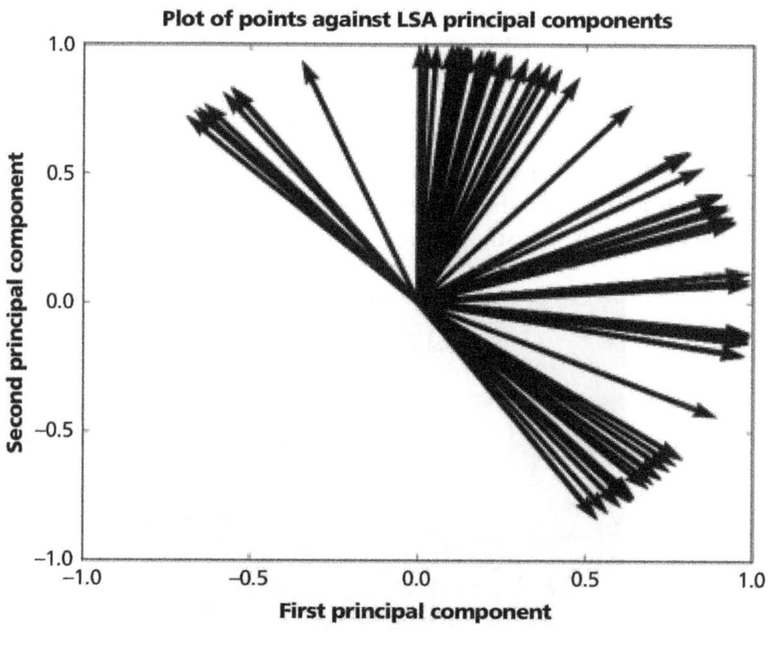

Figure 4.14 Attack data projected to the first and second principal components.

Attack	Similarity Score
From 118.193.241.192 on 2015-03-23	0.958453
From 222.186.190.157:56789 on 2015-03-23	0.996835
From 222.186.190.157:56789 on 2015-03-24	0.961000
From 117.21.176.79:333 on 2015-03-25	0.997087
From 222.186.190.157:56789 on 2015-03-25	0.946751
...	...
From 222.186.30.175:56789 on 2015-06-17	0.996835
From 61.160.247.42:1988 on 2015-06-17	0.996835
From 222.186.30.175:56789 on 2015-06-18	0.996835
From 61.160.247.42:1988 on 2015-06-18	0.996835

Figure 4.15 Attacks similar to attack from 61.160.212.21:5947 on 2015-03-23.

The similarity between attacks can be computed with the results of LSI, more specifically, by calculating the dot product of the attack-component matrix (Figure 4.15).

I connect two attacks if their similarity is above a certain threshold (e.g., 90%) and come up with a graph of connected attacks, shown in Figure 4.16.

There are a few big component subgraphs in the large graph. A component subgraph represents a group of attacks closely similar to each other. We can examine each of them in terms of what malware were deployed in the given attack group, what IP addresses were used, and how frequently the attacks were conducted.

I plotted the daily counts of attack for the two largest attack groups in Figure 4.17 and Figure 4.18. Both of them show that attacks happened more often on weekdays than on weekends. These attacks may have targeted different geo-located honeypots in the system and could be viewed as a widely expanded search for victims.

We can easily find out where those attackers' IPs were located (latitude and longitude), and the who-is data associated with the IPs. But it's much more difficult to fully investigate the true identity of the attackers.

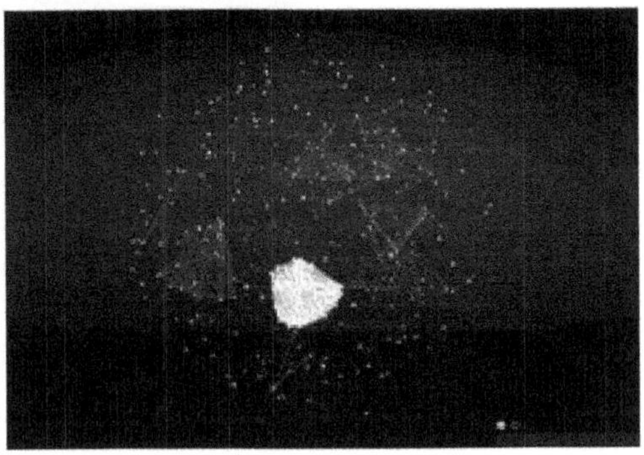

Figure 4.16 Visualization of attacks connected by similarity.

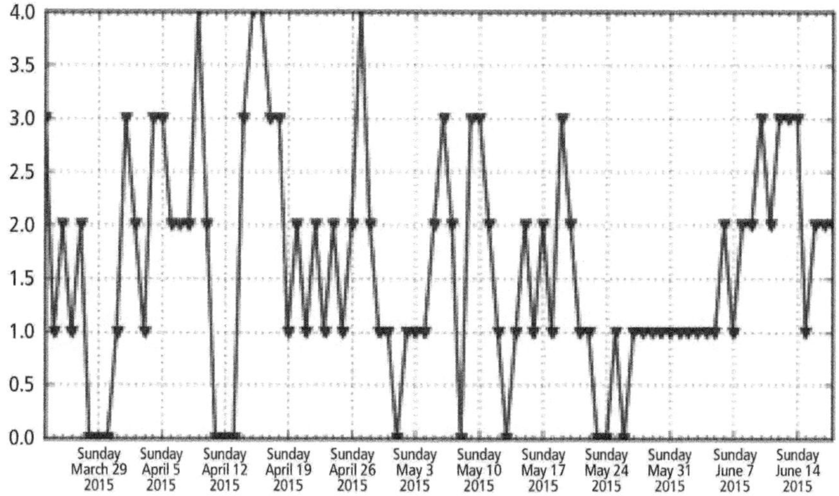

Figure 4.17 Daily counts of attack in one group.

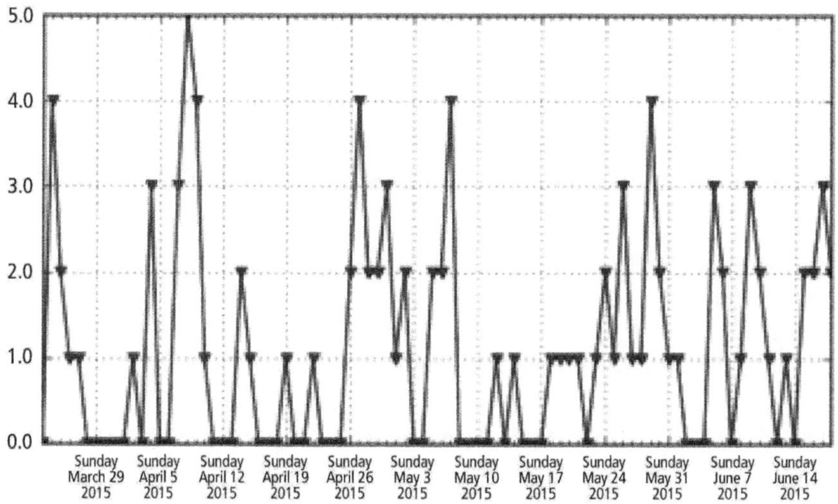

Figure 4.18 Daily counts of attack in another group.

SUMMARY

In this section, I explained how to apply data science techniques to identify honeypot attackers. Mathematically, I framed the problem as an Attack-Malware matrix, and used fuzzy hashing to represent files and compute the similarity between files. I then employed latent semantic indexing methods to calculate the similarity between attacks based on file similarity values. Finally, I constructed a network graph where similar attacks are linked so that I could apply SNAs to cluster the attacks.

REFERENCES

Antonakakis, M., Perdisci, R., Lee, W., Vasiloglou, N., & Dagon, D. (2011). Proceedings from USENIX Security Symposium: *Detecting malware domains at the upper DNS Hierarchy*. Berkeley, CA: University of California.

De Meo, P., Ferrara, E., Fiumara, G., & Provetti, A. (2011). Generalized louvain method for community detection in large networks. *Proceedings of the 11th International Conference on Intelligent Systems Design And Applications* (pp. 88–93). Ithaca, NY: Cornell University Library. doi:10.1109/ISDA.2011.6121636

Kirsch, A., & Mitzenmacher, M. (2008). *Less hashing, same performance: Building a better bloom filter.* Wiley InterScience. doi:10.1002/rsa.20208

Kornblum, J. (2006). Proceedings from the Digital Forensic Research Conference: *Identifying almost identical files using context triggered piecewise hashing.* Lafayette, IN.

Meer, H., & Slaviero, M. (2015, August 28). *Bring back the HoneyPots* [Video file]. Retrieved from https://www.youtube.com/watch?v=W7U2u-qLAB8

Rosario, B. (2000, Spring). *Latent Semantic Indexing: An overview.* Paper presented at INFOSYS 240.

van der Maaten, L., & Hinton, G. (2008). Visualizing data using t-SNE. *Journal of Machine Learning Research, 9*(November), 2575–2605.

Xiang, S., & Yang, J. (2012, December). Block-based image hashing with restricted blocking strategy for rotational robustness. *EURASIP Journal on Advances in Signal Processing.* doi:10.1186/1687-6180-2012-77

CHAPTER 5

ASSESSING LEARNER-DRIVEN CONSTRUCTS IN INFORMAL LEARNING ENVIRONMENTS

Synergies Created by the Nexus of Psychometrics, Learning Analytics, and Educational Data Mining

Lori C. Bland
George Mason University

In this chapter, I suggest that the processes and outcomes resulting from participation in informal learning environments (ILEs), including online informal learning environments (OILEs), are changed by the learner-driven nature of participation in such environments. I present a theoretical framework to understand and interpret the constructs embodied within all ILEs. I address key validity issues related to assessing learning and other constructs within such environments. I also suggest that a team science approach is necessary for meaningful examination, interpretation, and use of the data collected from all ILEs including the big data collected in OILEs.

Data Analytics and Psychometrics, pages 129–176

Results derived solely from operational definitions of constructs are difficult to interpret (Williams, 1999). Theory and methods from the learning, psychological, and pedagogical sciences and educational data mining, learning analytics, and computer science must be integrated to support research about learning in ILEs and OILEs. To develop these arguments, I will: (a) position educational and psychological theory and psychometric methods as integral to understanding processes and outcomes in ILEs and OILEs, (b) situate and define the concept of "learner-driven construct" within ILEs and OILEs, (c) develop a theoretical framework for assessment and data use, and (d) discuss the synergies created by a team science approach to develop measures and gather evidence of valid decision-making to support learners in ILEs and OILEs.

PROCESSES AND OUTCOMES IN INFORMAL LEARNING ENVIRONMENTS

We learn more outside of school than we do in school. Informal learning accounts for about 60% of our learning across the lifespan (Stevens, Bransford, & Stevens, 2005). Informal learning experiences can be transformative and memorable (Anderson & Gosselin, 2008; Brown, 2017). Informal learning has been shown to positively impact varied aspects of an individual's life, including cognition, metacognition, and interpersonal relationships, especially if that learning is acknowledged (Anderson & Thomas, 2014; Ehret & Hollett, 2016; Mezirow, 2000; Quintana & Morales, 2015; Stromquist, 2015; Thomas & Anderson, 2012). Understanding and assessing processes and outcomes related to informal learning is important, but can be challenging.

The key challenge is that the learner directs the nature, quantity, intensity, and quality of the participatory processes, products of engagement, and implicit and realized personal outcomes. This key challenge impacts all other challenges related to assessment of the learner and research on learning. The learner-driven nature of ILEs and OILEs also represents a philosophical challenge for assessment in ILEs and OILEs. Standardizing assessment of processes and outcomes may be considered antithetical to the nature of participation within all ILEs. How much does the act of observation change the observed and that which is observed, fundamentally impacting the informal nature of the environment?

The openness of ILE and OILE communities and the open-ended and nonlinear nature of individual and group participation within the communities represent additional challenges. Issues with data collection and missing data may impact valid interpretation of cognitive and non-cognitive process enactment (National Research Council [NRC], 2009; 2015b). For

OILEs, massive amounts of data can be generated impacting inferences drawn from the data or how the learner and other stakeholders use the data (Yang et al., 2015). Such challenges present an opportunity to consider a structure to (a) establish a theoretical framework to assess the learner-driven nature of the processes and outcomes within ILEs and OILEs, (b) gather validation evidence, and (c) choose appropriate analytical methods to draw valid inferences for learner data use.

Learner-Driven Constructs in Informal Learning Environments

Before defining a "learner-driven construct," I will draw on Taba's (1962) structure for concept development by (a) defining the concept of a construct, (b) explaining what a construct is not, (c) discussing the characteristics of a construct and types of constructs, (d) providing examples of constructs, and (e) drawing generalizations about constructs. Cronbach and Meehl (1955) defined a construct as "some postulated attribute of people, assumed to be reflected in test performance" (p. 283). Constructs are not concrete objects that can be observed through the senses. Rather, constructs are intangible experiences that describe the human condition. They are essentially defined by the philosopher, theoretician, or researcher. They can only be examined, defined, and discussed through indirect observation. Researchers have developed theory to understand and examine the processes and outcomes related to constructs. However, only inferences about constructs can be made from data collected, whether the data are small or big.

Constructs are important because they provide the means for us to think about, examine, understand, and make decisions about the cognitive and noncognitive characteristics, features, or qualities of individuals and groups. There are different types of constructs that are currently studied within the pedagogical, learning, and psychological sciences. Such constructs have been grouped into two categories: cognitive and noncognitive (Lipnevich et al., 2013). In fact, the National Assessment of Educational Progress ([NAEP]; National Center for Educational Statistics [NCES], 2017) and the Program for International Student Assessment ([PISA]; OECD, 2017) have begun to assess noncognitive skills at the national and international levels because of their potential impact on outcomes (Hayes, 2013). However, many constructs that are sometimes grouped within the noncognitive category clearly involve cognition, such as self-regulation (Zimmerman & Schunk, 2001). Therefore, noncognitive is an insufficient term because it implies that thought is not involved.

I propose that a more descriptive construct typology as discussed within the psychological and educational literature will be more useful for studying ILEs and OILEs. The constructs include: affect, conation, cognition, and executive function (ACCE). The ACCE construct groups more specifically describe the learner within the learner-driven nature of ILEs and OILEs. It important to note that the ACCE construct typology is not universally accepted. For example, 21st century skills have been classified as cognitive, intrapersonal, and interpersonal (NRC, 2012). However, 21st century skills focus on competencies necessary for the workforce. It is also important to note that constructs can be cross-categorical, such as self-regulation, having components within affect and executive function, for example. Therefore, researchers must clearly define the ACCE constructs.

All constructs define a phenomenon within the human experience. "A construct is some postulated attribute of people, assumed to be reflected in test performance" (Cronbach & Meehl, 1955, p. 283). A theoretical construct is the "postulated attribute" and is defined by the researcher both conceptually and operationally (Cronbach & Meehl, 1955). Conceptual definitions are grounded within extant theory and research. Within a given research study, the conceptual definition represents the researchers' vision of the construct (Boorsboom, 2005). The purpose for a conceptual definition or framework enables the researcher to interpret the data to better describe the human condition.

The operational definition of a construct is how the researcher will observe the construct (Boorsboom, 2005). Cronbach and Meehl (1955) reference the operational definition as "reflected in test performance" (p. 283). The researcher provides an operational definition to communicate precisely how a construct will be or was measured. Researchers utilize the operational definition to extend, clarify, or refine other researchers definitions and measures. Researchers must make decisions about the balance between theoretical construct fidelity and measure feasibility (McNeil, 2013). It is important to note that the "operational definition is not intended to be the ultimate statement of what a construct represents" (Williams, 1999, p. 414). As measures are crafted, researchers may shift the complexity/feasibility balance. Thus, operational definitions are only intended to represent that aspect of the construct that was measured.

Affect

Affective constructs are important to study because of their influence on formal and informal learning and performance outcomes (Boekerts, 1999; Boekaerts & Pekrun, 2016; D'Mello, 2013). Affect is defined as "that which arouses emotion rather than cognition or thought," "the resulting diffuse mental condition," and "the fundamental controlling element in an emotional state" (Izard, 2000, p.88). Attitudes, beliefs, emotions, interests, and values are examples of broad categories of affective constructs (McCoach, Gable, & Madura, 2013; Rokeach, 1968). An example of an affective construct that is a belief is self-efficacy. Bandura (1977) defined self-efficacy as "the conviction that one can successfully execute the behavior required to produce the outcomes" (p. 193). Self-efficacy is a widely researched construct because it is experienced within a specific domain (Bandura, 1977), such as math or programming self-efficacy (e.g., Parker, Marsh, Ciarrochi, Marshall, & Abduljabbar, 2014; Yukselturk & Altiok, 2017). Within ILEs, affective constructs may operate as an affordance for learners to make decisions to remain on a STEM pathway.

Understanding how affect operates within an ILE is important. Affective constructs can act as predictors of multiple types of outcomes, or can be considered as outcomes (McCoach et al., 2013; Stankov & Lee, 2014). For example, self-efficacy may act as a predictor of learning within an ILE, as an outcome of ILE participation, or both as a reciprocal relationship. ILE participation has been found to reinforce experiences within formal education (e.g., Carberry, Lee, & Ohland, 2010; Schaffer, Chen, Zhu, & Oakes, 2012). Bathgate and Schunn (2017) found that participation in a STEM ILE increased the value that participants placed on formal STEM experiences and attenuated decreases in STEM interest over time. However, affect is often overlooked within ILEs (Ehret & Hollett, 2016). Understanding the role of affective constructs within ILEs may contribute to engaging more students on a STEM trajectory including students from diverse populations on a STEM pathway (National Science Board, 2010).

Conation

Conation is defined as inclination, instinct, desire, drive, will, wish, or craving to perform an action purposefully (Militello, Gentner, Swindler, & Beisner, 2006). Conative constructs describe the inclinations and subsequent agentive functions of the mind. Conation is a historical term that has been difficult to define and has evolved to classify the striving mental activities (Corno, 2006; Hilgard, 1980; Mitello et al., 2006). McDougall (1923) used conation, a Latin word, "to denote the striving aspect of mental process" and acts "of willing or of resolving, choosing, striving, purposing" as conative mental activities (p. 266). Maslow (1943) suggested that the desire to know and understand were human needs and "are themselves conative, i.e., have a striving character," and are as much needed as safety or food (p. 385). Will, volition, and grit are examples of conative constructs (Duckworth, 2016; Huitt & Cain, 2005; Oettingen, Schrage, & Gollwitzer, 2016).

Conative constructs are important to study as conation explains variance in success in both FLEs and ILEs beyond those accounted for by intelligence or personality (Alsop & Watts, 1997; Duckworth, Peterson, Matthews, & Kelly, 2007).

Conative constructs are often cross-categorical to describe complex phenomena. Corno (2006) discussed the term "AFFCON" (p. 262) to represent constructs that included both affective and conative components. For example, Richard Snow's work with aptitude addressed affect, conation, and cognition (Stanford Aptitude Seminar, 2002). Grit is another example of an "AFFCON." Grit includes passion, an affective construct, and perseverance, a conative construct (Duckworth, 2016). William James (1890) contended, "a strictly voluntary act has to be guided by an idea, perception, and volition throughout its whole course" (p. 115). Thus, the voluntary nature of participation in ILEs and OILEs necessitates examination of conative constructs.

Cognition

Cognition is the "acquisition, storage, transformation, and use of knowledge" and includes multiple mental processes (Matlin & Farmer, 2016, p. 2). Cognition includes those functions that are typically attributed to learning about the world through perception and experience. Cognition involves memory, knowledge, understanding, language, and thinking, such as judgment, reasoning, and problem solving (Reisberg, 2016). Examples of cognitive processes include summarizing and organizing information, identifying patterns in information, and deriving meaning from that information (Ormrod, 2017). Examples of broad categories of cognitive constructs include ability, aptitude, achievement, and creativity (Williams, 1999).

Ability is a common term and is often confused with other constructs. Carroll (1993) contended that ability is a "conceptual primitive," and is often undefined in research (p. 3). Ability is used to characterize attributes of human individuals and "refers to the possible variations over individuals in the liminal levels of task difficulty (or in derived measurements based on such liminal levels) at which, on any given occasion in which all conditions appear favorable, individuals perform successfully on a defined class of tasks" (Carroll, 1993, p. 8). Historically, ability has been considered to be the result of nature rather than nurture, and was often operationalized on measures of intelligence as verbal and mathematical ability. Spatial ability has recently been researched as an intellectual ability (Lubinsky & Kell, 2017). Ability is often measured within FLEs for placement purposes, such as placement within special education or gifted programs.

Aptitudes are all the characteristics that an individual integrates in a useful manner to perform in a given scenario, such as readiness to learn, ability, knowledge, experience, motivation, and regulatory processes (Shavelson et al., 2002; Snow, 1992). Thus, in Snow's conception, aptitude is cross-categorical encompassing all of the ACCE constructs. Examples of an aptitude test include the Iowa Algebra Aptitude Test™, 5th ed. ([IAAT]; Schoen & Ansley, 2006) and the Mechanical Aptitude Test ([Form MAT-3-C]; Ramsay, 2015). The purpose for the IAAT is as a decision-making tool related to secondary math placement (Schoen & Ansley, 2006). The purpose for the MAT-3-C is to evaluate the mechanical skills of job applicants related to work production and maintenance, hand and power tools, household objects, and school science and physics (Ramsay, 2015). Aptitude measures are often given in formal contexts and are used to measure proclivities and learning from informal learning experiences to make predictions about future performance (Cohen, Swerdlik, & Sturman, 2013).

Achievement is a construct that is most often examined within FLEs (Cohen et al., 2013). Achievement addresses acquisition, retention, recall, and understanding of domain knowledge and application of domain skills, typically within formal education, as demonstrated via academic performance such as grades or GPA (York, Gibson, & Rankin, 2015). Thus, in FLEs, learning is often operationalized as a given achievement measure.

Kuh and colleagues (2006) identified academic success within higher education as a broader construct that included cognitive outcomes (academic achievement; attainment of educational outcomes; and acquisition of content knowledge, skills, and competencies), and affective and conative behaviors and outcomes (persistence, engagement, and satisfaction), as well as, performance post-graduation (Kuh, Kinzie, Buckley, Bridges, & Hayek, 2006). Much research on academic achievement exists and meta-analyses and research syntheses have been conducted to develop more sophisticated understandings of achievement and its predictors (e.g., Berkowitz, Moore, Astor, & Benbenishty, 2016; Fan, Xu, Cai, He, & Fan, 2017).

Within content domains, constructs, such as numeracy in mathematics (NRC, 1990) or comprehension in reading (Snow, 2002) are deconstructed into more specific knowledge and skills. The knowledge and skills are typically measured formally in FLEs using standards-based, standardized assessments at defined grade levels, such as via the Partnership for Assessment of Readiness for College and Careers (PARCC, 2017) to measure the Common Core Standards (National Governors Association Center for Best Practices, Council of Chief State School Officers, 2010). Norm-referenced measures may be used to rank student achievement in comparison to the norm-referenced sample. Standardized assessment means that the administrative procedures and conditions under which a measure is given and the reporting procedures are standardized for all test-takers (Cohen et al., 2013). Informal assessment within FLEs is not standardized and includes formative assessments, such as quizzes or homework and summative assessments, such as a unit test or project. Teachers typically base their grades on informal assessments that they administer within a classroom (Brookhart & Nitko, 2015). Cognitive measures address a broad range of constructs and content. It is important to understand the role of cognitive constructs in relation to the other ACCE constructs in ILEs and OILEs. However, for ILEs and OILEs, I suggest that learning or aptitude be considered as the primary constructs assessed, rather than achievement of ability.

Executive Constructs

For this chapter, I suggest the executive constructs include, but are not limited to self-regulation (e.g., Zimmerman & Schunk, 2001), metacognition (e.g., Schraw, 1998), and executive function (e.g., Baggetta & Alexander, 2016). In a cogent review of the literature on executive function within academics, cognitive abilities, human performance, and social functioning, Bagetta and Alexandar (2016) analyzed the conceptual and operational definitions of executive function, extracted key common features across the research, characterized areas of divergence across conceptual models, and identified goals for moving the field forward. They defined executive function as "a set of cognitive processes that (a) guide action and behaviors essential to aspects of learning and everyday human performance tasks; (b) contribute to the monitoring or regulation of such tasks; and (c) pertain not only to the cognitive domain, but also socioemotional and behavioral domains of human performance" (Bagetta & Alexander, 2016, p. 24). They found that a small portion of the studies considered executive function to be developmental.

Researchers have conceptualized executive function as either a direct or indirect relationship to outcomes. For direct relationships, executive function was conceptualized as cognition, such as general cognitive processes or domain-specific strategies contributing to academic outcomes, such as mathematics (Cragg & Gilmore, 2014). For indirect relationships, executive function was conceptualized as a self-regulatory process. In both types of studies, executive function was considered to be a multidimensional construct. Attention, working memory, and inhibitory control were components studied by most researchers, though other executive functions exist (Bagetta & Alexander, 2006; Miyake et al., 2000).

Whether conceptualized as a direct or indirect relationship, executive function has been shown to play a key role in outcomes related to academics, social functioning, human performance, and cognitive abilities (Bagetta & Alexander, 2016; Ballhausen et al., 2017; Biernacki et al., 2013; Ma, Ma, Chen, Ran, & Zhang, 2017; Ribner et al., 2016). Bagetta and Alexander (2016) clearly outlined the need for precision in conceptual and operational definitions of executive function. For example, conceptual definitions of executive function, self-regulation, and metacognition overlapped and need to be differentiated in future research (Bagetta & Alexander, 2016; Dinsmore, Alexander, & Loughlin, 2008).

Bagetta and Alexander (2016) also found a clear lack of clarity with operational definitions of executive function. Across the 106 studies included in their review, they identified 109 different instruments. For most of the studies, the psychometric properties of the instruments was either not reported or insufficient, which undermined the validity of the inferences drawn from those studies. Further, due to the complex conceptual nature of executive function, many measures suffered from "task impurity," in which a single task was used to measure multiple processes (McNeil, 2013; Miyake et al., 2000). Task impurity is addressed by aligning a task to a process, which if done properly can increase the validity of the inferences drawn from the data. Thus, more work is needed for clear conceptual definitions of the constructs examined, as well as, measures that are developed in advance of data collection for ILEs and OILEs.

Constructs provide the means to describe, group, explain, predict, and understand patterns and variability in the human condition. A conceptual framework can provide an organizational and interpretive framework for the researcher to examine how the ACCE constructs are embodied and inter-related within ILEs and OILEs. Investigating how the ACCE constructs vary for learners within and between ILEs and OILEs is important. In addition, it is important to understand how the ACCE constructs vary uniquely for each learner at a given point in time, longitudinally, and by environment in order to develop adaptable, personal learning trajectories. Understanding how the ACCE constructs function as processes, outcomes, or processes that develop into outcomes (Bland, Hjalmarson, Nelson, & Samaras, 2017; Hayes, 2013; NRC, 2015b). Thus, a clear conceptual framework derived from theory coupled with precise operational definitions as related to the learner-driven nature of the processes and outcomes within ILEs and OILEs can improve assessment development, validation evidence, and improve data use for learners.

LEARNING AS THE PRIMARY CONSTRUCT

The primacy of the learning construct in ILEs and OILEs, rather than the achievement construct, represents a fundamental difference between ILEs and FLEs as learner-driven, rather than standards-, textbook-, or teacher-driven. Multiple theories have been developed to attempt to describe the learning phenomenon.[1] Mayer (2011) defined learning as a "change in knowledge attributable to experience" (p. 14). For Mayer, knowledge encompasses beliefs, as well as, more traditional conceptions, such as facts, concepts, procedures, and strategies. Knowledge changes cannot be observed directly. Rather, they can be inferred from assessment data. Learning occurs due to an interaction with the environment.

FLE philosophies have been historically grounded within behaviorism and cognitivism. Constructivism, a cognitivist theory, has posited that the learner is primary in creating meaning (O'Donnell, 2012). Constructivism has dominated formal schooling (Jones & Brader-Araje, 2002), and gave rise to the demand for more authentic assessment of student learning (Wiggins, 1993).

However, the requirements defined by the standards movement have bounded and regulated learning and standardized assessment of prescribed outcomes. The formal educational system has developed a plethora of standards, curricula, materials, tools, and instructional strategies to help students achieve the defined outcomes at the minimal passing level. In addition, the environmental pathways in which curricula and instruction are delivered, the participants within each pathway (or grade level), and the timeline for outcome acquisition have also been legislated or defined through policy. Achievement within K–12 FLEs is situated within expectations as defined by federal, state, and local institutional policy, as well as, resource constraints. The nature of achievement is directed by content standards and curricula. Achievement quantity is determined by accountability tests. Achievement quality is influenced by the instruction and other teacher traits (e.g., Hattie, 2009). The achievement timeline is constrained by the school year and corresponding accountability test timeline. The student's peer group is defined by state law for year of entry into kindergarten, with students expected to maintain their age-grade level throughout schooling. Finally, teacher assignment is defined by the principal and licensure and certification. The student has very little opportunity for choice within FLEs. The formal schooling system, the actors implementing the rules and instruction, and the students and their parents operate under a defined set of parameters and constraints, under which the student constructs meaning. Within FLEs, learning is clearly bounded by predefined expectations about achievement.

Achievement is most clearly bounded by the age of the child, not the sophistication of the knowledge acquired or the proficiency of skills demonstrated at any given time. The underlying assumption of age level grouping is that students of a given age are considered and expected to possess similar cognitive, executive, conative, affective, and behavioral characteristics and abilities. Within formal schooling, students are required to complete in-class and homework assignments, pass tests, and score with a certain level of proficiency on minimal competency examinations.

Variations in proficiency levels and scores are addressed in FLEs via supportive programs for students who have not acquired all of the knowledge and skills expected at a given grade level, such as services for students with special needs. For example, response to intervention (Fuchs & Fuchs, 2006) was a relatively recent development to prevent large numbers of students from being retained in a grade level given accountability requirements and the negative outcomes associated with grade retention (Huddleston, 2014). Transitional programs have provided flexibility in age/grade level requirements to support early childhood students, producing positive outcomes for literacy, numeracy, problem-solving, and self-regulation (Maniates, 2016; Manship et al., 2017). Thus, some supports exist for students who need extra time or practice.

Less support exists for advanced students. Acceleration for advanced students is rarely an option (Colangelo, Assouline, & Gross, 2004). Instead, school systems generally opt to retain students at their age-grade level, with limited programming despite research indicating greater proximal and distal affective and cognitive gains by participating in all day programs (Cornell, Delcourt, Goldberg, & Bland, 1994; Delcourt, Cornell, & Goldberg, 2007). Further, African American students, students with English as a second language, students with special needs, poor students, and rural students have historically been denied access to advanced programming (Aud, Fox, & KewalRamani, 2010). Within FLEs, the upper limits of achievement are bounded by age, especially for those students who need less practice and more challenge. ILEs and OILEs may support acquisition of advanced processes and outcomes for broader communities of learners.

The Nature of Learning Within Informal Learning Environments

ILEs existed for many centuries long before formal schooling and pedagogical structures were created. Stevens, Bransford, and Stevens (2005) estimated that individuals have spent more than 60% of their lives engaged in ILEs across the lifespan. For children, researchers estimated that about 80% of their waking hours are engaged in nonschool activities in which learning occurs implicitly and informally (Bransford et al., 2006b; National Research Council, 2000). Within ILEs, individuals can learn either implicitly or explicitly (Bransford et al., 2006a). Implicit learning is unconscious. Individuals observe and grasp patterns of "critical covariations" in the environment to develop representational or abstract knowledge and complex skills (Reber, 1989, p. 233) Implicit learning controls behavior and supports adaptation to new environments without awareness by listening, observing, and interacting with the objects and people encountered" (Bransford et al., 2006a, p. 20). Informal, implicit learning underlies everyday STEM learning (NRC, 2009). However, it is often difficult to deconstruct implicit outcomes from explicit informal learning due to the complex environments and dynamic nature of ILEs and OILEs.

Informal learning environments

ILE and OILE participatory structures are voluntary, bounded by choices designed into the environment (as with FLE design). However, unlike FLEs the learner makes decisions about the nature, quantity, and quality of participation. The learner also makes decisions about the processes engaged and the outcomes of participation. Designed ILEs and OILEs, such as STEM competitions and the Scratch computing community, provide explicit opportunities for learning that is not bounded in the same manner as FLEs.

There are many types of ILEs and OILEs, though they vary in the design of delivery structures. For example, museums provide changing thematic exhibits (NRC, 2009). Other ILEs are project- or problem-based, such as STEM competitions. The IAM3D Challenge (American Society of Mechanical Engineers, 2017) provides participants with a problem to solve by using 3D printing, given rules and constraints. Means, Bakia, and Murphy (2014) identified several types of interest-driven online learning, such as curiosity-based episodic learning, entertainment-based learning, and several categories of improvement-based learning. The nature of learning may be incidental to a problem encountered or may involve sustained participation in the community (Chowdury, Cameron, Blanehard, & Johri, 2015; Gelman, Beckley, Johri, Yang, & Domeniconi, 2016; Johri, 2016). Thus, learning is situated within the nature of the ILE.

Thorough discussions of several types of informal learning spaces, such as museums, out-of-school experiences, and maker-spaces have helped to define how processes and outcomes are examined within these types of ILEs (e.g., Halverson & Sheridan, 2014; National Research Council [NRC], 2009, 2015b). Compelling characteristics of ILEs that have demonstrated sustained learning changes have included: activities to cognitively, affectively, and socially engage participants; responsiveness to participants prior experiences, interests, and cultural identities; and support for connections across ILEs, FLEs, and the home. Importantly, the characteristics the learner brought to the ILE were critical for success (NRC, 2015b). These findings lend support to the conceptualization of the ACCE constructs as learner-driven.

The making, solving, and doing communities have become increasingly popular types of learner-driven communities and include the maker movement, competitions, or service learning. The making, doing, and solving communities develop products or solve compelling problems, often within a team. Halverson and Sheridan (2014) defined the maker movement as "the growing number of people who are engaged in the creative production of artifacts in their daily lives and who find physical and digital forums to share their processes and products with others" (p. 496).

They provide a thorough review of the origins of the maker movement, describing how the maker movement and project- and problem-based learning share similar origins within constructionism. Harel and Papert (1991) defined constructionism by building on constructivism, that is learners build knowledge structures by active engagement with hands-on (i.e., a sand castle) or minds-on experiences (i.e., development of a new theory). The Scratch programming language is an extension of Papert's pedagogy (Resnick et al., 2009). However, understanding the processes and outcomes and developing assessments associated with intensive, problem-based ILEs, such as engineering competitions, or OILEs, such as the Scratch community, are nascent.

Scratch is an online learning community initially developed for children to understand and practice the underlying logic of coding.

> Scratch is a programming language and online community where you can create your own interactive stories, games, and animations—and share your creations with others around the world. In the process of designing and programming Scratch projects, young people learn to think creatively, reason systematically, and work collaboratively. Scratch is a project of the Lifelong Kindergarten group at the MIT Media Lab. It is available for free at http://scratch.mit.edu (https://scratch.mit.edu/info/faq#permissions, "Liscensing and Permissions," para. 3)

While participants are not required to post their products, more than 24 million projects have been posted. Participants may also make their code available for others' reuse, known as "remixing" (Hill & Monroy-Hernández, 2013).

The Scratch environment, as with other designed, informal learning structures, are participant-focused and navigated at the discretion of the learner (NRC, 2009). The "sandbox" environment provides opportunities to learn and practice coding and create, share, and remix work. A programming sandbox can be a very effective, motivating, and safe learning environment to learn programming, experiment with creative ideas, and improve design and performance (Chao, 2016; Majgaard, 2014). The design of the Scratch environment allows the learner to increase the complexity of the engagement, the processes used, and the quantity of outcomes enacted by the learner. Learners have control over the frequency and duration of participation, as well as, their actions during participation. For each engagement event, the learner has the opportunity to make multiple types of decisions. In Scratch, the learner decides on the content of learning, the amount of self-instruction needed, the type of product developed, the timeline for product development, the degree of participation in the community, and the nature, quantity, and quality of continued engagement.

Learning within ILEs and OILEs that are making, solving, or doing extend the characteristics of project- and problem-based learning within

FLEs. Problems or projects are multidimensional within ILEs and OILEs, such as based on the level of structure and complexity (Jonassen & Hung, 2015), authenticity, time, materials, and space needed. That is, the learner or group must structure the learning, design, problem solving, and product spaces in order to address the problem or to provide a product (Chowdhury, Kusano, Johri, & Sharma, 2014; Hung, Jonassen, & Liu, 2008; Lehmann, Christensen, Du, & Thrane, 2008). FLEs and ILEs that used problem-based learning within different types of learning environments, such as capstone experiences and undergraduate research opportunities within engineering, identified different outcomes and different intensities of similar outcomes across different learning environments on a common measure (e.g., Pierrakos, Borrego, & Lo, 2007; Pierrakos, Borrego, & Lo, 2008). Thus, it is important to understand why learners experience different outcomes across different learning environments.

The moment to moment decision-making process of a learner within an ILE or OILE may be an important construct to examine. Examining decision-making implies an understanding of the learners cognitions, such as their evaluations of the parameters examined to make a final decision. Understanding the cognitions would supplement studies of choice behavior (e.g., Shwartz & Arena, 2013). Decision-making within an ILE or OILE requires learner agency. Agency within ILEs is an ACCE process which can be examined within a situated learning framework. Clapp, Ross, Ryan, and Tishman (2017) discussed agency as choice, intention, and action. Agency is part of the striving nature that sustains the individual's or group's capacity to solve problems and to create or reconstruct ideas and activities, identities and relationships, and tools and materials. Agency operates within a sociocultural context that propels individuals or groups to act in order to meet goals that will change some aspect of themselves, the group, or the intended environment over time (Ahearn, 2001; Barton & Tan, 2010; Damşa, Kirschner, Andriessen, Erkens, & Sins, 2010; Maslow, 1954; Moje & Lewis, 2007; Rappa & Tang, 2016; Scardamalia & Berieter, 2014). Children as young as kindergarten have been found to be agentive, self-directed, and self-regulated (Spector-Levy, Basilio, Zachariou, & Whitebread, 2017; Spink, Danby, Mallon, & Butler, 2010). Other ACCE cross-categorical constructs are also important, such as self-regulation and metacognition. However, agency addresses the voluntary nature of the initial engagement decision and sustained engagement decisions. Thus, both the voluntary and situative nature of the learning processes and outcomes within ILEs and OILEs compels examination of these constructs as learner-driven.

Situated Learning

Situated learning extends behaviorism, cognitivism, and experiential learning theory which are singly insufficient to describe the nature of learning within ILEs and OILEs (Johri, Olds, & O'Connor, 2014). Johri and colleagues (2014) provided a cogent analysis and synthesis of learning theories, differentiating situated learning from behaviorism and cognitivism. Situated learning has historical roots in environmental and or experiential learning, but is insufficient to describe all aspects of learning within ILEs (e.g., Harel & Papert, 1991; Vygotsky, 1978). Learning is situated within the activities and participatory interactions in which learners are engaged (Lave & Wenger, 1999). Learning is mediated by the symbolic representations, tools used, and artifacts created within the social and material context of the environment (Greeno & Hall, 1997; Johri & Olds, 2014; Pea, 1993). Thus, situated learning theory extends the individual's creation of meaning to understand how learning is mediated by participatory interactions within a learning community or the activities or objects within an environment.

Situated learning theory can be used as a theoretical framework to understand how the ACCE constructs function and are integrated within ILEs and OILEs. For example, ILEs have been found to encourage engagement, facilitate identity formation, and support metacognitive reflection (Johri, Olds, & O'Connor, 2014; Scribner & Cole, 1973; Xu, Bland, Kusano, & Johri, 2017). Communities of practice have mediated identity formation, supported learning trajectories, and facilitated expertise development (Carbonell, Stalmeijer, Konings, Segers, & Merrienboer, 2014; Dall'Alba, 2009; Hill & Monroy-Hernandez, 2013; Kusano, 2014; Kusano & Johri, 2014; Kusano & Johri, 2015; Teo & Johri, 2014). Situated learning theory provides a framework to examine the collaborative nature of learning and the nature of how a problem or project shapes the learner-driven processes and outcomes within ILEs and OILEs.

Learner-Driven Constructs

A learner-driven construct is an ACCE construct, in which the learner makes the decisions about the nature, quality, quantity, and intensity of the processes and outcomes within an ILE or OILE. The learner is agentive about learning needs and how to meet those needs within an ILE. The learner structures the participation and determines the degree of engagement in exploration, the duration of practice, problem-solving procedures, the nature of product development, and quality control. The learner determines the degree of interaction with the learning community, the activities, and the objects and tools as situated within the ILE. The learner determines personal goals and whether a goal ranges from mild curiosity to self-actualization. The learner may also contribute to community goals. In essence, the learner makes the instructional and learning decisions that are typically decided by others within an FLE. Thus, learner decision-making defines the nature of the ACCE constructs and their relationships to each other.

Agency and decision-making in learner-driven ILEs and OILEs create complexities when examining processes and outcomes. One set of challenges is related to the participants. ILE participants are essentially a sample who volunteer to participate in the intervention. Volunteer samples represent a sampling bias affecting external validity (Johnson & Christensen, 2017). Rosenthal and Rosnow (2009) identified 17 characteristics on which volunteer and non volunteer samples differed, determining that volunteers were more advantaged and privileged. Ill-defined populations can impact the reliability of inferences drawn from the data (National Academies of Sciences, Engineering, and Medicine [NASEM], 2017; NRC, 2015b). Thus, sampling nonparticipants who could have elected to participate on the ACCE constructs may lead to greater insights about learner characteristics and participation barriers.

The size, participation rate, demographics, or level of anonymity in the data may not have been identified or selected by the researcher in advance of participation within the ILE or OILE. The researcher may not be able to determine the population to be studied a priori to the intervention based on population demographics. For an OILE, the level of anonymity in the data limits the ability to draw inferences about the characteristics of a given population as traditionally defined, such as fourth graders. Anonymity also limits use of known demographic learning moderators, such as socioeconomic status. For example, within the Scratch community, the population consists of all Scratch users, which is comprised of multiple groups, varying by demographic characteristics such as age and location, as well as, knowledge, skills, and abilities. A Scratch sample may be defined based on an outcome, such as featured projects. Thus, participant decision-making defines the researched population. The blindness to demographics may act as an affordance for fairness in examining products. However, such blindness may also continue to serve as a barrier to historically underserved populations if opportunity is denied, but remains hidden.

Different learning experiences within ILEs and OILEs may lead to variation in processes and outcomes (NRC, 2015b). Participant decision-making also defines the learning processes and outcomes within the learning experiences. Therefore, the learner's underlying decisions must be examined. Understanding the nature of individual variation may lead to fuller understanding of processes and outcomes. Outcomes vary within and across ILEs making assessment of processes and outcomes challenging (NRC, 2009).

Applying Psychometric Theory and Methods to Informal Learning Environments

Researchers have spent more than 100 years developing theory, measures, and procedures to examine learning and other outcomes using tests and psychological measures within the context of schooling. Assessment development requirements have changed to improve the properties of the assessment, such as the manner in which questions are posed to students (Downing & Haladyna, 2009; Haladyna & Rodriguez, 2013) and methods for scale development and validation (DeVellis, 2017; Dmitrov, 2012). Psychometric analyses have also evolved, such as improving how reliability is examined (e.g., Briesch, Swaminathan, Welsh, & Chafouleas, 2014; Deng & Chan, 2016; Stemler, 2004) or how tests are equated (Kolen & Brennan, 2004). Such procedures ensure that the inferences made about individuals and groups are based on reliable data and that the decisions made from those inferences are valid.

Validity theory has also continued to evolve. Validity theory focuses on the inferences made about the learner from the data and the use of the data to make decisions about the learner, the learning group, the instructor, or the intervention based on evidence gathered from multiple sources. Multiple frameworks have been developed to support new understandings of validity, increasingly complex constructs, assessment of higher level thinking skills, and demand for quality in assessment development, scoring, and reporting (e.g., American Educational Research Association [AERA], American Psychological Association [APA], & National Council on Measurement in Education [NCME], 2014; Benson, 1998; Kane, 2008; Lissitz & Samuelsen, 2008; Messick, 1994). The research and statistical procedures providing evidence for validity have worked well within the PK20+ FLE. However, these frameworks are grounded within cognitivist theories of learning and are focused on identifying evidence related to predefined outcomes, in a prescribed learning environment on predefined expectations for knowledge and skills attained. It's important to consider whether or how the frameworks apply to measurement in ILEs and OILEs.

Measuring Constructs

Measures of the mind can only be obtained through indirect observation of a sample within a universe of possibilities. For example, individual items on a test represent only a sample of the content domain. For achievement measures, summed scores are calculated, and that summed score and the relationship to the items within the summed score is used to ensure that enough consistent observations have occurred to obtain reliable data about knowledge and skills (Cohen et al., 2013). Underlying those items are latent traits or constructs that are presumed to be measured (Dmitrov, 2012). In psychological testing, these traits are comprised of the theorized components of the construct to be measured, such as the MSLQ which measures cognitive strategy use and self-regulation as the latent traits (Pintrich & DeGroot,

1990). In educational assessment, the latent traits are typically components of the measured achievement. For example, the content domain is deconstructed into isolated knowledge and skills. Variations of diagnostic modeling have been used to identify underlying traits consisting of subordinate skills (e.g., Rupp & Templin, 2010; Tatsuoka, 2002; Tatsuoka, 2009).

An example is computational thinking, which is an analytical problem solving approach using computing concepts, such as symbolic abstractions of time and space in order to design complex systems or represent human behavior (Wing, 2006; 2008). Different measures of computational thinking have deconstructed the construct into different aspects, such as abstract thinking, computational modeling, debugging skills, logic, problem solving, or use of algorithms (Chowdhury, Cameron, Blanchard, & Johri, 2015; Fields, Searle, Kafai, & Min, 2012; Weintrop et al., 2014; Werner, Denner, Campe, & Kawamoto, 2012). However, Grover and Pea (2013) contended that there is a gap in the research related to examining such constructs within a situated learning framework. Their contention implies that the constructs are not only impacted by the learner, but also, by the design of the environment. Therefore, an assessment framework must address the learner-directed nature of the construct and its situativity in order to fully understand how the constructs function together to support learner processes and outcomes.

Multiple types of latent trait analyses exist. In educational and psychological testing, principal component analysis is used to reduce the number of latent traits (Tabachnik & Fidell, 2013). Several different factor analytic techniques may be used to understand the factors within the construct and whether they are aligned with the proposed theory or the underlying cognitive traits tested (Dmitrov, 2012). Thus, in factor analysis, the measure is examined to determine whether the items are interpreted by the participants in the manner in which the researcher or tester intended. For learner-driven constructs, it is important that the researcher interpret the data as the learner intended. Thus, understanding the response processes of the learner is a critical validation step for assessments used within ILEs.

Design for Assessment, Analyses, and Data Use for Informal Learning

Assessing processes and outcomes is complex within ILEs (NRC, 2015b). Several issues must be addressed. First, the ACCE constructs need to be assessed to represent the learner-driven nature of the ILE or OILE, including assessment events that occur at multiple points along the personal learning trajectory. Second, assessment must be administered in a manner consistent with the environment and activity. Third, the results must be communicated back to the learner for use by the learner, so that the learner receives a benefit from the assessment. The learner should be considered as the primary stakeholder of the data. These are minimal requirements to ensure that the assessment will not contaminate the characteristics of the ILE or OILE, have no negative impact on subsequent participation, and not attenuate positive effects. Ideally, the assessment might even contribute to future performance, which can be studied.

Learners can benefit from assessment. Roediger, Putnam, and Smith (2011) reviewed the research on the direct and indirect effects of testing and identified several cognitive benefits of testing. For example, learners retrieve more information during testing than the assessed content. In addition, testing provides an opportunity for the learner to focus on tested material, which can potentially support knowledge organization (e.g., Roedinger et al., 2011; Szpunar, McDermott, & Roedinger, 2007; Zaromb & Roedinger, 2010). Retrieval during assessment reinforces retention and subsequent retrieval (e.g., Thompson, Wenger, & Bartling, 1978). Assessment improves subsequent learning, knowledge transfer, and metacognitive monitoring (Ackerman & Leiser, 2013; Rohrer, Taylor, & Sholar, 2010; Szpunar, McDermott, & Roedinger, 2008; Thomas, Finn, & Jacoby, 2015). In a meta-analysis of testing effect studies, Rowland (2014) indicated that effortful processing requiring recall of information, such as prompted within an authentic assessment of performance, produced greater benefits for the examinee than assessments requiring recognition. Within OILEs, assessment can also provide learners with immediate feedback to identify misunderstandings or gaps in knowledge (Feng, Heffernan, & Koedinger, 2009). For ILEs in general, assessment may support retention, reinforce content and skills learned in FLEs, support learning transfer, and may contribute to the development of adaptive expertise (Bransford, 2007; Litzinger, Lattuca, Hadgraft, & Newstetter, 2011). Therefore, the benefits to assessment within ILEs and OILEs may outweigh the consequences, if designed and administered properly.

Within ILEs and OILEs, assessment poses multiple challenges due to the personal nature of the processes and outcome trajectory. Research is nascent related to learner decisions underlying choice of processes, behaviors, or products within ILEs and OILEs. Assessments of the ACCE constructs could be delivered prior to participation, during sense-making, then at multiple decision points, such as during practice, help-seeking, independent research, collaboration, and product development. In addition, the assessments need to mirror the structure of the activities and complexity of tasks within the environment (Hung et al., 2008). Longitudinal assessment can offer insight about how ILEs and OILEs contribute to attainment of formal learning standards, workplace competencies, career success, and other lifelong goals.

Assessments should be authentic. That is, they should mirror the experiences within the environment. Assessment should also address the situated nature of the learning within the environment by capturing key aspects of the environment, such as those that promote learner engagement (Gomez & Lee, 2015; Kearney, 2013; NRC, 2009). The assessment should be unobtrusive and occur naturally within the ILE, such as "stealth" assessments (Allen, 2002; Martin, 2004; NRC, 2015b; Shute & Kim, 2014). Stealth assessments are embedded within a game, for example, with performance data gathered over the course of the game (Shute, Ventura, Bauer, & Zapata-Rivera, 2009). Adaptive and dynamic assessments can offer a personalized assessment for learners at a given competency level (Davey, Pitoniak, & Slater, 2016; Huebner, 2010; Passig, Tzuriel, & Eshel-Kedmi, 2016). Schwartz and Arena (2013) contended that examining choice leads to discovery of the effect. Choice-based assessments act as stealth assessments by examining the selection behavior of learners as they attempt to uncover hidden patterns. Machine learning algorithms are used to identify patterns in the selection behavior. However, the drawbacks of such assessments is that they do not examine the evaluative criteria or underlying decision-making processes of the choice behavior. Many types assessments have been developed to measure a variety of outcomes in ILE (e.g., Lemke, Lecusay, Cole, & Michalchik, 2015; PEAR, 2017). A close examination of developed assessments is necessary to identify their psychometric properties, such as evidence of validity and reliability.

One of the most important aspects of any assessment is that learner assessment data must be useful to the learner. For example, within OILEs, such as game- or simulation-based learning environments, learners receive formative feedback (e.g., Gibson, 2007). Computer-based assessments have provided formative and summative feedback within FLEs, showing gains in student outcomes (Shute & Ramani, 2017). It may be important for researchers to assess processes, outcomes, and longitudinal impact of participation in ILEs and OILE. Researchers may need to consider how assessment in ILEs and OILEs may contribute to unintended, negative outcomes.

Integrated Framework to Examine Processes and Outcomes Within ILEs and OILEs

In ILEs, learning is not bounded by the data that could be collected. However, it is bounded by the inferences made from the data. The theoretical framework integrates four models that address the ACCE constructs, assessment, data analysis, and use processes within ILEs and OILEs. The assessment model is based on evidence-centered design ([ECD]; Mislevy, Almond, & Lukas, 2003). The analytical model relies on a range of psychometric, educational data mining, and learning analytic methods based on the purpose for the assessment and the research questions. The use processes are reinforced with a data-driven decision-making model, with the learner as the primary data user.

Examining the ACCE Constructs

The NRC (2009) created a "conceptual tool for organizing and assessing science learning" across FLEs and ILEs consisting of six strands to describe the learners' experiences within ILEs (p. 4). These strands address the learner from a cognitive, social, developmental, and affective perspective and address learner: (a) interest, motivation, and excitement; (b) cognitive skills applied in learning; (c) exploration, experimentation skills, and analytical skills for sense-making; (d) metacognition about the learner's own processes and epistemologies about science; (e) participation in science communities, praxis, and activities; and (f) identity within science communities. These strands are useful when considering the ACCE constructs as situated within an ILE or OILEs

However, the conceptual framework of the strands needs to be extended. As stated, the strands define skills expected within FLEs, overlooking the learner-driven aspect of ILEs. In addition, participation is equated to learning within an ILE, rather than discussed as an indicator that might predict the quality or quantity of learning. The NRC (2009) report focuses on out-of-school experiences, such as museums. Differentiated outcome changes due to the situated nature of learning within a given environment nor how the culture and values of the environment shape learning are not adequately addressed (Nasir, Roseberry, Warren, & Lee, 2006). For example, science identity might be formed or enacted differently within science clubs versus museums. Examination of the ACCE constructs within ILEs and OILEs should not mimic FLE standardization as the learner interacts and shapes the decision-making, activities, tasks, materials, and outcomes differently within the environment.

Assessment Model

Evidence-centered design (ECD) is comprehensive assessment model and can address the different types of assessments needed to measure the ACCE constructs and individual and group behaviors. ECD is a mechanism to provide a "sound chain of reasoning" about individual learning and program evaluation (Mislevy et al., 2003, p. 3.). Researchers can adapt ECD to construct validity arguments that support learners within an ILE or OILE. Reasoning within ECD is grounded within the sources of validity evidence gathered about the constructs of interest and the content assessed. Assessments must be developed based on clear descriptions of the desired performances and tasks grounded within theoretical constructs or specific content knowledge and skills (Gitomer & Bennett, 2002; Messick,

1994). Sufficient psychometric evidence, including evidence of reliability and validity needs to be gathered for each assessment (National Research Council, 2001). Such evidence also needs to be reported for any posteriori scales that are extracted from OILE environments based on the variables, or data features.

Reliability. Reliability is a necessary, but not sufficient condition, for validity. Reliability is an estimate of systematic observed variance within the population assessed. Reliability increases as variance due to error decreases (Boorsboom, 2005). In educational and psychological assessment, Cronbach's alpha is often used as an estimate of reliability. However, Cronbach's alpha lacks sensitivity to subtleties in variance components (Cronbach & Shavelson, 2004). Generalizability theory can be used to identify variance components and estimate the degree to which inferences can be made to support decision making about an individual based on a single score from a universe of possible scores (Gleser, Cronbach, & Rajaratnam, 1965, p. 395). For example, generalizability theory is used to examine error in performance assessment scoring (e.g., Briesch et al., 2014). In addition, other estimates of reliability have also been used to address issues with alpha, assessment dimensionality, and assessment format (Deng & Chan, 2016; Kolen & Lee, 2011; Stemler, 2004; Widhiarso & Ravand, 2014). Because reliability is not a fixed property of a measure, but a "population dependent property of scores," local reliability is a criterion for reporting when an extant instrument is used with a new population (Boorsboom, 2005, p. 47). Thus, within an ILE and OILE, it is important that reliability be reported each time a measure is used, especially as the population within an ILE or OILE can be fluid and ill-defined.

Validity involves the collection of multiple sources of evidence to make judgments about individuals or groups. Validity refers to how data are interpreted and results are used. There are multiple sources of validity evidence to support user decision-making that have been clearly delineated within the *Standards for Educational and Psychological Testing* (AERA, APA, & NCME, 2014). These include evidence derived from (a) measure[2] or test content, (b) response processes, (c) the internal structure of the measure or test, (d) relationships to other variables, and (e) consequences of testing. For ILEs and OILEs, I contend that situative validity is also an important validity concept to consider for ILEs and OILEs.

Content validity. Content validity is a fundamental requirement of all instruments (Lissitz & Samuelsen, 2007; Sireci, 1998). Content validity addresses the relationship between the content of the measure or test and the degree to which it represents the intended construct or content. Content validity includes the wording and format of items, questions, tasks, or themes within reading passages (AERA, APA, & NCME, 2014). Content validity is demonstrated in a test blueprint or measure specifications that are developed in advance. Content validity represents the degree to which the specifications or blueprint and the measure or test are representative of the content domain, such as for an accountability test. "Alignment" typically refers to the degree to which an accountability test assesses K–12 content standards (Fulmer & Polikoff, 2014).

Another source of content validity is subject matter expert (SME) judgments. SMEs can evaluate the content validity of a test by providing their judgments about the degree to which a content domain is represented by items on a test, such as for a licensure test (Sireci & Faulkner-Bond, 2014). Content validity can also be based on observations of behavior in situ, such as for a job analysis (Kurz et al., 2017). For ILEs and OILEs, content validity can refer to the degree to which the assessment content is aligned with STEM content standards (e.g., Pierrakos et al., 2008), expectations for the designed environment (e.g., Koh, 2013), or by expert review of a multidimensional ACCE construct measure (e.g., Hillman, Zeeman, Tilburg, & List, 2016).

Response processes. Response process validity addresses the assumptions about the cognitive processes engaged in an assessment. Thus, response process validity examines the responses processes of participants who take a given measure (AERA, APA, & NCME, 2014). Response process examination provides evidence that the cognition engaged and the cognitive nature of the performance is aligned with the construct as visualized by the assessor (Ercikan & Pellegrino, 2017). The learner answers questions about how they are thinking about a question or task while they are in the process of answering the question or doing the task, or soon after the learner has finished the question or task. This allows the assessor to determine whether learners are engaging in a targeted complex process, such as analysis, or simply recall. Categorization of this process within a cognitive hierarchy, such as the revised Bloom's taxonomy (Anderson & Krathwohl, 2001), is important for content validity. Response processes can be used to examine a novice–expert trajectory, as experts are more facile at applying analytical processes to novel situations (Carbonell et al., 2014). A key question in examining response process validity for traditional assessment is, "Did the learner understand the intention of the test question?"

Response process validity can also include other types of evidence. For example, evidence might include documentation of stages of work (such as written drafts for essays) or problem solving steps or strategies, knowledge and competencies applied to test items, behaviors (such as eye movements), analysis of responses to parts of the test in comparison to the whole test, use of test resources, guessing, and examinations of judges scoring, (AERA, NCME, & APA, 2014; Ercikan & Pellegrino, 2017). Within naturalistic and unobtrusive assessment, it is important that the researcher understand the nature of the construct from the learner's perspective (Lemke et al., 2015). Within ILEs and OILEs response process evidence can reveal the learner-driven nature of the ACCE constructs examined. Therefore, a key validity question in ILEs and OILEs is, "Did the researcher understand the intention of the learner's behavior or response?"

Collecting several forms of qualitative data can extend response process research. For example, extended observations of learners within the naturalistic environment and speaking with learners proximally to the observation of a performance task may extend response process data (Rossman & Rallis, 2012). Different qualitative approaches can frame data collection, analysis, and interpretation (e.g., Goldman, Pea, Barron, & Derry, 2006). For example, ethnography can be used to examine the cultures of learning communities (Sawchuck, 2008). Phenomenology has been applied to understand learner experiences of the problem-solving and product development processes within ILEs, OILEs, including within the professions (e.g., Adams, Yin, Madriz, & Mullen, 2014; Bland, Kusano, & Johri, 2016; van Manen, 2014). While these methods rely on self-report, researchers can use student reflections to identify the salient characteristics of the learning experience to create more authentic assessment tools (Bland, Kusano, Xu, & Johri, 2017). In addition, metacognitive reflection can augment evidence about learner processes and outcomes offering evidence about the nature of metacognitive influences on conceptual development and content processing within STEM (Anderson, Nashon, & Thomas, 2007; De Backer, Van Keer, & Valke, 2017; Schraw, 1998; Schraw & Dennison, 1994; Xu, Bland, Kusano, & Johri, 2017). Response process validity provides evidence related to inferences about learner's cognitions. Thus, learner explanation gathered in a response process study reduces the number of links in the researcher's chain of inferences.

Internal structure. Internal structure validity focuses on the measure as a gestalt of the construct assessed and how sub-constructs and individual items support the gestalt of the construct. Internal structure validity addresses the degree to which the researcher's operationalization of the construct and the participants' interpretation of the items on the measure are related to the construct as conceptualized by the researcher. Thus, internal structure validity examines how the "relationships among test items and test components conform to the construct on which the proposed test score interpretations are based" (AERA, APA, & NCME, 2014, p. 16). Principal components analysis is used for data reduction (Tabachnik & Fidell, 2013). Exploratory factor analyses are used to explore the underlying nature of the construct and to identify latent traits (Costello & Osborne, 2005; Courtney, 2013).

Evidence of validity about the internal structure of a measure or test should also involve more complex analyses. For example, confirmatory factor analyses are grounded in theory and are used to confirm the number of expected factors, the variables associated with the factors, and the nature of the relationships across the factors (Thompson, 2004). Internal structure analysis should also address measurement invariance, or the degree to which the measure assesses the construct similarly for different groups or by occasions (Van De Schoot, Schmidt, De Beuckelaer, Lek, & Zondervan-Zwijnenburg, 2015). For ILEs and OILEs, measurement invariance is critically important to ensure that measures can apply to a wide variety of participants across groups, time, and learning environment to attain NRC (2015b) evaluation goals. Item response theory (Reise & Revicki, 2015), multidimensional item response theory ([MIRT]; Reckase, 2009), and Rasch modeling (Englehard, 2013) can be used to examine internal structure validity, including measurement invariance (see Engelhard, 2013; Reckase, 2009). MIRT may be especially important within ILEs and OILEs because MIRT addresses the characteristics a person brings to the test (e.g., knowledge, skills, or ACCE constructs) and multiple item characteristics including "the sensitivity of the test item to differences in the characteristics of person" (Reckase, 2009, p. v). MIRT provides the means to examine measures that include different latent traits or different composite scores of different latent traits (Ackerman, 1994), which is an important analysis for cross-categorical ACCE constructs.

Relations to other variables. Validity in terms of relations to other variables addresses the need for a new measure and use of a given measure, such as how the construct is related to the variables intended for external use (AERA, APA, & NCME, 2014; Breaux et al., 2017). Convergent and discriminant validity evidence support the need for a new measure. Convergent evidence implies that measures assess similar constructs. For example, grit scores would be expected to be related to self-regulation scores (Muenks, Wigfield, Yang, & O'Neal, 2017). Discriminant evidence implies that different constructs are measured (e.g., Kosovich, Hulleman, Barron, & Getty, 2015).

Criterion-related validity, such as concurrent and predictive validity, provides evidence of the assessment can predict performance on an outcome that is not measured by the test (AERA, APA, & NCME, 2014). Concurrent validity is examined when measures are administered simultaneously (e.g., Martin et al. 2010). Predictive validity provides evidence of a relationship between the test and a future outcome (e.g., Mandelman, Barbot, & Grigorenko, 2016). For example, assessment in a voluntary engineering competition might be used to predict future performance in a required internship.

Validity generalization refers to the degree to which "evidence of validity in one situation can be generalized to another situation without further study of validity in the new situation" (Rafilson, 1991, p. 1.). Facets, such as sample, sample size, time period, criterion measure used, or situativity can vary, resulting in differences in criterion correlations. Thus, accumulated research about a measure and meta-analyses of test-criterion studies support evidence of validity generalization (AERA, APA, & NCME, 2014). For ILEs and OILEs, different types of criterion-relation evidence can provide evidence of the relationship between informal learning experiences and achievement in FLEs or competency in the workplace (NRC, 2009; 2015b). Validity generalization is important when drawing inferences about different samples across diverse ILE environments.

Consequences. Consequential validity addresses issues related to test score use. Three concerns dominate the consequential validity conversation within the psychometric community: (a) alignment of interpretation and use of test scores with those intended by the test developers, (b) arguments about test use unrelated to test score interpretations, and (c) unintended consequences of testing (AERA, APA, & NCME, 2014). For example, an unintended consequence of early ability testing for entry into gifted programs is potentially denial of access for learners from poverty who may not have had an opportunity to develop the skills as measured on the test (e.g., Kaya, Stough, & Juntune, 2016). Consequential validity is important because it may provide evidence of a systemic problem, beyond simply the test score (AERA, APA, & NCME, 2014). The notion of an opportunity missed is an important aspect of consequential validity for ILEs and OILEs.

Situative validity. I propose situative validity as a new type of validation evidence for assessment within ILEs and OILEs. Another source of evidence critical for ILEs and OILEs is situative validity. Situative validity is grounded within psychology, education, and the learning sciences. For example, within psychological research, ecological validity refers to the degree to which inferences about laboratory behavior can be generalized to the real world (Schmuckler, 2001). Within educational research, ecological validity refers to the degree to which a measure aligns to learning opportunities (Moss, Pullin, Gee, Haertel, & Young, 2008; NRC, 2009). Moss and colleagues (2008) contended that many children do not have the opportunity to access those informal environments that support development of a broader competency base necessary for a competent citizenry. Thus, opportunity to learn (OTL) is critical when considering the ACCE constructs in underrepresented and under-served individuals and groups (Greeno & Gresalfi, 2008; Pullin, 2008; Pullin & Haertel, 2008).

Greeno and Gresalfi (2008) conceptualized OTL as a set of affordances that support learning by enabling entry into the system, providing access to practices and resources, and facilitating legitimate peripheral participation within the community. Legitimate peripheral participation is the means for novices to engage with experts in communities of practice, develop sociocultural identity, and understand and engage in community practices (Lave & Wenger, 1991). Lave and Wenger (1991) contended that the nature of situativity could not be empirically represented as everyday activities. Rather, the gestalt of agent, activity, and environment form communal situativity.

Intention and engagement become the means for social processes to embody content learning (Lave & Wenger, 1991). Thus, assessment of learning within ILEs and OILEs must be examined within a situative learning framework.

Situative validity reflects the degree to which an assessment acts as an authentic experience within an ILE or OILE as represented by the learner's access to activities, legitimate peripheral participation, and opportunity to learn. Situative validity evidence represents the intersection of (a) an affordance/barrier range within ILEs and OILEs; (b) the enactment of that range as embodied by learner participation, engagement, and apprenticeship within the community; and (c) evidence of the concomitant effects on learner processes and outcomes. Therefore, situative validity must offer evidence that stakeholders, can make inferences about personal learning trajectories within the context of access and sociocultural practices.

Multiple sources of validity evidence must be gathered from assessments used within ILEs and OILEs. Validity evidence supports inferences drawn from data for the given purpose, can support arguments for data use, and must be aligned to the values as situated within ILEs and OILEs (Messick, 1989; 1994). Integrating multiple sources of reliability and validity evidence is key to creating arguments about individual or group performance from a priori or posteriori measures and tests within ILEs and OILEs.

Synergies Created by the Nexus of Psychometrics and Educational Data Mining

Integrating psychometric principles with educational data mining and learning analytics can improve valid decision-making about learning from the big data gathered within OILEs or ILEs. The nature of validity can be very challenging in OILEs. Large educational data repositories may have high dimensionality, with more predictors than outcomes (Romero, Romero, & Ventura, 2014). Features or variables may exceed sample size, potentially resulting in noise, bias, or spurious correlations. Additionally, each educational problem has specific characteristics and objectives necessitating adaptations because data have different levels of granularity and formats (Romero & Ventura, 2012). Thus, examining big data in OILEs demands adherence to statistical principles (NASEM, 2017).

Several techniques can be used to address dimensionality reduction. Principal components analysis (PCA) while sufficient for smaller data sets, can be highly influenced by outliers and noise. Multiple adaptations of PCA have been developed (Jolliffe & Cadima, 2016). In addition, multiple latent variable models can be used to understand the latent traits and their relationships to each other (Kline, 2016). Sparse latent multifactor models can address issues of nonlinearity (Mayrink & Lucas, 2013). Results from such studies can offer evidence of construct validity.

Environmental context is highly variable across and within different types of STEM ILEs and OILEs. For example the Scratch environment includes different types of users which affect environmental context. Users may include undergraduate students assigned to engage in an online environment to complete a class project. Kindergartners may engage with Scratch to learn coding for fun. Middle school students may want to increase coding skills. Such a wide variety of learners affects learner interactions within the community and the types of products created. Dimensionality reduction along behavioral trajectories can identify significant differences in experiential pathways and temporal progressions for different learning levels and skills acquisition (Yang et al., 2015). However, huge differences in learning progressions within OILEs may support the advanced learners, but not the new learners.

Created products that are featured, such as in the Scratch environment, may impact participation due to the big-fish–little pond effect (Marsh, 1987). For example, highly able learners may develop lower academic self-concept when participating in environments with high ability peers as they make social comparisons to their peers (Salchegger, 2016; Zell, Strickhouser, & Alicke, 2017). Lack of social support within an OILE was especially damaging to self-concept (Bane, Haymayker, & Zinchuk, 2005). Thus, the situativity of the data within an OILE ecosystem affects the ACCE constructs and requires understanding of the distributed nature of cognition and other applicable ACCE constructs within the community (Madhavan & Richey, 2016). However, without more understanding of the underlying ACCE processes, such as by gathering response process validity evidence, the researcher cannot assume that behaviors within an OILE embody thought as Madhavan and Richey (2016) assert. Therefore, more research probing learner thought in relation to the context of the environment will lead to improved judgments about the nature of the ACCE constructs and decision-making within an OILE.

The benefit of big data in educational environments can be enhanced by integrating data from many sources, such as FLE input, process, and outcome data (Ikemoto & Marsh, 2007). However, effective data integration implies that identifiers need to be collected within OILEs that can be matched to identifiers in FLE data. Researchers can also examine big data to gain insight into the broader effects of community, schooling, and informal or personalized learning. For example, causal discoveries may emerge by examining health data, academic performance, and participation in after-school activities. In addition, researchers can use data visualization to illustrate complexities within and across social networks. Data visualization can also be used to show temporal and spatial learning trajectories (NASEM, 2017).

The computer science and educational data mining communities have made key contributions to learner data use, creating actionable knowledge for learners within OILEs. Many educational data mining methods are applied to formative assessment within cognitive tutors (which may be used formally or informally). For example, Bayesian knowledge tracing can be used to either predict student learning of a given skill or application of a skill (Corbett & Anderson, 1995; Van de Sande, 2013). Latent knowledge estimation can be used to identify learner knowledge and skills. In response, the cognitive tutor adjusts the learning level (Baker & Inventado, 2014). Other types of latent knowledge estimation includes performance factor analysis and learning factors transfer analysis which examines knowledge transfer (Pavlik, Cen, & Koedinger, 2009; Pavlik, Yudelson, & Koedinger, 2011). These types of models support learner pathways through online environments, providing an opportunity for the learner to benefit from the analyzed data.

EDM models have typically been applied to formative assessment within cognitive tutors. Psychometric models have been typically used for measure development for research and test development for individual summative assessment and program accountability. However, producing actionable information from big data in OILEs requires reliability of inferences based on the applied statistical models, else the result may be spurious relationships and erroneous conclusions (NRC, 2013). Inference remains a significant challenge in big data analysis (NASEM, 2017). Resolving these issues requires transdisciplinary collaboration across the education, learning, and psychological sciences and the computer science, educational data mining, and learning analytics communities.

One key issue in examining OILE big data is that the processes in which factors are gathered, envisioned, or constructed remain largely undiscussed (Marquez-Vera, Cano, Romero, & Ventura, 2013). The ability of informal learning systems to capture data from a large number of participants presents multiple challenges when attempting to examine educational and psychological constructs posteriori (Cuzzocrea, Song, & Davis, 2011). For example, interestingness is the degree to which data patterns have utility for the user (Geng & Hamilton, 2006). Interestingness implies an atheoretical posteriori conceptualization of the constructs discovered (Liu, Hsu, Chen, & Ma, 2000). Thus, measures are created by how variables are combined and analyzed as single scores to represent constructs, but may lack theoretical or empirical validation evidence. The key challenge is to build models that enable data to be filtered and processed into useful information (NASEM, 2014) as grounded within conceptual and operational definitions of ACCE constructs.

Therefore, collaboration between domain experts and methodologists is crucial. Collaborative efforts should include planning the OILE and potential studies, examining the assumptions made during data analysis, verifying the validity of inferences from the analyses, and creating actionable knowledge and intelligent insights for stakeholders (Madhavan & Richey, 2016; Mandinach, Honey, Light, & Brunner, 2008; NASEM, 2017). Knowledge and insights must be useful for the learner, as the primary stakeholder within ILEs and OILEs. A team science approach can address the challenges posed by the increasing complexity of assessing learning and making inferences about the ACCE constructs situated within ILEs and OILEs (NRC, 2015a).

CONCLUSION

Interdisciplinary research, while increasing, has been rare given the siloed nature of the Academy (NRC, 2005). Shepard (2016) contended that deep understanding of the contexts in which learning occurs and the constructs associated with learning is necessary to make lasting contributions. Deep understanding of the ACCE constructs as situated within ILEs and OILEs is critical for adequate assessment of learner-driven constructs. Bridging the academic silos across domain exports, methodologists, and computer scientists to assess the ACCE constructs within learning progressions has enormous potential. Shifting the role of assessment from the methodological lens to epistemological and ontological lens is critical to fully understand the processes and outcomes in ILEs and OILEs. Finally, the researcher must understand the ACCE constructs phenomenologically, with the axiological focus on the learner as the primary actor and stakeholder within an ILE and OILE.

Maslow (1943) suggested that the desire to know and understand were human needs that had a "striving character" (p. 385). Perhaps, informal learner-driven making, doing, and solving communities, such as Scratch, STEM competitions, and service-learning communities indicate that higher order thinking skills, such as problem-solving and making are components of that striving condition beyond basic needs contributing to self-actualization. Maslow (1954) contended: "Growth, self-actualization, the striving toward health, the quest for identity and autonomy, the yearning for excellence... the striving 'upward' must by now be accepted beyond question as a widespread and perhaps universal human tendency" (pp. xii–xiii). Maslow (1954) defined self-actualization as: "the full use and exploitation of talents, capacities, potentialities, etc. Such people seem to be fulfilling themselves and to be doing the best that they are capable of doing..." (p. 150). Without knowledge boundaries, perhaps ILEs and OILEs are the most significant contributors to the individual's longitudinal capacity for self-actualization.

ACKNOWLEDGMENTS

This work is partly based upon research supported by U.S. National Science Foundation (NSF) Award EEC #1424444. Any opinions, findings, and conclusions or recommendations expressed in this material are those of the authors and do not necessarily reflect the views of the National Science Foundation.

NOTES

1. It is beyond the scope of this chapter to address all of them. See Mayer and Alexander (2017) and Sawyer (2014) for different perspectives on learning and other ACCE constructs.
2. In this chapter, I use "measure" to refer to a psychological measure, such as self-efficacy, and the affective, conative, and executive constructs. I use "test" to refer to a measure of the cognitive constructs, such as ability or content knowledge or skills.

REFERENCES

Ackerman, R., & Leiser, D. (2014). The effect of concrete supplements on metacognitive regulation during learning and open-book test taking. *British Journal of Educational Psychology, 84,* 329–348. doi:10.1111/bjep.12021

Ackerman, T. A. (1994). Using multidimensional item response theory to understand what items and tests are measuring. *Applied Measurement in Education, 7,* 255–278. doi:10.1207/s15324818ame0704_1

Adams, C., Yin, Y., Madriz, L. F. V., & Mullen, C. S. (2014). A phenomenology of learning large: The tutorial sphere of xMOOC video lectures. *Distance Education, 35,* 202–216. doi:10.1080/01587919.2014.917701

Ahearn, L. M. (2001). Language and agency. *Annual Review of Anthropology, 30,* 109–137. doi:10.1146/annurev.anthro.30.1.109

Allen, S. (2002). Looking for learning in visitor talk: A methodological exploration. In G. Leinhardt, K. Crowley, & K. Knutson (Eds.), *Learning conversations in museums* (pp. 259–303). Mahwah, NJ: Erlbaum.

Alsop, S., & Watts, M. (1997). Sources from a Somerset village: A model for informal learning about radiation and radioactivity. *Science Education, 81,* 633–650. doi:10.1002/(SICI)1098-237X(199711)81:6<633::AID-SCE2>3.0.CO;2-J

American Educational Research Association, American Psychological Association, & National Council on Measurement in Education. (2014). *Standards for educational and psychological testing.* Washington, DC: American Educational Research Association.

American Society of Mechanical Engineers. (2017). *ASME IAM3D 2017: Upgraded to Optimize Impact.* Retrieved from https://www.asme.org/events/competitions/iam3d-challenge

Anderson, D., & Gosselin, V. (2008). Private and public memories of Expo 67: A case study of recollections of Montreal's World's Fair, 40 years after the event. *Museum & Society, 6*(1), 1–21.

Anderson, D., Nashon, S., & Thomas, G. (2007). Predators of knowledge construction: Interpreting students' metacognition in an amusement park physics program. *Science Education, 91,* 298–320. doi:10.1002.sce.20176

Anderson, D., & Thomas, G. (2014). 'Prospecting for metacognition' in a science museum—A metaphor reflecting hermeneutic inquiry and questioning into metacognition in a new context. *Issues in Educational Research, 24,* 1–20.

Anderson, L. W., & Krathwohl, D. R. (Eds.). (2001). *A taxonomy for learning, teaching, and assessing: A revision of Bloom's taxonomy of educational objectives, complete edition.* New York, NY: Longman.

Aud, S., Fox, M., & KewalRamani, A. (2010). *Status and trends in the education of racial and ethnic groups (NCES 2010-015).* U.S. Department of Education, National Center for Education Statistics. Washington, DC: U.S. Government Printing Office. Retrieved from http://nces.ed.gov/pubs2010/2010015.pdf

Baggetta, P., & Alexander, P. A. (2016). Conceptualization and operationalization of executive function. *Mind, Brain, and Education, 10*(1), 10–33. doi:10.1111/mbe.12100

Baker, R. S., & Inventado, P. S. (2014). Educational data mining and learning analytics. In J. A. Larusson & B. White (Eds.), *Learning analytics: From research to practice* (pp. 61–75). New York, NY: Springer. doi:10.1007/978-1-4614-3305-7_4

Ballhausen, N., Mahy, C. E. V., Hering, A., Voigt, B., Schnitzspahn, K. M., Lagner, P., & Kliegel, M. (2017). Children's planning performance in the zoo map task (BADS-C): Is it driven by general cognitive ability, executive functioning, or prospection? *Applied Neuropsychology: Child, 6,* 138–144. doi:10.1080/21622965.2015.1124276

Bandura, A. (1977). Self-efficacy: Toward a unifying theory of behavioral change. *Psychological Review, 84,* 191–215. doi:10.1037/0033-295X.84.2.191

Bane, C. M. H., Haymaker, C. M. B., & Zinchuk, J. (2005). Social support as a moderator of the big-fish-in-a-little-pond effect in online self-help support groups. *Journal of Applied Biobehavioral Research, 10,* 239–261. doi:10.1111/j.1751-9861.2005.tb00015.x

Barton, A. C., & Tan, E. (2010). We be burnin'! Agency, identity, and science learning. *Journal of the Learning Sciences, 19,* 187–229. doi:10.1080/10508400903530044

Bathgate, M., & Schunn, C. (2017). Factors that deepen or attenuate decline of science utility value during the middle school years. *Contemporary Educational Psychology, 49,* 215–225. doi:10.1016.j.cedpsych.2017.02.005

Benson, J. (1998). Developing a strong program of construct validation: A test anxiety example. *Educational Measurement: Issues and Practice, 17,* 10–17. doi:10.1111/j.1745-3992.1998.tb00616.x

Berkowitz, R., Moore, H., Astor, R. A., & Benbenishty, R. (2017). A research synthesis of the associations between socioeconomic background, inequality, school climate, and academic achievement. *Review of Educational Research, 87,* 425–469. doi:10.3102/0034654316669821

Biernacki, M. P., Tarnowski, A., Lengsfeld, K., Lewkowicz, R., Kowalczuk, K., & Dereń, M. (2013). +Gz load and executive functions. *Aviation, Space, and Environmental Medicine, 84,* 511–515. doi:10.3357/ASEM.3224.2013

Bland, L. C., Hjalmarson, M., Nelson, J. K., & Samaras, A. P. (2017, June). Applying conjecture mapping as a design-based research method to examine the design and implementation of a teaching development project for STEM faculty. *Proceedings of American Society for Engineering Education Annual Conference and Exposition.* Columbus, OH. Retrieved from https://peer.asee.org/27602

Bland, L. C., Kusano, S. M., & Johri, A. (2016, June). Engineering competitions as pathways to development of professional engineering skills. *Proceedings of American Society for Engineering Education Annual Conference and Exposition.* New Orleans, LA. doi:10.18260/p.26629

Bland, L. C., & Kusano, S. M., Xu, X., & Johri, A. (2017, June). Examining learner-driven constructs in co-curricular engineering environments: The role of student reflection in assessment development. *Proceedings of American Society for Engineering Education Annual Conference and Exposition.* Columbus, OH. Retrieved from https://peer.asee.org/28315

Boekaerts, M. (1999). Coping in context: Goal frustration and goal ambivalence in relation to academic and interpersonal goals. In E. Frydenberg (Ed.), *Learning to cope: Developing as a person on complex societies* (pp. 175–197). Oxford, England: Oxford University Press.

Boekaerts, M., & Pekrun, R. (2016). Emotions and emotion regulation in academic settings. In L. Corno & E. M. Anderman (Eds.), *Handbook of educational psychology* (3rd ed.; pp. 76–90). New York, NY: Routledge.

Boorsboom, D. (2005). *Measuring the mind: Conceptual issues in contemporary psychometrics.* New York, NY: Cambridge University Press.

Bransford, J. (2007). Preparing people for rapidly changing environments. *Journal of Engineering Education, 96,* 1–3.

Bransford, J., Barron, B., Pea, R. D., Meltzoff, A., Kuhl, P., Bell, P., . . . Sabelli, N. H. (2006a). Foundations and opportunities for an interdisciplinary science of learning. In R. K. Sawyer (Ed.), *The Cambridge handbook of the learning sciences* (pp. 19–34). New York, NY: Cambridge University Press.

Bransford, J., Barron, B., Pea, R. D., Meltzoff, A., Kuhl, P., Bell, P., . . . Sabelli, N. H. (2006b). Learning theories and education: Toward a decade of synergy. In P. Alexander & P. Winne (Eds.), *Handbook of educational psychology,* (2nd ed.; pp. 209–244). New York, NY: Routledge.

Breaux, K. C., Avitia, M., Koriakin, T., Bray, M. A., DeBiase, E., Courville, T., . . . Grossman, S. (2017). Patterns of strengths and weaknesses on the WISC-V, DAS-II, and KABC-II and their relationship to students' errors in oral language, reading, writing, spelling, and math. *Journal of Psychoeducational Assessment, 35*(1–2), 168–185. doi:10.1177/0734282916669657

Briesch, A. M., Swaminathan, H., Welsh, M., & Chafouleas, S. M. (2014). Generalizability theory: A practical guide to study design, implementation, and interpretation. *Journal of School Psychology, 52,* 13–35. doi:10.1016/j.jsp.2013.11.008

Brookhart, S. M., & Nitko, A. J. (2015). *Educational assessment of students.* New York, NY: Pearson.

Brown, J. (2017). Exploring the transformative potential of recognition of prior informal learning for learners: A case study in Scotland. *Journal of Further Higher Education, 41,* 80–78. doi:10.1080/0309877X.2015.1862850

Carberry, A. R., Lee, H.-S., & Ohland, M. W. (2010). Measuring engineering design self-efficacy. *Journal of Engineering Education, 99,* 71–79. doi:10.1002/j.2168-9830.2010.tb01043.x

Carbonell, K. B., Stalmeijer, R. E., Könings, K. D., Segers, M., & van Merriënboer, J. J. G. (2014). How experts deal with novel situations: A review of adaptive expertise. *Educational Research Review, 12,* 14–29. doi:10.1016/j.edurev.2014.03.001

Carroll, J. B. (1993). *Human cognitive abilities: A survey of factor-analytic studies.* New York, NY: Cambridge University Press.

Chao, P. (2016). Exploring students' computational practice, design and performance of problem-solving through a visual programming environment. *Computers & Education, 95,* 202–215. doi:10.1016/j.compedu.2016.01.010

Chowdhury, B., Cameron, K., Blanchard, S., & Johri, A. (2015, June). SeeMore: An interactive kinetic sculpture designed to teach parallel computational thinking. *Proceedings of American Society for Engineering Education Annual Conference and Exposition.* Seattle, WA. doi:10.18260/p.24697

Chowdhury, B., Kusano, S., Johri, A., & Sharma, A. (2014). Student experiences in an interdisciplinary studio-based design course: The role of peer scaffolding. *Proceedings of American Society for Engineering Education Annual Conference and Exposition.* Indianapolis, IN. Retrieved from https://peer.asee.org/23046

Clapp, E. P., Ross, J., Ryan, J. O., & Tishman, S. (2017). *Maker-centered learning: Empowering young people to shape their worlds.* San Francisco, CA: Wiley.

Cohen, R. J., Swerdlik, M. E., & Sturman, E. (2013). *Psychological testing and assessment: An introduction to tests and measurement* (8th ed.). New York, NY: McGraw-Hill.

Colangelo, N., Assouline, S. G., & Gross, M. U. M. (2004). *A nation deceived: How schools hold back America's brightest students. The Templeton national report on acceleration. Volume 1.* Iowa City, IA: University of Iowa. Connie Belin & Jacqueline N. Blank International Center for Gifted Education and Talent Development.

Corbett, A. T., & Anderson, J. R. (1994). Knowledge tracing: Modeling the acquisition of procedural knowledge. *User Modeling and User-Adapted Interaction, 4,* 253–278. doi:10.1007/BF01099821

Cornell, D. G., Delcourt, M. A. B., Goldberg, M. D., & Bland, L. C. (1992). Characteristics of elementary students entering gifted programs: The learning outcomes project at the University of Virginia. *Journal for the Education of the Gifted, 15,* 309–331. doi:10.1177/016235329201500402

Corno, L. (2006). Commentary on Vollmeyer and Rheinberg: Putting the teacher in research on self-regulated learning. *Educational Psychology Review, 18,* 261–266.

Costello, A. B., & Osborne, J. (2005). Best practices in exploratory factor analysis: Four recommendations for getting the most from your analysis. *Practical Assessment Research & Evaluation, 10*(7). Retrieved from http://pareonline.net/getvn.asp?v=10&n=7

Courtney, M. G. R. (2013). Determining the number of factors to retain in EFA: Using the SPSS R-Menu v2.0 to make more judicious estimations. *Practical Assessment, Research & Evaluation, 18*(8). Retrieved from http://pareonline.net/getvn.asp?v=18&n=8

Cragg, L., & Gilmore, C. (2014). Skills underlying mathematics: The role of executive function in the development of mathematics proficiency. *Trends in Neuroscience and Education, 3*(2), 63–68. doi:10.1016/j.tine.2013.12.001

Cronbach, L. J., & Meehl, P. E. (1955). Construct validity in psychological tests. *Psychological Bulletin, 52,* 281–302.

Cronbach, L. J., & Shavelson, R. J. (2004). My current thoughts on coefficient alpha and successor procedures. *Educational and Psychological Measurement, 64,* 391–418. doi:10.1177/0013164404266386

Cuzzocrea, A., Song, I., & Davis, K. C. (2011, October). Analytics over large-scale multidimensional data: The big data revolution! *Proceedings of the ACM 14th*

International Workshop on Data Warehousing and OLAP, Glasgow, Scotland, p. 101–104. doi:10.1145/2064676.2064695

Dall'Alba, G. (2009). *Learning to be professionals.* New York, NY: Springer.

Damşa, C. I., Kirschner, P. A., Andriessen, J. E. B., Erkens, G., & Sins, P. H. M. (2010). Shared epistemic agency: An empirical study of an emergent construct. *Journal of the Learning Sciences, 19,* 143–186. doi:10.1080/10508401003708381

Davey, T., Pitoniak, M. J., & Slater, S. C. (2016). Designing computerized adaptive tests. In S. Lane, M. R. Raymond, & T. M. Haladyna (Eds.), *Handbook of test development,* (pp. 467–484). New York, NY: Routledge.

De Backer, L., Van Keer, H., & Valcke, M. (2017). Is collaborative learners' adoption of metacognitive regulation related to students' content processing strategies and the level of transactivity in their peer discussions? *European Journal of Psychology of Education, 32,* 617–642. doi:10.1007/s10212-016-0323-8

Delcourt, M. A. B., Cornell, D., & Goldberg, M. D. (2007). Cognitive and affective learning outcomes of gifted elementary school students. *Gifted Child Quarterly, 51,* 359–381. doi:10.1177/0016986207306320

Deng, L., & Chan, W. (2016). Testing the difference between reliability coefficients alpha and omega. *Educational and Psychological Measurement, 77,* 185–203. doi:10.1177/0013164416658325

DeVellis, R. F. (2017). *Scale development: Theory and application* (4th ed.). Thousand Oaks, CA: SAGE.

Dinsmore, D. L., Alexander, P. A., & Loughlin, S. M. (2008). Focusing the conceptual lens on metacognition, self-regulation, and self-regulated learning. *Educational Psychology Review, 20,* 391–409. doi:10.10071s10648-008-9083-6

D'Mello, S. (2013). A selective meta-analysis on the relative incidence of discrete affective states during learning with technology. *Journal of Educational Psychology, 105,* 1082–1099. doi:10.1037/a0032674

Dmitrov, D. M. (2012). *Statistical methods for validation of assessment scale data in counseling and related fields.* Alexandria, VA: American Counseling Association.

Downing, S. M., & Haladyna, T. M. (1997). Test item development: Validity evidence from quality assurance procedures. *Applied Measurement in Education, 10,* 61–82. doi:10.1207/s15324818ame1001_4

Duckworth, A. (2016). *Grit: The power of passion and perseverance.* New York, NY: Scribner.

Duckworth, A. L., Peterson, C., Matthews, M. D., & Kelly, D. R. (2007). Grit: Perseverance and passion for long-term goals. *Journal Of Personality And Social Psychology, 92,* 1087–1101. doi:10.1037/0022-3514.92.6.1087

Ehret, C., & Hollett, T. (2016). Affective dimensions of participatory design research in informal learning environments: Placemaking, belonging, and correspondence. *Cognition and Instruction, 34,* 250–258. doi:10.1080/07370008.2016.1169815

Engelhard, G. (2013). *Invariant measurement: Using rasch models in the social, behavioral, and health sciences.* New York, NY: Routledge.

Ercikan, K., & Pellegrino, J. W. (2017). *Validation of score meaning for the next generation of assessments: The use of response processes.* New York, NY: Routledge.

Fan, H., Xu, J., Cai, Z., He, J., & Fan, X. (2017). Homework and students' achievement in math and science: A 30-year meta-analysis, 1986–2015. *Educational Research Review, 20,* 35–54. doi:10.1016/j.edurev.2016.11.003

Fields, D. A., Kafai, Y. B., Searle, K. A., & Min, H. S. (2012, March). Debuggems to assess student learning in e-textiles. Poster presented at the annual meeting of the ACM Special Interest Group on Computer Science Education (SIGCSE), Raleigh, NC.

Feng, M., Heffernan, N., & Koedinger, K. (2009). Addressing the assessment challenge with an online system that tutors as it assesses. *User Modeling and User-Adapted Interaction, 19,* 243–266. doi:10.1007/s11257-009-9063-7

Fuchs, D., & Fuchs, L. S. (2006). Introduction to response to intervention: What, why, and how valid is it? *Reading Research Quarterly, 41,* 93–99. doi:10.1598/RRQ.41.1.4

Fulmer, G. W., & Polikoff, M. S. (2014). Tests of alignment among assessment, standards, and instruction using generalized linear model regression. *Educational Assessment, Evaluation, and Accountability, 26,* 225–240. doi:10.1007/s11092-014-9196-z

Gelman, B., Beckley, C., Johri, A., Yang, S., & Domeniconi, C. (2016, April). Online urbanism: Interest-based subcultures as drivers of informal learning in an online community. *Proceedings of the Third ACM Conference on Learning @ Scale Conference.* Edinburgh, Scotland. Retrieved from https://dl.acm.org/citation.cfm?id=2876052

Gibson, D. (2007). Sim school and the conceptual assessment framework. In D. Gibson, C. Aldrich, & M. Prensky (Eds.), *Games and simulations in online learning: Research and development frameworks* (pp. 308–322). Hershey, PA: Information Science.

Gitomer, D. H., & Bennett, R. E. (2002). *Unmasking constructs through new technology, measurement theory, and cognitive science.* RM-02-01. Princeton, NJ: Educational Testing Service. Retrieved from https://www.ets.org/Media/Research/pdf/RM-02-01-Gitomer.pdf

Gleser, G. C., Cronbach, L. J., & Rajaratnam, N. (1965). Generalizability of scores influenced by multiple sources of variance. *Psychometrika, 30,* 395–418. doi:10.1007/BF02289531

Goldman, R., Pea, R., Barron, B., & Derry, S. J. (2006). *Video research in the learning sciences.* New York, NY: Routledge.

Gomez, K., & Lee, U. (2015). Situated cognition and learning environments: Implications for teachers on- and offline in the new digital media age. *Interactive Learning Environments, 23,* 634–652. doi:10.1080/10494820.2015.1064447

Greeno, J. G., & The Middle-School Mathematics through Applications Project Group. (1997). Theories and practices of thinking and learning to think. *American Journal of Education. 106,* 85–126. doi:10.1086/444177

Greeno, J. G., & Gresalfi, M. S. (2008). Opportunities to learn in practice and identity. In P. A. Moss, D. C. Pullin, J. P. Gee, E. H. Haertel, & L. J. Young, (Eds.), *Assessment, equity, and opportunity to learn* (pp. 170–199). New York, NY: Cambridge University Press.

Greeno, J. G., & Hall, R. P. (1997). Practicing representation: Learning with and about representational forms. *Phi Delta Kappan, 78,* 361–367.

Grover, S., & Pea, R. (2013). Computational thinking in K–12. *Educational Researcher, 42*(1), 38–43. doi:10.3102/0013189X12463051

Haladyna, T. M., & Rodriguez, M. C. (2013). *Developing and validating test items.* New York, NY: Routledge.

Halverson, E. R., & Sheridan, K. M. (2014). The maker movement in education. *Harvard Educational Review, 84,* 495–504.

Harel, I. E., & Papert, S. E. (1991). *Constructionism.* Norwood, NJ: Ablex.

Hattie, J. (2009). *Visible learning: A synthesis of over 800 meta-analyses relating to achievement.* New York, NY: Routledge.

Hayes, A. F. (2013). *Introduction to mediation, moderation, and conditional process analysis: A regression-based approach.* New York, NY: Guilford.

Hilgard, E. R. (1980). The trilogy of mind: Cognition, affection, and conation. *Journal of the History of the Behavioral Sciences, 16,* 107–117. doi:10.1002/1520-6696/(198004)16:2<107::AID-JHBS2300160202>3.0.CO;2-Y

Hill, B. M., & Monroy-Hernández, A. (2013). The remixing dilemma: The trade-off between generativity and originality. *American Behavioral Scientist, 57,* 643–663. doi:10.1177/0002764212469359oi:10.1177/0002764212469359

Hillman, S. J., Zeeman, S. I., Tilburg, C. E., & List, H. E. (2016). My attitudes toward science (MATS): The development of a multidimensional instrument measuring students' science attitudes. *Learning Environments Research, 19,* 203–219. doi:10.1007/s10984-016-9205-x

Huddleston, A. P. (2014). Achievement at whose expense? A literature review of test-based grade retention policies in U.S. schools. *Education Policy Analysis Archives, 22*(18). doi:10.14507/epaa.v22518.2014

Huebner, A. (2010). An overview of recent developments in cognitive diagnostic computer adaptive assessments. *Practical Assessment, Research, & Evaluation, 15*(3). Retrieved from http://pareonline.net/getvn.asp?v=15&n=3

Huitt, W. G., & Cain, S. C. (2005). *An overview of the conative domain.* Educational Psychology Interactive. Valdosta, GA: Valdosta State University. Retrieved from http:/www.edpsycinteractive.org /brilstar/chapters/conative.pdf

Hung, W., Jonassen, D. H., & Liu, R. (2008). Problem-based learning. In J. M. Spector, M. D. Merrill, J. Van Merrienboer, & M. P. Driscoll (Eds.), *Handbook of research on educational communications and technology* (3rd ed.; pp. 485–506). Mahwah, NJ: Erlbaum.

Ikemoto, G. S., & Marsh, J. A. (2007). Chapter 5: Cutting through the "data-driven" mantra: Different conceptions of data-driven decision making. *Yearbook of the National Society for the Study of Education, 106,* 105–131. doi:10.1111/j.1744-7984.2007.00099.x

Izard, C. (2000). Affect. In A. E. Kazdin, (Ed.), *Encyclopedia of psychology* (Vol. 1; p. 88). Washington, DC: American Psychological Association. doi:10.1037/10516-026

James, W. (1890). *The principles of psychology.* New York, NY: Holt.

Johri, A., Olds, B. M., & O'Connor, K. (2014). Situative frameworks for engineering learning research. In A. Johri & B. Olds (Eds.), *Cambridge Handbook of Engineering Education Research* (pp. 47–66). New York, NY: Cambridge University Press.

Johri, A. (2015, June). Sociomaterial bricolage: Engineering learning as the practice of making sense by making do. *Proceedings of the 11th Conference on Computer Supported Collaborative Learning* (pp. 691–692). Gothenburg, Sweden.

Johri, A. (2016). Makers and making online: Situated informal learning in online communities of engineering enthusiasts. *Proceedings of Australasian Association for Engineering Education Annual Conference.* Coffs Harbour, Australia.

Johnson, R. B., & Christensen, L. (2017). *Educational research: Quantitative, qualitative, and mixed approaches* (6th ed.). Los Angeles, CA: SAGE.

Jolliffe, I. T., & Cadima, J. (2016). Principal component analysis: A review and recent developments. *Philosophical Transactions of the Royal Society A: Mathematical, Physical and Engineering Sciences, 374*(2065). Retrieved from https://www.ncbi.nlm.nih.gov/pmc/articles/PMC4792409/

Jonassen, D. H., & Hung, W. (2015). All problems are not equal: Implications for problem-based learning. In A. Walker, H. Leary, C. E. Hmelo-Silver, & P. A. Ertmer (Eds.), *Essential readings in problem-based learning: Exploring and extending the legacy of Howard S. Barrows* (pp. 17–41). West Lafayette, IN: Purdue University Press.

Jones, M. G., & Brader-Araje, L. (2002). The impact of constructivism on education: Language discourse, and meaning. *American Communication Journal, 5*(3), 1.

Kane, M. T. (2008). Terminology, emphasis, and utility in validation. *Educational Researcher, 37,* 76–82. doi:10.3102/0013189X08315390

Kaya, F., Stough, L. M., & Juntune, J. (2016). The effect of poverty on the verbal scores of gifted students. *Educational Studies, 42,* 85–97. doi:10.1080/03055698.2016.1148585

Kearney, S. (2013). Improving engagement: The use of 'authentic self and peer-assessment for learning' to enhance the student learning experience. *Assessment & Evaluation in Higher Education, 38,* 875–891. doi:10.1080/02602938.2012.751963

Kline, R. B. (2016). *Principles and practice of structural equation modeling* (4th ed.). New York, NY: Guilford.

Koh, K. (2013). Adolescents' information-creating behavior embedded in digital media practice using Scratch. *Journal of the American Society for Information Science and Technology, 64,* 1826–1841. doi:10.1002/asi.22878

Kolen, M. J., & Brennan, R. L. (2004). *Test equating, scaling, and linking: Methods and practices* (2nd ed.). New York, NY: Springer.

Kolen, M. J., & Lee, W.-C. (2011). Psychometric properties of raw and scale scores on mixed-format tests. *Educational Measurement: Issues and Practice, 30,* 15–24. doi:10.1111/j.1745-3992.2011.00201.x

Kosovich, J. J., Hulleman, C. S., Barron, K. E., & Getty, S. (2015). A practical measure of student motivation: Establishing validity evidence for the expectancy-value-cost scale in middle school. *The Journal of Early Adolescence, 35*(5–6), 790–816. doi:10.1177/0272431614556890

Kuh, G. D., Kinzie, J., Buckley, J. A., Bridges, B. K., & Hayek, J. C. (2006). *What matters to student success: A review of the literature.* Commissioned report for the National Symposium on Postsecondary Student Success: Spearheading a Dialog on Student Success. Washington, DC: National Postsecondary Education Cooperative. Retrieved from https://nces.ed.gov/npec/pdf/Kuh_Team_Report.pdf

Kurz, R. S., Yager, C., Yager, J. D., Foster, A., Breidenbach, D. H., & Irwin, Z. (2017). Advancing the certified in public health examination: A job task analysis. *Public Health Reports, 132,* 518–523. doi:10.1177/0033354917710015

Kusano, S. (2014). *Beyond the classroom: Understanding the educational significance of non-curricular engineering design experiences* (Unpublished doctoral dissertation). Virginia Polytechnic Institute and State University, Blacksburg, VA.

Kusano, S., & Johri, A. (2014, June). A sense of autonomy: Students' self-assessment of design-based informal learning experiences in engineering. *Proceedings of American Society for Engineering Education Annual Conference and Exposition.* Indianapolis, IN.

Kusano, S., & Johri, A. (2015, June). Developing global engineering competency through participation in "Engineers Without Borders." *Proceedings of American Society for Engineering Education Annual Conference and Exposition.* Seattle, WA.

Lave, J., & Wegner, E. (1991). *Situated learning: Legitimate peripheral participation.* New York, NY: Cambridge University Press.

Lehmann, M., Christensen, P., Du, X., & Thrane, M. (2008). Problem-oriented and project-based learning (POPBL) as an innovative learning strategy for sustainable development in engineering education. *European Journal of Engineering Education, 33,* 283–295. doi:10.1080/03043790802088566

Lemke, J., Lecusay, R., Cole, M., & Michalchik, V. (2015). *Documenting and assessing learning in informal and media-rich environments.* Cambridge, MA: MIT Press.

Lipnevich, A. A., MacCann, C., & Roberts, R. D. (2013). Assessing non-cognitive constructs in education: A review of traditional and innovative approaches. In D. H. Saklofske, C. R. Reynolds, & V. Schwean (Eds.), *The Oxford Handbook of Child Psychological Assessment* (pp. 750–772). doi:10.1093/oxfordhb/9780199796304.013.0033

Lissitz, R. W., & Samuelsen, K. (2007). A suggested change in terminology and emphasis regarding validity and education. *Educational Researcher, 36,* 437–448. doi:10.3102/0013189X07311286

Litzinger, T. A., Lattuca, L. R., Hadgraft, R. G., & Newstetter, W. C. (2011). Engineering education and the development of expertise. *Journal of Engineering Education, 100,* 123–150. doi:10.1002/j.2168-9830.2011.tb00006.x

Liu, B., Hsu, W., Chen, S., & Ma, Y. (2000). Analyzing the subjective interestingness of association rules. *IEEE Intelligent Systems and their Applications, 15*(5), 47–55. doi:10.1109/5254.889106

Lubinski, D., & Kell, H. J. (2018). Three crucial dimensions for students with intellectual gifts: It is time to stop talking and start thinking. In S. I. Pfeiffer, E. Shaunessy-Dedrick, & M. Foley-Nicpon (Eds.), *APA Handbooks in Psychology. APA Handbook of Giftedness and Talent* (pp. 479–496). Washington, DC: Americam Psychological Association. doi:10.1037/0000038-031

Ma, Y., Ma, H., Chen, X., Ran, G., & Zhang, X. (2017). Do attachment patterns predict aggression in a context of social rejection? An executive functioning account. *Aggressive Behavior, 43,* 408–418. doi:10.1002/ab.21700

Madhavan, K., & Richey, M. C. (2016). Problems in big data analytics in learning. *Journal of Engineering Education, 105,* 6–14. doi:10.1002/jee20113

Majgaard, G. (2014). The playful and reflective game designer. *Electronic Journal of E-Learning, 12,* 271–280.

Mandelman, S. D., Barbot, B., & Grigorenko, E. L. (2016). Predicting academic performance and trajectories from a measure of successful intelligence. *Learning and Individual Differences, 51,* 387–393. doi:10.1016/j.lindif.2015.02.003

Mandinach, E. B., Honey, M., Light, D., & Brunner, C. (2008). A conceptual framework for data-driven decision making. In E. B. Mandinach & M. Honey, (Eds.), *Data-driven school improvement: Linking data and learning* (pp. 13–31). New York, NY: Teachers College Press.

Maniates, H. (2016). Transitional kindergarten: an opportunity to explore the intersection between early childhood and kindergarten practice. *Early Childhood Development and Care, 186,* 750–763. doi:10.1080/03004430.2015.1057580

Manship, K., Holod, A., Quick, H., Ogat, B., Brodziakdelos Reyes, I., Anthony, J., . . . , & Anderson, E. (2017). *The impact of transitional kindergarten on California students: Final report from the study of California's Transitional Kindergarten Program.* Washington, DC: American Institutes for Research.

Márquez-Vera, C., Cano, A., Romero, C., & Ventura, S. (2013). Predicting student failure at school using genetic programming and different data mining approaches with high dimensional and imbalanced data. *Applied Intelligence, 38,* 315–330. doi:0.1007/s10489-012-0374-8

Marsh, H. W. (1987). The big-fish-little-pond effect on academic self-concept. *Journal of Educational Psychology, 79,* 280–295. doi:10.1037/0022-0663.79.3.280

Martin, L. M. (2004). An emerging research framework for studying informal learning and schools. *Science Education, 88,* S71–S82. doi:10.1002/sce.20020

Martin, P. A., Daley, D., Hutchings, J., Jones, K., Eames, C., & Whitaker, C. J. (2010). The teacher–pupil observation tool (T-POT): Development and testing of a new classroom observation measure. *School Psychology International, 31,* 229–249. doi:10.1177/0143034310362040

Maslow, A. H. (1943). A theory of human motivation. *Psychological Review, 50,* 370–396. doi:10.1037/h0054346

Maslow, A. H. (1954). *Motivation and personality.* New York, NY: Harper & Row.

Matlin, M. W., & Farmer, T. A. (2016). *Cognition* (9th ed.). Hoboken, NJ: Wiley.

Mayer, R. E. (2011). *Applying the science of learning.* Boston, MA: Pearson.

Mayer, R. E., & Alexander, P. A. (Eds.). (2017). *Handbook of research on learning and instruction* (2nd ed.). New York, NY: Routledge.

Mayrink, V., & Lucas, J. (2013). Sparse latent factor models with interactions: Analysis of gene expression data. *The Annals of Applied Statistics, 7,* 799–822. Retrieved from http://www.jstor.org/stable/23566413

McCoach, D. B., Gable, R. K., & Madura, J. P. (2013). Affective characteristics in school and corporate environments: Their conceptual definitions. In D. B. McCoach, R. K. Gable, & J. P. Madura (Eds.), *Instrumental development in the affective domain: Schools and corporate applications* (3rd ed., pp. 1–32). New York, NY: Springer.

McDougall, W. (1923). *An outline of psychology.* London, England: Methuen.

McNeil, M. (2013). *Developing good tasks and the task impurity problem in cognitive and linguistic research.* Retrieved from http://cred.pubs.asha.org/article.aspx?articleid=2195461

Means, B., Bakia, M., & Murphy, R. (2014). *Learning on-line: What research tells us about whether, when, and how.* New York, NY: Routledge.

Messick, S. (1994). The interplay of evidence and consequences in the validation of performance assessments. *Educational Researcher, 23*(2), 13–23. doi:10.3102/0013189X023002013

Mezirow, J. (2000). *Learning as transformation: Critical perspectives on a theory in progress.* San Francisco, CA: Jossey-Bass.

Mislevy, R. J., Almond, R. G., & Lukas, J. F. (2003, July). *A brief introduction to evidence-centered design* (Research Report RR-03-16). Princeton, NJ: Educational Testing Service. Retrieved from https://www.ets.org/Media/Research/pdf/RR-03-16.pdf

Militello, L., Gentner, F. C., Swindler, S. D., & Beisner, G. I. (2006, May). Conation: Its historical roots and implications for future research. *Proceedings of the 2006 International Symposium on Collaborative Technologies and Systems, CTS 2006* (pp. 240–247). Las Vegas, NV. doi:10.1109/CTS.2006.31

Miyake, A., Friedman, N. P., Emerson, M. J., Witzki, A. H., Howerter, A., & Wager, T. D. (2000). The unity and diversity of executive functions and their contributions to complex frontal lobe tasks: A latent analysis. *Cognitive Psychology, 41,* 49–100. doi:10.1006/cogp.1999.0734

Moje, E. B., & Lewis, C. (2007). Examining opportunities to learn literacy: The role of critical sociocultural literacy research: Reframing sociocultural research on literacy. In C. Lewis, P. Enciso, & E. Moje (Eds.), *Identity, agency, and power: Reframing sociocultural research on literacy* (pp. 15–48). New York, NY: Routledge.

Moss, P. A., Pullin, D. C., Gee, J. P., Haertel, E. H., & Young, L. J., (Eds.). (2008). *Assessment, equity, and opportunity to learn.* New York, NY: Cambridge University Press.

Muenks, K., Wigfield, A., Yang, J. S., & O'Neal, C. R. (2017). How true is grit? Assessing its relations to high school and college students' personality characteristics, self-regulation, engagement, and achievement. *Journal of Educational Psychology, 109,* 599–620. doi:10.1037/edu0000153

Nasir, N. S., Rosebery, A. S., Warren B., & Lee, C. D. (2006). Learning as a cultural process: Achieving equity through diversity. In R. K. Sawyer (Ed.), *The Cambridge Handbook of the Learning Sciences* (pp. 489–504). New York, NY: Cambridge University Press.

National Academies of Sciences, Engineering, and Medicine. (2014). *Complex operational decision making in networked systems of humans and machines: A multidisciplinary approach.* Committee on Integrating Humans, Machines, and Networks: A Global Review of Data-to-Decision Technologies; Board on Global Science and Technology; Policy and Global Affairs; National Research Council. Washington, DC: The National Academies Press. doi: 10.17226/18844

National Academies of Sciences, Engineering, and Medicine. (2017). *Refining the concept of scientific inference when working with big data: Proceedings of a workshop.* Washington, DC: The National Academies Press. doi:10.17226/24654

National Center for Education Statistics. (2017). *NAEP technical documentation: Contextual variables (Survey questionnaires).* Retrieved from http://nces.ed.gov/nationsreportcard/tdw/instruments/noncog.aspx

National Governors Association Center for Best Practices, Council of Chief State School Officers. (2010). *Common Core state standards.* Washington, DC: Author.

National Research Council. (1990). *On the shoulders of giants: New approaches to numeracy.* Washington, DC: The National Academies Press. doi:10.17226/1532

National Research Council. (2000). *How people learn: Brain, mind, experience, and school* (expanded edition). Washington, DC: National Academy Press. Retrieved from http://www.nap.edu/html/howpeople1/

National Research Council. (2001). *Knowing what students know: The science and design of educational assessment.* Committee on the Foundations of Assessment. Pelligrino, J., Chudowsky, N., and Glaser, R. (Eds.). Board on Testing and Assessment, Center for Education. Division of Behavioral and Social Sciences and Education. Washington, DC: National Academy Press.

National Research Council. (2005). *Facilitating interdisciplinary research.* Washington, DC: National Academies Press.

National Research Council. (2009). *Learning science in informal environments: People, places, and pursuits.* Committee on Learning Science in Informal Environments. Philip Bell, Bruce Lewenstein, Andrew W. Shouse, and Michael A. Feder (Eds.). Board on Science Education, Center for Education. Division of Behavioral and Social Sciences and Education. Washington, DC: The National Academies Press.

National Research Council. (2012). *Education for life and work: Developing transferable knowledge and skills in the 21st century.* Committee on Defining Deeper Learning and 21st Century Skills, J. W. Pellegrino and M. L. Hilton (Eds.). Board on Testing and Assessment and Board on Science Education, Division of Behavioral and Social Sciences and Education. Washington, DC: The National Academies Press.

National Research Council. (2015a). *Enhancing the Effectiveness of Team Science.* Committee on the Science of Team Science, N. J. Cooke and M. L. Hilton (Eds). Board on Behavioral, Cognitive, and Sensory Sciences, Division of Behavioral and Social Sciences and Edu cation. Washington, DC: The National Academies Press.

National Research Council. (2015b). *Identifying and supporting productive STEM programs in out-of-school settings.* Committee on Successful Out-of-School STEM Learning. Board on Science Education, Division of Behavioral and Social Sciences and Education. Washington, DC: The National Academies Press.

National Science Board. (2010). *Preparing the Next Generation of STEM Innovators: Identifying and Developing Our Nation's Human Capital.* Arlington, VA: Author.

O'Donnell, C. L. (2008). Defining, conceptualizing, and measuring fidelity of implementation and its relationship to outcomes in K–12 curriculum intervention research. *Review of Educational Research, 78*(1), 33–84. doi:10.3102/0034654307313793

Oettingen, G., Schrage, J., & Gollwitzer, P. M. (2016). Volition. In L. Corno & E. M. Anderman (Eds.), *Handbook of educational psychology* (3rd ed.; pp.104–117). New York, NY: Routledge.

Ormrod, J. E. (2017). *How we think and learn: Theoretical perspectives and practical implications.* New York, NY: Cambridge University Press.

Parker, P. D., Marsh, H. W., Ciarrochi, J., Marshall, S., & Abduljabbar, A. D. (2014). Juxtaposing math self-efficacy and self-concept as predictors of long-term achievement outcomes. *Educational Psychology, 34,* 29–48. doi:10.1080/01443410.2013.797339

Partnership for Assessment of Readiness for College and Careers. (2017). *PARCC end-of-year assessment.* Retrieved from http://parcc-assessment.org

Passig, D., Tzuriel, D., & Eshel-Kedmi, G. (2016). Improving children's cognitive modifiability by dynamic assessment in 3D Immersive Virtual Reality environments. *Computers & Education, 95,* 296–308. doi:10.1016/j.compedu.2016.01.009

Pea, R. (1993). Learning scientific concepts through material and social activities: Conversational analysis meets conceptual change. *Educational Psychologist, 28,* 265–277. doi:10.1207/s15326985ep2803_6

PEAR. (2017). *Assessment tools in informal science (ATIS): Ratings and reviews.* Retrieved from pearweb.org/atis

Pierrakos, O., & Borrego, M., & Lo, J. (2007, June). Assessing learning outcomes of a senior mechanical engineers in a capstone design experience. *Proceedings of American Society for Engineering Education Annual Conference and Exposition.* Honolulu, Hawaii. Retrieved from https://peer.asee.org/1953

Pierrakos, O., & Borrego, M., & Lo, J. (2008, June). Assessing students' learning outcomes during summer undergraduate research experiences. *Proceedings of American Society for Engineering Education Annual Conference and Exposition.* Pittsburgh, Pennsylvania. Retrieved from https://peer.asee.org/3668

Pintrich, P. R., & DeGroot, E. V. (1990). *Motivated Strategies for Learning Questionnaire* [Database record]. Retrieved from PsycTESTS. doi:10.1037/t09161-000

Pullin, D. C. (2008). Assessment, equity, and opportunity to learn. In P. A. Moss, D. C. Pullin, J. P. Gee, E. H. Haertel, L. J. Young, (Eds.), *Assessment, equity, and opportunity to learn* (pp. 333–352). New York, NY: Cambridge University Press.

Pullin, D. C., & Haertel, E. H. (2008). Assessment through the lens of "Opportunity to Learn." In P. A. Moss, D. C. Pullin, J. P. Gee, E. H. Haertel, & L. J. Young, (Eds.), *Assessment, equity, and opportunity to learn* (pp. 17–41). New York, NY: Cambridge University Press.

Pavlik, P. I., Cen, H., & Koedinger, K. R. (2009, July). Performance factors analysis: A new alternative to knowledge tracing. In V. Dimitrova, R. Mizoguchi, B. du Boulay, & A. Graesser (Eds.), *Proceedings of the 2009 conference on Artificial Intelligence in Education: Building Learning Systems that Care: From Knowledge Representation to Affective Modelling* (pp. 531–538). Amsterdam, Netherlands: IOS Press.

Pavlik, P. I., Yudelson, M., & Koedinger, K. R. (2011, June–July). Using contextual factors analysis to explain transfer of least common multiple skills. In G. Biswas, S. Bull, J. Kay, & A. Mitrovic (Eds.), *Artificial Intelligence in Education: 15th International Conference, AIED 2011, Auckland, New Zealand, June 28—July 2011* (pp. 256–263). Berlin, Heidelberg: Springer Berlin Heidelberg. doi:10.1007/978-3-642-21869-9_34

PEAR Institute. (2017). *A guide to PEAR's STEM tools: Common instrument suite and dimensions of success.* Retrieved from https://docs.wixstatic.com/ugd/e45463_cba72f96380742d39fefe40cc271de56.pdf

Quintana, M., & Morales, A. (2015). Learning from listservs: Collaboration, knowledge exchange, and the formation of distributed leadership for farmers' markets and the food movement. *Studies in the Education of Adults, 47,* 160–175.

Rafilson, F. (1991, November). The case for validity generalization. *Practical Assessment, Research, & Evaluation, 2*(13). pareonline.net/getvnasp?v=2+n=13

Ramsay, R. (2015). *Mechanical Aptitude Test.* Retrieved from Mental Measurements Yearbook with Tests in Print. Ipswich, MA.

Rappa, N. A., & Tang, K. (2017). Student agency: An analysis of students' networked relations across the informal and formal learning domains. *Research in Science Education, 47,* 673–684. doi:10.1007/s11165-016-9523-0

Reber, A. S. (1989). Implicit learning and tacit knowledge. *Journal of Experimental Psychology: General, 118,* 219–235. doi:10.1037/0096-3445.118.3.219

Reckase, M. D. (2009). *Multidimensional item response theory.* New York, NY: Springer.

Reisberg, D. (2016). *Cognition: Exploring the science of the mind* (6th ed.). New York, NY: Norton.

Reise, S. P., & Revicki, D. A., Eds. (2015). *Handbook of item response theory modeling: Applications to typical performance assessment.* New York, NY: Routledge.

Resnick, M., Maloney, J., Monroy-Hernández, A., Rusk, N., Eastmond, E., Brennan, K., . . . Kafai, Y. (2009). Scratch: Programming for all. *Communications of the ACM, 52,* 60–67. doi:10.1145/1592761.1592779

Ribner, A. D., Willoughby, M. T., Blair, C. B., & The Family Life Project Key Investigators. (2017). Executive function buffers the association between early math and later academic skills. *Frontiers in Psychology, 8.* doi:10.3389/fpsyg.2017.00869

Roedinger, H. L., Putnam, A. L., & Smith, M. A. (2011). Ten benefits of testing and their applications to educational practice. In J. Mestre & B. H. Ross (Eds.), *The Psychology of Learning and Motivation: Cognition in Education (Vol. 55*; pp. 1–pp. 36). San Diego, CA: Elsevier Science. doi:10.1016/B978-0-12-387691-1.00001-6

Rohrer, D., Taylor, K., & Sholar, B. (2010). Tests enhance the transfer of learning. *Journal of Experimental Psychology: Learning, Memory, and Cognition, 36,* 233–239. doi:10.1037/a0017678

Rokeach, M. (1968). A theory of organization and change within value-attitude systems. *Journal of Social Sciences, 24*(1), 13–33. doi:10.1111/j.1540-4560.1968.tb01466.x

Romero, C., Romero, J. R., & Ventura, S. (2014). A survey on pre-processing educational data. In A. Peña-Ayala (Ed.), *Educational Data Mining: Applications and Trends* (pp. 29–64). Cham, Switzerland: Springer. doi:10.1007/978-3-319-02738-8_2

Romero, C., & Ventura, S. (2013). Data mining in education. *WIREs Data Mining and Knowledge Discovery, 3,* 12–27. doi:10.1002/widm.1075

Rosenthal, R., & Rosnow, R. L. (2009). Characteristics of the volunteer subject. In R. Rosenthal & R. L. Rosnow (Eds.), *Artifacts in behavioral research* (pp. 677–744). New York, NY: Oxford University Press.

Rossman, G. B., & Rallis, S. F. (2012). *Learning in the field: An introduction to qualitative research* (3rd ed.). Thousand Oaks, CA: SAGE.

Rowland, C. A. (2014). The effect of testing versus restudy on retention: A meta-analytic review of the testing effect. *Psychological Bulletin, 140,* 1432–1463. doi:10.1037/a0037559

Rupp, A. A., & Templin, J. (2010). *Diagnostic measurement: Theory, methods, and applications.* New York, NY: Guilford.

Salchegger, S. (2016). Selective school systems and academic self-concept: How explicit and implicit school-level tracking relate to the big-fish–little-pond effect across cultures. *Journal of Educational Psychology, 108,* 405–423. doi:10.1037/edu0000063

Sawchuk, P. H. (2008). Theories and methods for research on informal learning and work: Towards cross-fertilization. *Studies in Continuing Education, 30,* 1–16. doi:10.1080/01580370701628474

Sawyer, R. K., (Ed.). (2014). *The Cambridge Handbook of the Learning Sciences* (2nd ed.). New York, NY: Cambridge University Press.

Scardamalia, M., & Bereiter, C. (2014). Knowledge building and knowledge creation: Theory, pedagogy, and technology. In K. Sawyer (Ed.), *Cambridge Handbook of the Learning Sciences* (2nd ed.; pp. 397–417). New York, NY: Cambridge University Press.

Schaffer, S. P., Chen, X., Zhu, X., & Oakes, W. C. (2012). Self-Efficacy for cross-disciplinary learning in project-based teams. *Journal of Engineering Education, 101,* 82–94. doi:10.1002/j.2168-9830.2012.tb00042.x

Schmuckler, M. A. (2001). What is ecological validity? A dimensional analysis. *Infancy, 2,* 419–436. doi:10.1207/S15327078IN0204_02

Schoen, H. L., & Ansley, T. N. (2006). *Iowa Algebra Aptitude Test™, 5th ed.* Retrieved from Mental Measurements Yearbook with Tests in Print. Ipswich, MA.

Schraw, G., & Dennison, R. S. (1994). Assessing metacognitive awareness. *Contemporary Educational Psychology, 19,* 460–475.

Schraw, G. (1998). Promoting general metacognitive awareness. *Instructional Science, 26*(1–2), 113–125.

Schwartz, D. L., & Arena, D. A. (2013). *Measuring what matters most: Choice-based assessments for the digital age.* Cambridge, MA: MIT Press.

Scribner, S., & Cole, M. (1973). Cognitive consequences of formal and informal education. *Science, 182*(4112), 553–559. http://www.jstor.org/stable/1737765

Shavelson, R. J., Roeser, R. W., Kupermintz, H., Lau, S., Ayala, C., Haydel, A., . . . Quihuis, G. (2002). Richard E. Snow's remaking of the concept of aptitude and multidimensional test validity: Introduction to the special issue. *Educational Assessment, 8,* 77–99. doi:10.1207/S15326977EA0802_01

Shepard, L. A. (2016). Testing and assessment for the good of education: Contributions of AERA Presidents, 1915–2015. *Educational Researcher, 45*(2), 112–121. doi:10.3102/0013189X16639599

Shute, V. J., & Kim, Y. J. (2014). Formative and stealth assessment. In J. M. Spector, M. D. Merrill, J. Elen, & M. J. Bishop (Eds.), *Handbook of Research on Educational Communications and Technology* (pp. 311–321). New York, NY: Springer New York. doi:10.1007/978-1-4614-3185-5_25

Shute, V. J., & Rahimi, S. (2017). Review of computer-based assessment for learning in elementary and secondary education. *Journal of Computer Assisted Learning, 33,* 1–19. doi:10.1111/jcal.12172

Shute, V. T., Ventura, M., Bauer, M., & Zapata-Rivero, D. (2009). Melding the power of serious games and embedded assessment to monitor and foster learning: Flow and grow. In G. Ritterfeld, M. Cody, & P. Vorderer (Eds.), *Serious games: Mechanisms and effects* (pp. 295–321). New York, NY: Routledge.

Sireci, S. G. (1998). The construct of content validity. *Social Indicators Research, 45,* 83–117. doi:10.1023/A:1006985528729

Sireci, S., & Faulkner-Bond, M. (2014). Validity evidence based on test content. *Psicothema [en linea], 26.* Retrieved from http://www.redalyc.org/articulo.oa?id=72729538016

Snow, C. (2002). *Reading for understanding: Toward an R&D program in reading comprehension.* Santa Monica, CA: RAND. Retrieved from https://www.rand.org/pubs/monograph_reports/MR1465.html

Snow, R. E. (1992). Aptitude theory: Yesterday, today, and tomorrow. *Educational Psychologist, 27,* 5–32. doi:10.1207/s15326985ep2701_3

Spektor-Levy, O., Basilio, M., Zachariou, A, & Whitebread, D. (2017). Young children's spontaneous manifestation of self-regulation and metacognition during constructional play tasks. *Teachers College Record, 119,* 13. Retrieved from http://www.tcrecord.org

Spink, A., Danby, S., Mallan, K., & Butler, C. (2010). Exploring young children's web searching and technoliteracy. *Journal of Documentation, 66*(2), 191–206. doi:http://dx.doi.org.mutex.gmu.edu/10.1108/00220411011023616

Szpunar, K. K., McDermott, K. B., & Roediger, H. L. (2007). Expectation of a final cumulative test enhances long-term retention. *Memory & Cognition, 35,* 1007–1013. doi:10.3758/BF03193473

Szpunar, K. K., McDermott, K. B., & Roediger, H. L. (2008). Testing during study insulates against the buildup of proactive interference. *Journal of Experimental Psychology: Learning, Memory, and Cognition, 34,* 1392–1399. doi:10.1037/a0013082

Stanford Aptitude Seminar. (2002). *Remaking the concept of aptitude: Extending the legacy of Richard E. Snow.* Mahwah, NJ: Erlbaum.

Stankov, L., & Lee, J. (2014). Quest for the best non-cognitive predicto of academic achievement. *Educational Psychology, 34,* 1–8. doi:10.1080/01443410.2013.858908

Stemler, S. E. (2004). A comparison of consensus, consistency, and measurement approaches to estimating inter-rater reliability. *Practical Assessment, Research, and Evaluation, 9*(4), 1–11. Retrieved from http://pareonline.net/getvn.asp?v=9&n=4

Stevens, R., Bransford, J., & Stevens, A. (2005). *The LIFE Center's Lifelong and Lifewide Diagram.* Seattle, WA: University of Washington, The LIFE Center. Retrieved from http://life-slc.org

Stromquist, N. P. (2015). Gender structure and women's agency: Toward greater theoretical understanding of education for transformation. *International Journal of Lifelong Education, 34,* 59–75. doi:10.1080/02601370.2014.991524

Taba, H. (1962). *Curriculum development: Theory and practice.* New York, NY: Harcourt, Brace, & World.

Tabachnick, B. G., & Fidell, L. S. (2013). *Using multivariate statistics* (6th ed.). Boston, MA: Pearson.

Tatsuoka, C. (2002). Data analytic methods for latent partially ordered classification models. *Journal of the Royal Statistical Society. Series C (Applied Statistics), 51,* 337–350. Retrieved from http://www.jstor.org/stable/3592656

Tatsuoka, K. K. (2009). *Cognitive assessment: An introduction to the rule space method.* New York, NY: Routledge.

Teo, H. J., & Johri, A. (2014, February). Fast, functional, and fitting: Expert response dynamics and response quality in an online newcomer help forum. *Proceedings of the 17th ACM conference on computer supported cooperative work and social computing.* Baltimore, MD. doi:10.1145/2531602.2531731

Thomas, G., & Anderson, D., (2012). Parents' metacognitive knowledge: Influences on parent-child interactions in a science museum setting. *Journal of Research in Science Education, 43,* 1245–1265.

Thomas, R. C., Finn, B., & Jacoby, L. L. (2016). Prior experience shapes metacognitive judgments at the category level: The role of testing and category difficulty. *Metacognition and Learning, 11,* 257–274. doi:10.1007/s11409-015-9144-4

Thompson, B. (2004). *Exploratory and confirmatory factor analysis: Understanding concepts and applications.* Washington, DC: American Psychological Association. doi:10.1037/10694-000

Thompson, C. P., Wenger, S. K., & Bartling, C. A. (1978). How recall facilitates subsequent recall: A reappraisal. *Journal of Experimental Psychology: Human Learning and Memory, 4,* 210–221. doi:10.1037/0278-7393.4.3.210

Van De Sande, B. (2013). Properties of the Bayesian knowledge tracing model. *Journal of Educational Data Mining, 5*(2), 1–10. Retrieved from https://jedm.educationaldatamining.org/index.php/JEDM/article/view/35/pdf_27

Van De Schoot, R., Schmidt, P., De Beuckelaer, A., Lek, K., & Zondervan-Zwijnenburg, M. (2015). Editorial: Measurement Invariance. *Frontiers in Psychology, 6,* 1064. doi:10.3389/fpsyg.2015.01064

van Manen, M. (2014). *Phenomenology of practice.* Walnut Creek, CA: Left Coast Press.

Vygotsky, L. S. (1978). *Mind in society: The development of higher psychological processes.* Cambridge, MA: Harvard University Press.

Weintrop, D., Beheshti, E., Horn, M. S., Orton, K., Trouille, L., Jona, K., & Wilensky, U. (2014, July). Interactive assessment tools for computational thinking in high school STEM classrooms. In D. Reidsma, I. Choi, & R. Bargar (Eds.), *Intelligent Technologies for Interactive Entertainment: 6th International Conference, INTETAIN 2014, Chicago, IL, Proceedings* (pp. 22–25). Cham, Switzerland: Springer International. doi:10.1007/978-3-319-08189-2_3

Werner, L., Denner, J., Campe, S., & Kawamoto, D. C. (2012, February–March). The fairy performance assessment: Measuring computational thinking in middle school. SIGSE '12. *Proceedings of the 43rd ACM technical symposium on computer science education* (pp. 215–220). Raleigh, NC. doi:10.1145/2157136.2157200

Widhiarso, W., & Ravand, H. (2014). Estimating reliability coefficient for multidimensional measures: A pedagogical illustration. *Review of Psychology, 21,* 111–121.

Wiggins, G. (1993). *Assessing student performance: Exploring the limits of testing.* San Francisco, CA: Jossey-Bass.

Williams, R. L. (1999). Operational definitions and assessment of higher-order cognitive constructs. *Educational Psychology Review, 11,* 411–427. doi:10.1023/A:1022065517997

Wing, J. M. (2006). Computational thinking. *Communications of the ACM, 49,* 33–35.

Wing, J. M. (2008). Computational thinking and thinking about computing. *Philosophical Transactions of the Royal Society A, 366,* 3717–3725. doi:10.1098/rsta.2008.0118

Xu, X., & Bland, L. C., & Kusano, S. M., & Johri, A. (2017, June). The development of engineering students' metacognitive skills in informal engineering learning activities. *Proceedings of American Society for Engineering Education Annual Conference and Exposition.* Columbus, OH. Retrieved from https://peer.asee.org/28959

Yang, S., Domeniconi, C., Revelle, M., Sweeney, M., Gelman, B., Beckley, C., & Johri, A. (2015, March). Uncovering trajectories of informal learning in large online communities of creators. *Proceedings of the Second ACM Conference on Learning at Scale 2015* (pp. 131–140). Vancouver, Canada. doi:10.1145/2724660.2724647

York, T. T., Gibson, C., & Rankin, S. (2015). Defining and measuring academic success. *Practical Assessment, Research, and Evaluation, 20*(5). Retrieved from http://pareonline.net/getvn.asp?v=20&n=5

Yukselturk, E., & Altiok, S. (2017). An investigation of the effects of programming with Scratch on the pre-service IT teachers' self-efficacy perceptions and attitudes toward computer programming. *British Journal of Educational Technology, 48,* 789–801. doi:10.1111/bjet.12453

Zaromb, F. M., & Roediger, H. L. (2010). The testing effect in free recall is associated with enhanced organizational processes. *Memory & Cognition, 38,* 995–1008. doi:10.3758/MC.38.8.995

Zell, E., Strickhouser, J., & Alicke, M. (2017). Local dominance effects on self-evaluations and intrinsic motivation. *Self and Identity, 16,* 629–644. doi:10.1080/15298868.2017.1295100

Zimmerman, B. (2005). Attaining self-regulation: A social-cognitive perspective. In M. Bockaerts, P. R. Pintrich, & M. Zeidner (Eds.), *Handbook of self-regulation* (pp. 13–39). New York, NY: Elsevier.

Zimmerman, B., & Schunk, S. (Eds.). (2001). *Self-regulated learning and academic achievement: Theoretical perspectives.* Mahwah, NJ: Erlbaum.

CHAPTER 6

MEASURING RATER EFFECTIVENESS

New Uses of Value-Added Modeling in Competency-Based Education

B. Brian Kuhlman
Western Governors University

ABSTRACT

Raters are effective to the extent that they are unbiased yet helpful. This chapter demonstrates a novel way for institutions to monitor the levels of bias and helpfulness among raters without requiring multiple ratings of task submissions. The ability to work with single ratings is crucial in settings where the volume and velocity of task submissions is high. While bias and helpfulness require separate models and different outcome variables they can be measured using the same basic approach: a variation of value-added modeling where the "teacher effect" is translated into the "rater effect." Understood within this framework a rater's bias is the extent to which her pass rate tends to be higher or lower than expected (given other factors), and a rater's helpfulness is the extent to which his students' growth rates tend to be faster or slower than expected (given other factors). The result of each model is a measure

Data Analytics and Psychometrics, pages 177–193

of effectiveness that competency-based institutions can use to evaluate their raters. My goal in this chapter is to provide an overview of the methods and outputs of this approach at a conceptual rather than technical level. To this end, the chapter uses examples from fictional raters and students at Western Governors University (WGU). After the conceptual models are established, analyses of over 800 actual raters at WGU (whose actual Evaluation Department rates thousands of task submissions every day) across 2 months demonstrates: (a) the rater bias model, trained on 1 month of data, correctly predicts about three-fourths (*AUC* = 0.749) of the following month's testing outcomes; (b) the rater helpfulness model, also trained on 1 month of data, explains about two-thirds of the variance (*R-sqd* = 0.64) in the following month's score increases; and (c) bias and helpfulness measures are uncorrelated among the raters which suggests that they indicate distinct abilities.

Leaders in competency-based education have a duty to measure rater effectiveness, and to do so fairly using the best information. This is true anywhere high-stakes assessments are administered, but truer yet at institutions which heavily depend on constructed-response tasks to assess professional competencies. For example, at WGU (whose Evaluation Department manages nearly 900 raters and 2,500 task submissions every day) 68% of the assessments are constructed-response format. While these numbers will certainly shift across time as WGU grows, it is safe to assume that rating task submissions will remain a very big piece of its operations. That said, rater effectiveness is important to measure not only because of the operational scale but also because of its regular impact on the progress of each student.

At competency-based institutions like WGU, students submit their constructed-response tasks to a team of raters who (a) decide whether those students are required to revise and resubmit before progressing and (b) send written feedback to students regarding the decision. These ratings are effective to the extent that (a) the decisions are unbiased and (b) the feedback is helpful. Students deserve to be rated fairly and need our help to improve. The most effective raters make unbiased decisions, provide helpful feedback, and do so consistently. In other words, there are really two aspects of rater effectiveness: bias and helpfulness.

The goal of this chapter is to demonstrate a fair, accurate, comprehensive, and efficient way to measure rater effectiveness. The measures are fair and accurate because they are drawn from the ideal information source (actual ratings) and they accurately predict testing outcomes. The approach is comprehensive and efficient because it uses multiple information sources (multiple predictors) but does not require any extra processes or resources. There are no self-report forms or subjective performance reviews. More importantly multiple ratings are not necessary. This last point is worth addressing further.

To my knowledge, all existing approaches to measuring rater effects require each task submission to be evaluated by multiple raters. For example, generalizability theory (Cronbach, Nageswari, & Gleser, 1963) and inter-rater reliability (e.g., Cohen's [1960] *Kappa*) approaches can both measure rater effects but they require multiple ratings in order to do so. This multiple ratings requirement imposes a trade-off between efficiency and accuracy. On the one hand, you could increase efficiency by using a small subsample of task submissions. This sampling approach is what WGU uses to calibrate teams of raters; all raters on a team rate the same few task submissions and then team dialogue is used to build a mutual understanding of the submissions' strengths and weaknesses (see process description here: Gunnell, Fowler, & Colaizzi, 2016). This process is useful for team calibration but not for performance evaluation; this is because sampling error reduces the accuracy of rater effect measurements. On the other hand, it would yield high measurement accuracy if a team provided multiple ratings of *every* task submission, but doing so would incur extreme operation costs (especially in a high-volume/high-velocity context like WGU's Evaluation Department). This trade-off is unnecessary.

VALUE-ADDED MODELING

Rater effectiveness can be measured in much the same way that teacher effectiveness is measured: via regression-based models of student outcomes. Eric Hanushek (1971) was the first to demonstrate how such models could provide efficient measures of teacher effectiveness. These models are built as linear regression equations where each testing outcome is a function of its weighted-factors. The basic idea is that testing outcomes (e.g., pass/fail, score improvements) are caused by the student's baseline ability (i.e., prior testing outcomes), current status (e.g., grade level), and learning environment (e.g., teacher, school, district). Hanushek's approach was later dubbed value-added modeling (VAM) because it yielded a "value-add" weight for each teacher. Since other factors are controlled for, these weights are considered a precise measure of the teacher's effect on testing outcomes.

It is beyond the scope of this chapter to provide a detailed account of VAM methodology, but a couple bits are worth noting. First, VAMs fit under the hierarchical linear modeling (HLM; aka multilevel modeling) umbrella because factors like teacher and school are modeled as hierarchical. Students are typically nested within teachers. Teachers are nested within schools. Second, HLM and VAM require that a long data format—in which each row represents a single testing outcome—be altered so that teacher IDs (and other hierarchical variables) are dummy-coded. After dummy-coding it is important to check the table's row:column ratio and to make sure the analysis will have an acceptable level of statistical power. Third, HLM is often misunderstood and thus VAM is considered "controversial" because the models employ fancy techniques, such as shrinkage estimation and restricted maximum likelihood estimation, to control for sources of measurement bias (e.g., multicollinearity, missing data, kurtosis). To be fair, the controversy is not usually couched in these terms; however, critiques of VAM generally reflect a misunderstanding of its techniques. If readers want to dig deeper into these topics, I recommend Koedel, Mihaly, and Rockoff's (2015) review of VAM as well as Bryk and Raudenbush's (1992) technical introduction to HLM.

How could VAM, an approach used across many states and counties to measure teacher effectiveness, be used to measure rater effectiveness at competency-based institutions? In the sections below I focus first on how VAM translates into a model of rater bias and then demonstrate how VAM translates into a model of rater helpfulness.

RATER BIAS

A rater's bias is the extent to which her pass rate tends to be higher or lower than expected (given other factors). As illustrated in Figure 6.1, there are really two types of rater bias: positive and negative. Positive bias would colloquially be known as leniency and is exhibited anytime a rater's pass rate is higher than expected. Negative bias is typically called strictness and is evident whenever a rater's pass rate is lower than expected. Raters are supposed to be unbiased and so the closer this measure is to zero the better.

Why Rater Bias Matters

Rater bias is a topic that touches on a perennial issue with so-called subjective assessments: the issue of fairness. Imagine students Fry and Bender are required to write a poem about Mars. Fry and Bender do not get to select their raters; the raters are randomly assigned to them. It would be unfair if Fry's poem is rated strictly while Bender's is rated with much lenience. For this reason, the institution should make the rating process more objective by curbing both strictness and leniency among its raters.

Perhaps the most important way to safeguard the fairness of this process is for all ratings to be made according to a standard scoring guide: a rubric. The elements and scoring rules of the rubric should be specified clearly so each rater interprets them the same way. At institutions that manage a high volume of task submissions, like WGU, much effort goes into creating and maintaining precise rubrics. And yet, most rubrics contain one or more

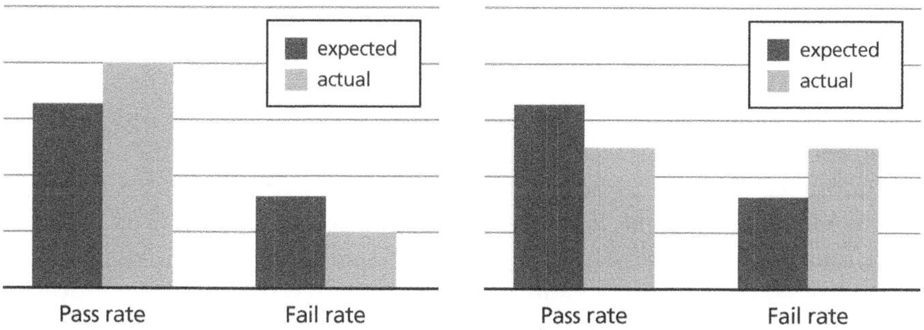

Figure 6.1 Examples of positive (left) and negative (right) rater bias.

points of ambiguity. So, while adhering to best practices in rubric development is crucial, more should be done to increase the objectivity of ratings.

Another way to reduce bias is to hold raters accountable to a target pass rate. This approach has the advantage of being very direct and simple to monitor. When a rater's pass rate goes too high or too low some feedback/accountability mechanism can encourage the rater to self-correct. The tricky part for the institution is selecting appropriate targets. Looking at the Figure 6.1 graphs, one wonders how the institution selected 66% as the expected pass rate. A simple way to select these targets is normative: Base the expectation on the team's recent pass rate. For example, if the team's pass rate was 66% in Quarter 1 then 66% becomes the target for each team member in Quarter 2. While this approach is reasonable it leaves a problematic (and rather obvious) margin of error.

Imagine that Leela is meeting with her manager, Professor Farnsworth. The focus of the meeting turns to Leela's numbers.

Professor: The team's target pass rate was 66%. Your pass rate was 44%. What happened?

Leela: I know it seems like I was being very strict, but the reality is more complicated than that. Let me explain why the 66% target was too high for my particular circumstances. First of all, most of my ratings this quarter were submissions of our most difficult tasks. Second, my students this quarter were lower-than-normal performers. Third, the majority of my ratings this quarter were done on first submissions. For these reasons, 44% is a good pass rate. Perhaps I have even been a bit lenient.

At this point, Professor Farnsworth can either (a) dismiss Leela's arguments and hold her accountable to the 66% target, (b) dig through all of Leela's submissions to see if her arguments are correct, or (c) believe Leela's arguments and let her off the hook. Each of these options is undesirable: In all likelihood they (a) will make Leela resentful, (b) will make Professor Farnsworth resentful, and (c) will make both of them doubt the validity of this accountability system. There is a way to set these targets which would avoid these problems.

Before we discuss this better way, we need to revisit the very savvy arguments Leela made. First, her pass rate was low because most of her ratings were on submissions of very difficult tasks. Some tasks are more demanding than others. At WGU, for example, there is a bell-shaped distribution of pass rates among tasks; the most difficult tasks have pass rates below 40% and the easiest tasks have pass rates above 90%. If Leela rated more difficult tasks than the rest of the team, then her pass rate really should be lower. Second, her pass rate was low because her students were poor performers. Some students are consistently better performers than others. At WGU, for example, there is a bell-shaped distribution of pass rates among students; the lowest performers have pass rates below 30% and the highest performers have pass rates above 90%. If Leela's students were lower-than-normal performers, then her pass rate really should be lower. Third, her pass rate was low because she rated first submissions. Because competency-based education requires failing submissions to be revised and resubmitted, a student's first submission of a task is by definition less likely to pass than his second or third or fourth submission of that task. This is discussed in more detail in the "Rater Helpfulness" section. If Leela's ratings were all done on early submissions, then her pass rate would suffer. Given these factors, how could Leela's bias be measured with any accuracy?

How to Measure Rater Bias

Pass rate expectations should be individualized to each rater, controlling for the effects of task difficulty, student ability, and submission count. Upon each submission, information should be recorded about task difficulty (i.e., the task's pass rate), student ability (i.e., the student's pass rate), submission count (i.e., how many times this student has submitted this task), and the rater's ID. If you treat each submission as an observation and each of those variables as a predictor, then you can build a model that will predict the outcome of each submission. These predicted outcomes would be used to set individualized expectations for each rater, and VAM would be used to measure exactly how far the raters' actual pass rates are from their individualized targets.

Some of the VAM specification details depend on the statistical package. If using HLM, then the model would specify both Level 1 (task difficulty, student ability, submission count) and Level 2 (rater ID) predictors. If using SAS (e.g., PROC MIXED or PROC GLIMMIX) or *R* (e.g., lme4), then the model would specify both fixed (task difficulty, student ability, submission count) and random (rater ID) factors. Regardless of the stats package, this is a binary logistic model that predicts the final outcome (pass or fail).

How to Interpret a Rater Bias VAM

With proper coaching, Professor Farnsworth's raters should be able to interpret VAM output. As mentioned in the previous section, VAM is considered opaque and confusing because it employs maximum likelihood and shrinkage estimation procedures. There is no magic to these estimation procedures; they are complicated but not deceptive. More importantly, nonexperts can accurately interpret VAM output without understanding statistical estimation. All that needs to be known is that the models produce optimal weights (or multipliers) for each of the predictors in the model. If that is understood then Tables 6.1–6.4 should be digestible to folks like Hermes and Leela.

On Tables 6.1–6.4, we see the effects of Hermes's very negative (strict) bias and Leela's slightly positive (lenient) bias. If Fry's submission had gone to a perfectly unbiased rater, he would have had a 74% likelihood of passing rather than 43%. Basically, we would expect an unbiased rater to pass Fry but we expect Hermes to fail him. In contrast, the likelihood of Bender's submission passing was not much affected by the fact that Leela was the rater. The expected outcome for Fry's submission is defined as the 74% likelihood of

TABLE 6.1 Example Observations—Bias VAM

				Rater	
Student_ID	Task_PRate	Student_PRate	Subm_Count	Hermes	Leela
Fry	0.75	0.92	1	1	0
Bender	0.75	0.43	3	0	1

TABLE 6.2 Example Output—Bias VAM

Intercept = 0.023

Predictor	Weight
Task_PRate	0.412
Student_PRate	0.324
Subm_Count	0.112
Hermes	–0.311
Leela	0.081

TABLE 6.3 Interpretation—Bias VAM—Fry's Submission

Predictor	Weight	Value	Product	
Task_PRate	0.412	0.75	0.309	
Student_PRate	0.324	0.92	0.298	
Subm_Count	0.112	1	0.112	
Hermes	–0.311	1	–0.311	
Leela	0.081	0	0.000	
		Sum of Products =	0.408	
			+ 0.023	(intercept)
			0.431	→ Fry has a 43% likelihood of passing

TABLE 6.4 Interpretation—Bias VAM—Bender's Submission

Predictor	Weight	Value	Product	
Task_PRate	0.412	0.75	0.309	
Student_PRate	0.324	0.43	0.139	
Subm_Count	0.112	3	0.336	
Hermes	–0.311	0	0.000	
Leela	0.081	1	0.081	
		Sum of Products =	0.865	
			+ 0.023	(intercept)
			0.888	→ Bender has a 89% likelihood of passing

passing which was calculated by adding together the intercept and all the predictor-products except for Hermes' effect. Whenever this rater-less likelihood of passing is above 50% we expect a pass, but when it is below 50% a fail is expected. So, a rater's individualized target pass rate would be the proportion of submissions in which the rater-less likelihood of passing is above 50%. With this system, it is not impossible for a rater's expected pass rate to be 0%; this could happen if all the rater-less likelihoods fell below 50% (e.g., if he exclusively rated first submissions of low performers on very difficult tasks). On the other hand, it is possible for the individualized target to be 100%; this could happen if all of the rater-less likelihoods fell above 50% (e.g., if he exclusively rated later submissions of high performers on tasks much easier than the Mars poem). In other words, the target entirely depends on the mix of factors represented among the submissions.

Imagine that Hermes' actual pass rate was higher than Leela's (as in Figure 6.2). Leela's bias (0.081) is slightly positive because her pass rate (44%) was slightly higher than expected. Hermes' actual pass rate (66%) matched

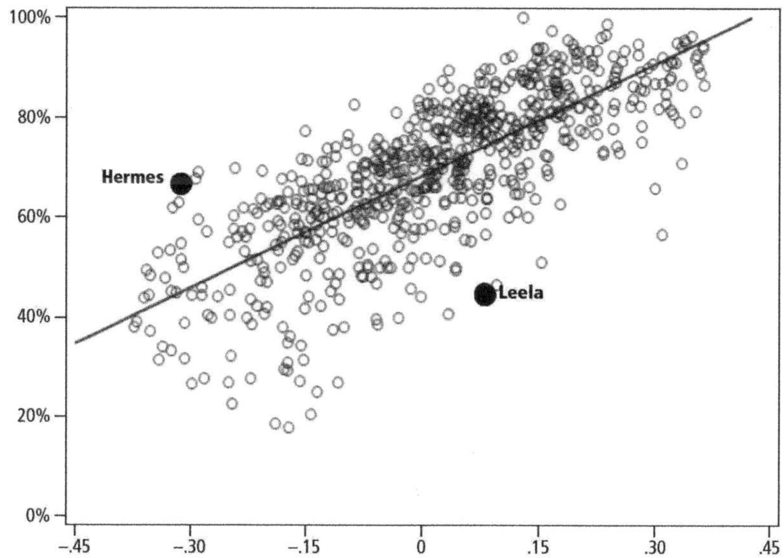

Figure 6.2 Relationship of rater pass rates (*Y*) to rater biases (*X*). *Note:* Each dot represents a different rater. Except for the fictional Hermes and Leela dots, the rest of this data represents actual raters at WGU.

the team's prior average and yet VAM revealed that it was much lower than his individualized target (*Bias* = –0.311). These counter-intuitive results are exactly what makes this approach so useful. With Figure 6.2 (and perhaps Tables 6.1–6.4) in hand, Professor Farnsworth has information that should not cause resentment and that everyone can trust.

This section has not addressed whether rater bias VAM measurements are stable across time. Given that Leela was slightly-lenient in this window of time, is it reasonable to expect she will be slightly-lenient in the next? Also, since the model predicts the outcome of each submission, one wonders how accurate these predictions are. These topics will be addressed in the "Predictive Validity" section below. But first we should turn our attention to the second aspect of rater effectiveness.

RATER HELPFULNESS

A rater's helpfulness is the extent to which his students' growth rates tend to be faster or slower than expected (given other factors). Because it deals with growth rates instead of pass rates, this second aspect of rater effectiveness resembles teacher effectiveness more closely than the first. As with the students of effective teachers, the students of helpful raters tend to improve faster than they would under other conditions. And students of unhelpful raters tend to improve slower than they would otherwise. Like teachers, raters are supposed to be helpful and so the more positive this measure is the better.

Why Rater Helpfulness Matters

While rater helpfulness is an underappreciated topic in psychometric research, there are a variety of contexts in which it clearly matters. In competency-based education, for example, students cannot graduate until they pass each assessment. Whenever a student fails a task she is required to revise and resubmit. Because of this requirement, the quality of rater feedback is key. When Hermes decides to fail a submission, he provides feedback detailing the submission's strengths and areas of improvement. On the one hand, if Hermes's feedback is ambiguous, terse, jargony or otherwise unhelpful, we can reasonably expect that student growth will be retarded. On the other hand, student growth should be accelerated following clear and helpful feedback.

Figure 6.3 helps explain student growth metrics. Recall that Bender is required to submit a poem about Mars. Figure 6.3 compares Bender's actual scores with a standard model of student growth. Amy scored Bender's first submission at 50% (a failing score); then Bender revised and resubmitted

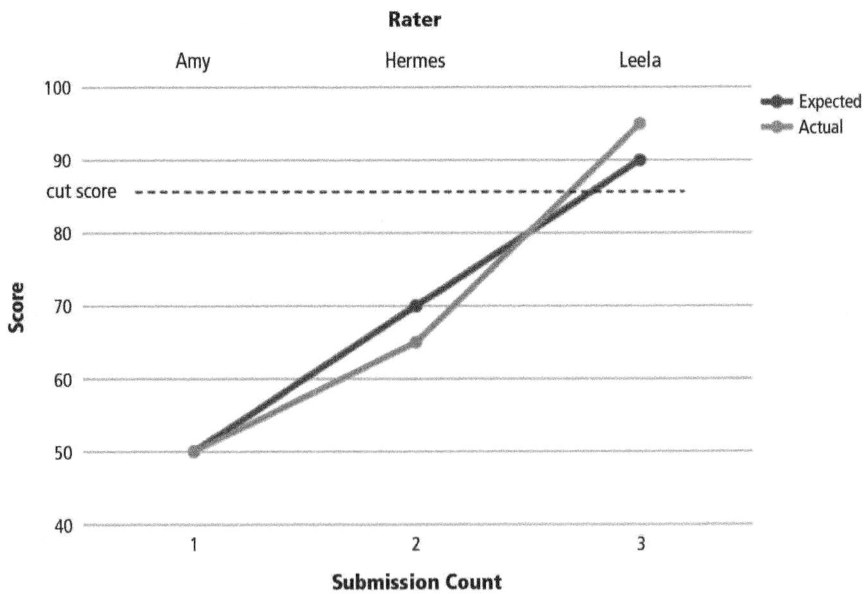

Figure 6.3 Bender's growth on the Mars poem task.

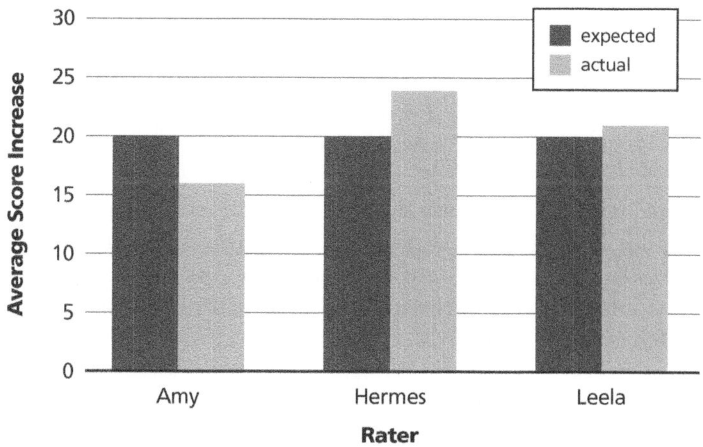

Figure 6.4 Growth rates for three raters.

and Hermes gave this second submission a 65% (also a failing score); finally Leela gave his third submission a 95% (a passing score).

A simple helpfulness measure is the average of score increases associated with a rater's fail decisions (see Figure 6.4). In the Figure 6.3 example, we would associate Amy with a 15 point increase (65%–50%) and we would associate Hermes with a 30 point increase (95%–65%). Because Leela passed the submission, this example would not affect her measure of helpfulness. Once these raters have failed a good number of submissions, and once those failed submissions have been revised and resubmitted, we can calculate the average score increase (growth rate) associated with each rater.

Again when using a system like this the tricky part for the institution is selecting appropriate targets. Looking at Figures 6.3 and 6.4, one wonders how the institution selected 20% as the expected score increase. A simple way to select these targets is normative: base the expectation on the team's recent growth rate. For example, if the team's average score increase was 20% in Quarter 1 then 20% becomes the target for each team member in Quarter 2. While this approach is reasonable it leaves a problematic (and rather obvious) margin of error.

Imagine that Amy is meeting with her manager, Professor Farnsworth. The focus of the meeting turns to Amy's numbers.

Professor: The team's target growth rate was 20%. Your growth rate was 16%. What happened?

Amy: I know it seems like my feedback was unhelpful, but the reality is more complicated than that. Let me explain why the 20% target was too high for my particular circumstances.

> First of all, most of my failing scores fell just below the cut score; this left very little room for these students to demonstrate growth. Second, the raters who followed me were unusually strict. For these reasons, 16% is a good growth rate. Perhaps I have even been a bit helpful.

Here we go again. At this point, none of Professor Farnsworth's options are very good. This simple measure of helpfulness is too simple; it does not reflect the particular circumstances of each rater. As with rater bias, a better approach would be to set individualized targets for each rater. So, how can Professor Farnsworth do that?

How to Measure Rater Helpfulness

To be clear, I am not suggesting that each rater's target be set at his previous average. The chase-your-tail approach would be worse than setting the target at the team's previous average. Instead, to provide individualized targets, Professor Farnsworth needs to do some math that controls for known correlates of the outcome. As Amy argued above, two correlates of score increase are (a) how close the first score is to the cut and (b) the second rater's bias level. Obviously, Professor Farnsworth cannot know the values of these correlates ahead of time; it is impossible to know how close Amy's future scores will be to the cut or how biased the raters will be who immediately follow her. To individualize the targets, Professor Farnsworth needs to wait until after the fact. An advantage of VAM is that it does not require a separate model to specify the individualized targets. As demonstrated in the "Rater Bias" section, the individualized target for each submission is the sum of all VAM-weighted variables minus the rater effect. In other words, Professor Farnsworth will not be able to specify the individualized targets until he is able to measure rater helpfulness.

To measure rater helpfulness, Professor Farnsworth will set up a linear VAM predicting score increase (second score minus first score). Each observation will represent a failing submission that was revised and resubmitted. Level 1 fixed factors will include distance from the cut (cut score minus first score) and second rater's bias (preferably measured by VAM instead of by pass rate). Level 2 random factors will include all the first rater IDs.

How to Interpret Rater Helpfulness VAM

As a good manager, Professor Farnsworth will help his raters understand the VAM output by showing how it applies to individual observations.

On Tables 6.5–6.8, we see that Amy was wrong about her effectiveness; she has indeed been slowing (not accelerating) student progress. For example, if Bender's first submission of the Mars poem task had gone to a rater with a 0.0 helpfulness score, the model would have predicted a 23%

TABLE 6.5 Example Observations—Helpfulness VAM

Student_ID	Score		Increase	Cut	Dist_ to_Cut	Rater2 _Bias	First Rater	
	1st	2nd					Amy	Hermes
Bender	50	65	15	85	35	−0.311	1	0
Bender	65	95	30	85	20	0.081	0	1

Note: This data reflects Figure 6.3, and the Rater2_Bias values are from Table 6.2.

TABLE 6.6 Example Output—Helpfulness VAM

Intercept = 17.211

Predictor	Weight
Dist_to_Cut	0.212
Rater2_Bias	6.324
Amy	−8.112
Hermes	2.921

TABLE 6.7 Interpretation—Helpfulness VAM—Amy's Rating

Predictor	Weight	Value	Product	
Dist_to_Cut	0.212	35	7.420	
Rater2_Bias	6.324	−0.311	−1.967	
Amy	−8.112	1	−8.112	
Hermes	2.921	0	0.000	
		Sum of Products =	−2.669	
			+ 17.211	(intercept)
			14.542	→ predicted 15% score increase

TABLE 6.8 Interpretation—Helpfulness VAM—Hermes's Rating

Predictor	Weight	Value	Product	
Dist_to_Cut	0.212	20	4.420	
Rater2_Bias	6.324	0.081	0.512	
Amy	−8.112	0	0.000	
Hermes	2.921	1	2.921	
		Sum of Products =	7.673	
			+ 17.211	(intercept)
			24.884	→ predicted 25% score increase

rather than a 15% score increase. Note that the expected score increase following Amy's rating is this 23% calculated using all weighted predictors except the rater effect. A rater's individualized target would be the average of these rater-less predictions. Amy's helpfulness score of –8.122 indicates that her students' actual average score increase (16%; see Figure 6.4) was 8.122% lower than her individualized target. In contrast, Hermes' rate was about 3% (*helpfulness* = 2.921) higher than his individualized target.

PREDICTIVE VALIDITY

To test the validity of these models, I collected 2 months of data from WGU whose Evaluation Department rates thousands of task submissions every day. Each month of this sample (872 raters) contained nearly 70,000 submissions. Whereas the rater bias model uses all observations, the rater helpfulness model uses only failed submissions that have been revised and resubmitted. So, the helpfulness model's *N* counts were a bit smaller: (10,923 in the first month and 11,231 in the second month).

Using a supervised machine learning framework, the first month of data was used as a training set and the second month as a testing set. To be clear: These were completely independent data sets. Weights like those shown in Tables 6.2 and 6.6 were calculated using the first month's data. Those weights were applied to the second month's data, yielding predicted pass/fail outcomes (from the rater bias VAM) and predicted score increases (from the rater helpfulness VAM) for each observation. Figures 6.5 and 6.6 display the results of these analyses.

For those unaccustomed to ROC plots, the most important piece of Figure 6.5 is the number on top which indicates that 74.87% of the graph's area is "under the curve." The higher this number is the better. Of the 69,923 predictions made by this model 51,743 (74%) were correct. Sensitivity (91%) was higher than specificity (35%) which means the model did a better job predicting passing than failing outcomes. Overall, these numbers are impressively high, which suggests (a) we have included good predictors of the pass/fail outcome and (b) the predictors work similarly month to month. More specifically, rater biases are stable month to month.

As Figure 6.6 shows, there is a very strong correlation between the actual score increases and those predicted by the rater helpfulness model. The predicted values explain about two-thirds of the variance (*R-sqd* = 0.64) in the actual values. Again, because these predictions were made using the prior month's data, and because the outcomes are impressively strong, it is reasonable to assume that (a) we have included good predictors of the outcome and (b) the predictors work similarly month to month. More specifically, rater helpfulness is stable month to month.

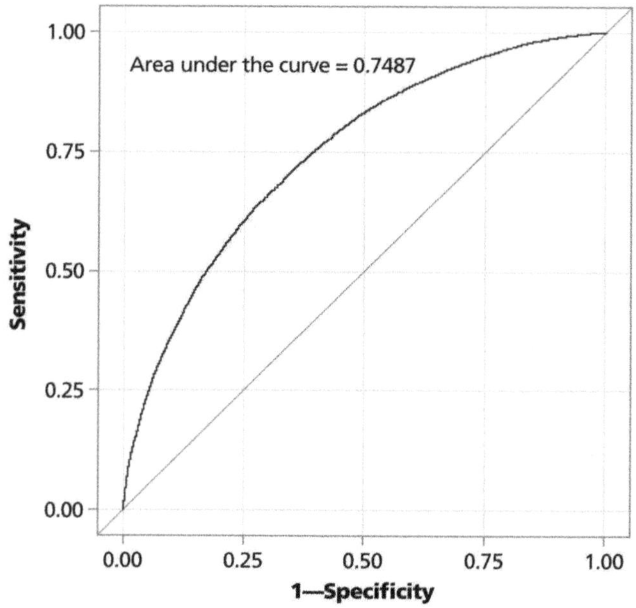

Figure 6.5 Receiver operating curve showing predictive validity of rater bias model.

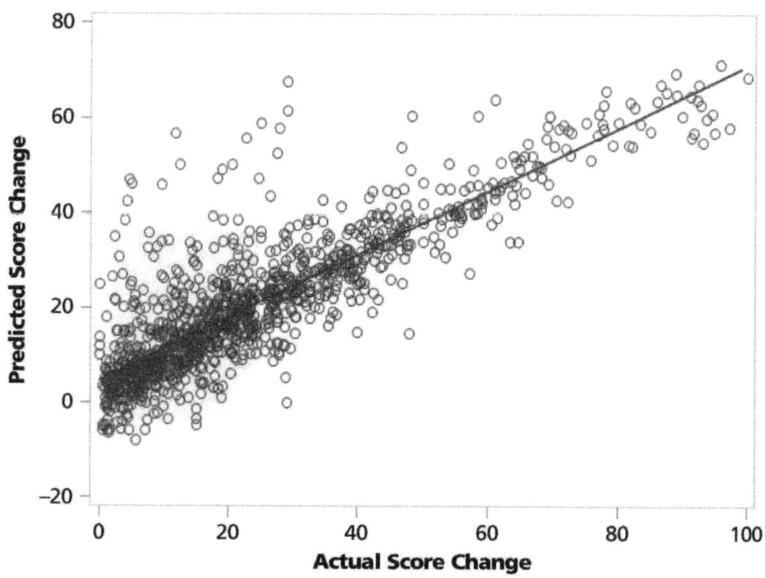

Figure 6.6 Scatterplot showing predictive validity of rater helpfulness model.

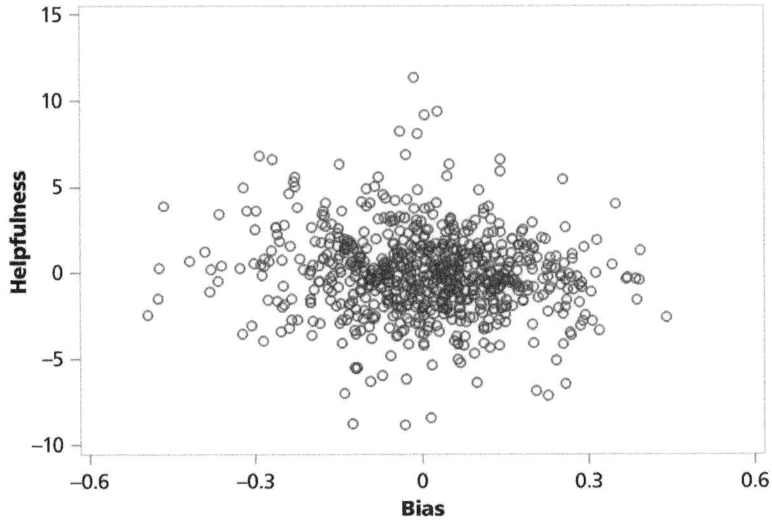

Figure 6.7 Two aspects of rater effectiveness are uncorrelated. *Note:* Each dot represents a different WGU rater. $N = 872$.

How predictive of her helpfulness is a rater's bias, and vice versa? If we know a rater's level of helpfulness, how much can we say about his level of bias? Not much, according to the data in Figure 6.7. At WGU, across the 2-month period investigated here, rater bias was uncorrelated ($r = 0.014$, $p = 0.231$) with rater helpfulness. It appears that these traits are orthogonal, which suggests that the most effective raters—those with zero bias and positive helpfulness scores—are rare treasures.

FUTURE DIRECTIONS

The results of this analysis suggest that in places like WGU—a high-volume high-velocity competency-based institution where all task submissions are rated according to carefully crafted rubrics—a rater's bias and helpfulness levels one month are very good predictors of her bias and helpfulness levels the next month. To learn more about these aspects of rater effectiveness future researchers should compare positively and negatively biased (or helpful and unhelpful) raters; I suggest in vivo methods such as think-aloud protocols or screen recordings to capture differences in their rating processes, computational linguistic methods to uncover differences in the content of their feedback, and survey-based methods to test for differences in their personalities. This line of research could inform ongoing efforts to improve intelligent tutoring systems and automated essay scoring tools.

While fostering effectiveness among robot raters would be great, educational leaders might take more interest in human raters. It might be possible for raters to become more effective. Bias and helpfulness could be either dispositions or competencies or a mixture of both. To the extent that they are competencies and not dispositions, bias and helpfulness levels could be controlled. Researchers should ask questions such as: how frequently should bias and helpfulness measures be taken and how should they be fed back to raters? One good approach would be to randomly assign raters to one of two-or-more promising interventions. Another would be an ABAB longitudinal design, where A is business-as-usual and B is a promising feedback mechanism regarding the rater's performance.

The most effective raters—those with zero bias and positive helpfulness scores—may indeed be rare, but we should try to make them less so.

ACKNOWLEDGMENTS

This work would not have been possible without support from Jason Levin, Sarah DeMark, and Shelley Ragland. I am very grateful for this collaboration with WGU's Evaluation Department leadership: Debbie Fowler, Maureen O'Brien, Kirk Welter, and the Senior Managers.

REFERENCES

Bryk, A. S., & Raudenbush, S. W. (1992). *Hierarchical Linear Models.* Newbury Park, CA: SAGE.

Cohen, J. (1960). A coefficient for agreement for nominal scales. *Education and Psychological Measurement, 20,* 37–46.

Cronbach, L. J., Nageswari, R., & Gleser, G. C. (1963). Theory of generalizability: A liberation of reliability theory. *The British Journal of Statistical Psychology, 16,* 137–163.

Gunnell, K. L., Fowler, D., & Colaizzi, K. (2016). Inter-rater reliability calibration program: Critical components for competency-based education. *The Journal of Competency-Based Education, 1,* 36–41.

Hanushek, E. A. (1971). Teacher characteristics and gains in student achievement: Estimation using micro-data. *American Economic Review, 61*(2), 280–288.

Koedel, C., Mihaly, K., & Rockoff, J. E. (2015). Value-added modeling: A review. *Economics of Education* Review, *47,* 180–195.

CHAPTER 7

RANKING DOCUMENTS IN ONLINE ENTERPRISE SOCIAL NETWORK

Alex H. Wang and Umeshwar Dayal
Hitachi America, Ltd.

Social media applications, such as Jive, Salesforce.com, and Yammer, have been widely adopted by enterprises. The importance of a document posted in the Enterprise Social Network (ESN) applications is different from traditional document collections or Web pages. More importantly, it is different from public social networks, such as Facebook, Twitter, which view the entire social network as a "flat" graph. In most enterprise social network applications, the documents are organized in a hierarchical structure, which may include "group," "space," "project," and so on. Also, the authors of the documents play a critical role in the importance of a document. In this work, we take advantage of the unique structure of ESN applications to propose a novel method to rate the importance of every document posted in ESN objectively.

To rate the importance of a document posed in ESN, we consider two major factors, which are "who posted it" and "where it was posted." The

Data Analytics and Psychometrics, pages 195–203

document posted by a famous or influential user may get a better chance to be viewed by others. At the same time, if the document is posted in a popular place, it may also have a higher probability to be viewed.

Depending on the implementation of the ESN, the place where authors can post their documents may have different names, such as "space," "group," "community," "project," and so on. In this work, we use the term *space*. When ranking documents, users, and spaces, we use the terms document *importance*, user *influence*, and space *popularity*.

RELATED WORK

Ranking algorithms for social network in general have been well studied. In Kwak, Lee, Park, and Moon (2010), Twitter, a microblogging service, is studied to learn its topological characteristics and its power as a new media. The users are ranked by the number of followers and by PageRank. These two rankings are found to be similar. The authors also rank the users by retweets, which shows differences from the previous two rankings. This indicates the need for a comprehensive and reliable influence ranking algorithm.

Bian, Liu, Agichtein, and Zha (2008) proposes a machine learning based ranking framework for social media to vote spam in particular. The ranking algorithm integrates user interactions and content relevance. The results show that the ranking is significantly more robust to vote spam compared to existing works.

Instead of ranking the users, Liu, Hua, Yang, Wang, and Zhang (2009) rank the relevance of tags associated with a given image. The authors first estimate the initial scores for the tags based on probability density estimation, and then perform a random walk over a tag similarity graph to recalculate the relevance scores.

This work is different from existing works in three aspects. First, most existing work, such as research done by Google, Microsoft, and Facebook, mainly focus on public social networks, such as Facebook and Twitter. Meanwhile the structure of ESN is different from most popular public social networks. Secondly, most existing works focus on ranking the users in the social network. In this work, we can provide not only a rank of users in ESN, but also a rank of posted documents. For an enterprise, it cares more about the influence of a posted document, which may contain important notification or promoted special events, than the influence of a particular user. Finally, most existing works only utilize the social connections among users to calculate a rank. The unique structure of ESN is largely overlooked by exiting works.

DOCUMENT RANKING FRAMEWORK IN ESN

The importance of a document posted in ESN is affected by two major factors, which are the author of the document and the space where the document posted. Here we assume that each document has only one author and was posted in only one space. If the document has been posted in multiple spaces, we consider them as different documents. Figure 7.1 shows the relationships among author, document, and space in ESN.

First, each individual author may post multiple documents. We assume that there is a mutually reinforcing relationship between authors and documents that could be reflected in the rankings. In particular, the more popular an author is, the more likely it is that his/her document will be viewed. Meanwhile, influential documents will bring more acknowledgements to their authors.

Secondly, depends on various implementations of ESN, the place where authors can post their documents may be called by different names, such as space, group, community, project, and so on. In this work, we refer to them all as space. As shown in Figure 7.1, a space may contain multiple documents. Similarly, we assume a mutually reinforcing relationship between spaces and documents that could be reflected in the rankings. In other

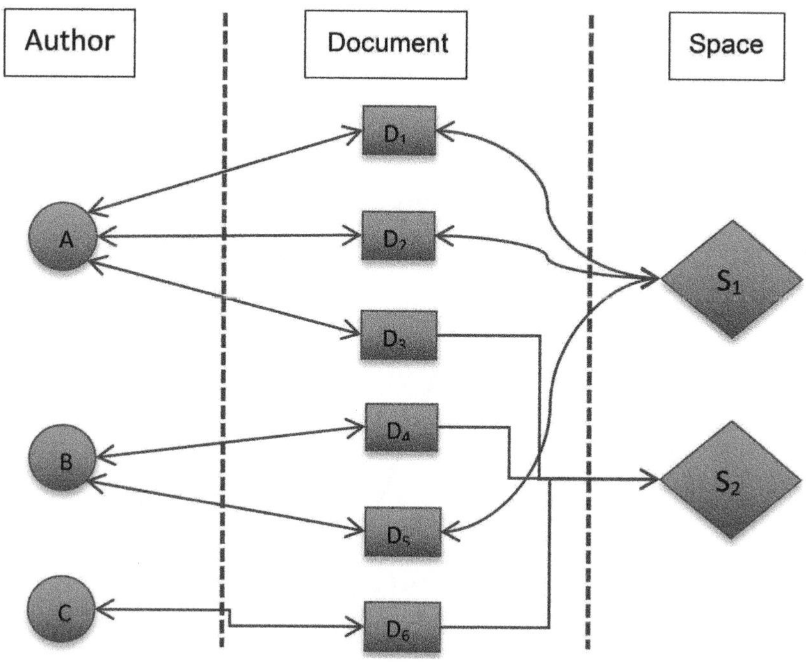

Figure 7.1 Relationships between author, document, and space.

words, the more popular a space is, the more likely it is that the document posted in this space will be viewed. At the same time, an influential document will boost the popularity of the space where it is posted.

DOCUMENT RANKING CALCULATION

To calculate the importance of the documents in ESN, we need to evaluate the initial ranking of the users and spaces in the ESN. First, we evaluate the initial influence of the author of a document. The ESN is modeled as a directed graph based on the following relationships between users as shown in Figure 7.2. The graph $G = (V, A)$ consists of a set V of nodes (vertices) representing user accounts and a set A of arcs (directed edges) that connect nodes. Each arc is an ordered pair of distinct nodes; a directed arc (i, j) from user i to user j represents that i is following j.

In this graph, the in-degree $d_I(i)$ of a node v_i, which is the number of arcs *into* i, is equal to the number of followers of user i. A real example of a social graph is shown in Figure 7.3. The graph is built based on a real large ESN. The data set is collected using Jive software REST API. The social graph contains a total of 1,654 nodes (numbers of users) and 10,045 edges (numbers of following relationships), and the average degree (numbers of followers + numbers of following) in this graph is six.

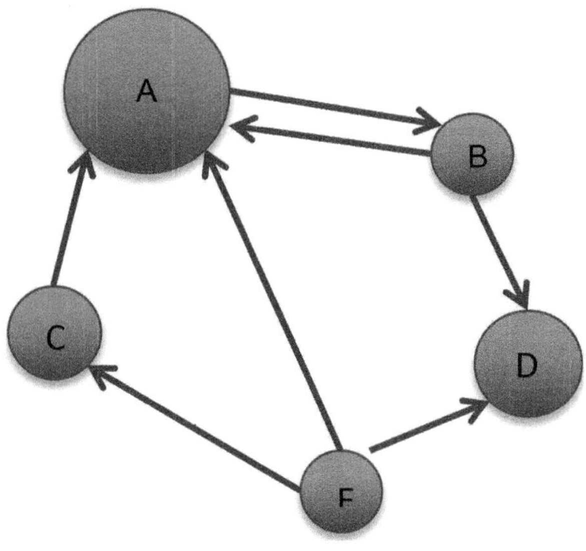

Figure 7.2 Social graph.

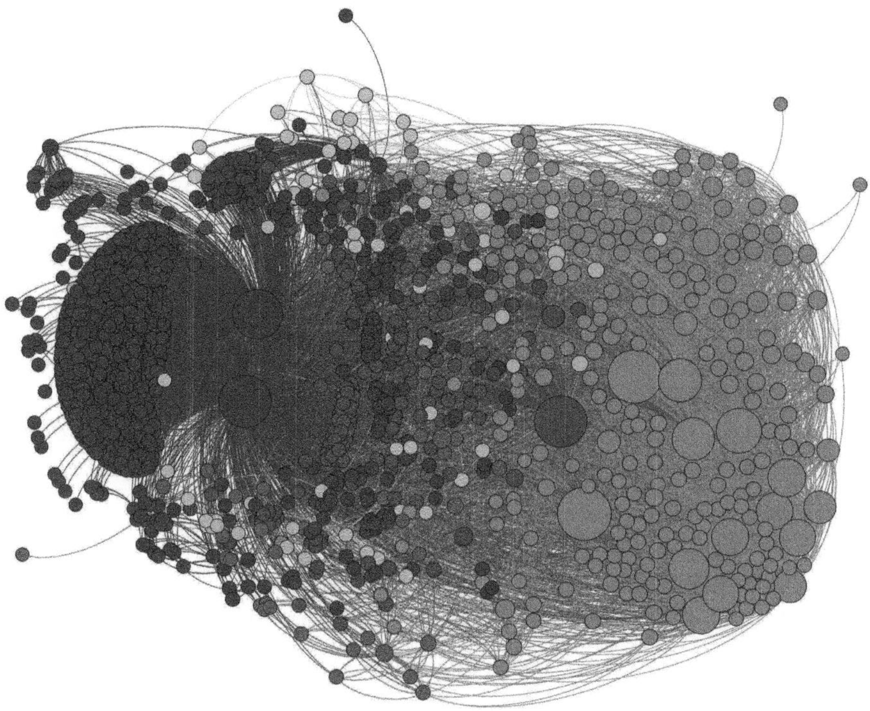

Figure 7.3 Social graph.

To calculate the initial ranking of users, let N_u be the total number of arcs in this graph, and define the initial influence of user i as $y_i^0 = d_I(i) / N_u$. The flowchart of the algorithm of calculating initial user ranking is shown in Figure 7.4.

To calculate the document rankings, initially, we assume that the more documents are posted in a space, the more popular the space is. Let N_d denote the total number of documents posted in the ESN and N_s the number of documents posted in space s. The initial normalized popularity of space s is $z_s^0 = N_s / N_d$.

We define the document importance x_d, user influence y_i, and space popularity z_s as the solution to the following system of equations:

$$x_d = w y_{\text{author}(d)} + (1-w) z_{\text{space}(d)} \tag{7.1}$$

$$y_i = \alpha \left[\sum_{\text{author}(d)=s} x_d \right] + (1-\alpha) y_i^0 \tag{7.2}$$

$$z_s = \beta \left[\sum_{\text{space}(d)=i} x_d \right] + (1-\beta) z_s^0 \tag{7.3}$$

where w, α, and β are given numbers between 0 and 1.

Equation 7.1 formalizes the notion that the importance x_d of a document depends on *who* posted it as well as *where* it is posted. It states that x_d is a weighted average of $y_{\text{author}(d)}$, the influence of the author of that document and $z_{\text{space}(d)}$, the popularity of the space containing that document.

Similarly, Equation 7.2 states that the user influence y_i is the weighted average of the total importance of all the documents authored by that user and the initial influence y_i^0.

Lastly, Equation 7.3 states that the space popularity z_s is the weighted average of the total importance of all the documents in that space and the initial popularity z_s^0.

We now introduce the following notation, which allows us to rewrite the above equations in a compact manner. Let M be the matrix where the (i,d) element is 1 if user i is the author of document d, and 0 otherwise. Let N be

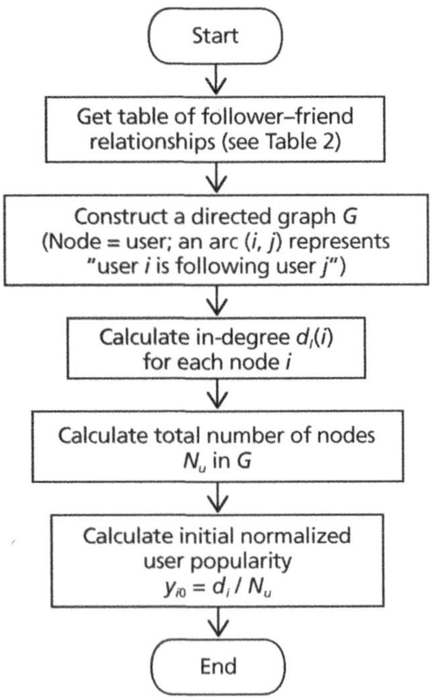

Figure 7.4 Algorithm of calculating the initial user ranking.

the matrix where the (s,d) element is 1 if space s contains document d, and 0 otherwise. Then equations 7.1–7.3 can be rewritten as

$$x = wM^T y + (1-w)N^T z$$

$$y = \alpha Mx + (1-\alpha)y^0$$

$$z = \beta Nx + (1-\beta)z^0$$

By substituting the last two equations into the first, we get

$$Ax = b,$$

where

$$A = I - w\alpha M^T M - (1-w)\beta N^T N$$

$$b = w(1-\alpha)M^T My^0 + (1-w)(1-\beta)N^T Nz^0$$

The document importance is then given by the solution to the above linear equation, namely

$$x = A^{-1}b.$$

The user influence y_i and space popularity z_s can then be obtained from Equation 7.2 and 7.3.

When the matrix A is singular, there may not be a solution to the original system of Equations 7.1–7.3. In that case, we may adopt an alternative approach, such as defining x to be the minimizer of $\|Ax - b\|$, where $\|\cdot\|$ is a vector norm, such as the L_1 or L_2 norm. We may also choose to use such an alternative approach in other cases, such as when A is close to singular or when the dimension of A makes the computation of the exact solution impractical. The algorithm is shown in Figure 7.5.

CONCLUSION

ESN has been widely adopted by enterprises, especially large companies. This work can be used in the following two scenarios:

1. Integrated into existing ESN platforms: Currently the popular ESN platforms, such as Jive, Saleforce.com, and Yammer, have not provided an effective solution for ranking the documents posted in the network. This work can be integrated into the existing systems as a component to provide a better ranking result.

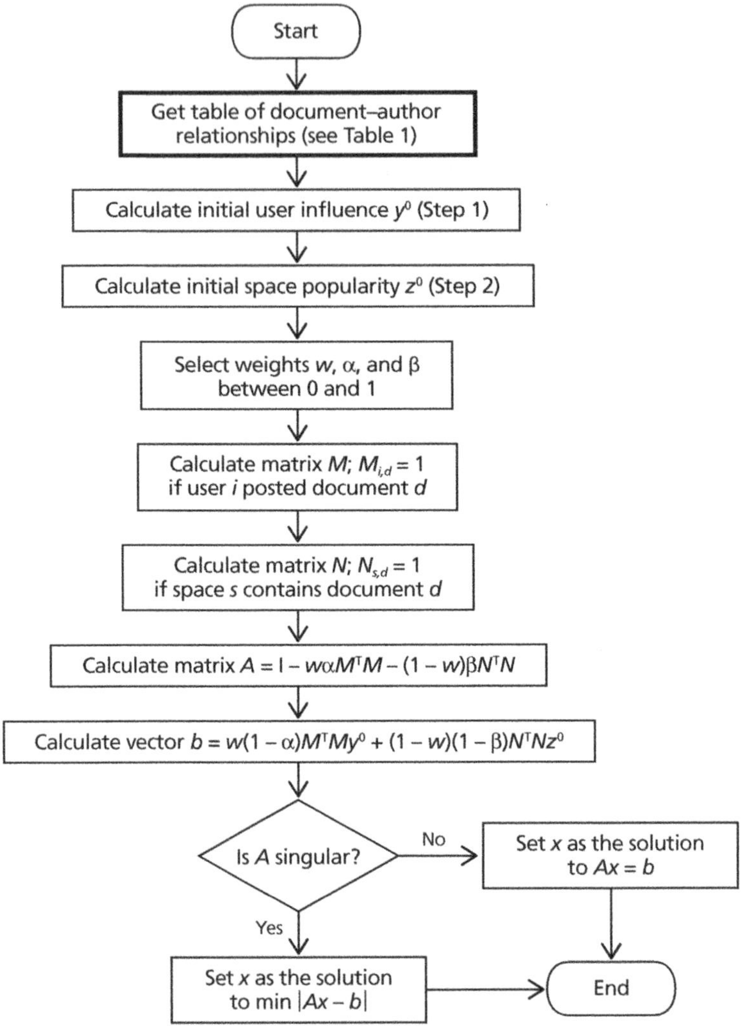

Figure 7.5 Algorithm of calculating the document ranking.

2. Providing an independent service: This work does not rely on a particular ESN platform. It can be implemented as an independent service to rank documents in different ESNs.

REFERENCE

Bian, J., Liu, Y., Agichtein, E., & Zha, H. (2008, April). A few bad votes too many?: Towards robust ranking in social media. In C. Catillo, K. Chellapilla, & D. Fetterly (Eds.), *Proceedings of the 4th international workshop on Adversarial information retrieval on the Web (AIRWeb '08)* (pp. 53–60). New York, NY: ACM.

Kwak, H., Lee, C., Park, H., & Moon, S. (2010, April). What is Twitter, a social network or a news media? In *Proceedings of the 19th international conference on World Wide Web (WWW '10)* (pp. 591–600). New York, NY: ACM.

Liu, D., Hua, X.-S., Yang, L., Wang, M., & Zhang, H.-J. (2009, October). Tag ranking. In *Proceedings of the 18th international conference on World Wide Web (WWW '09)* (pp. 351–360). New York, NY: ACM.

CHAPTER 8

METHODS FOR MEASURING LEARNING EVALUATION IN THE CONTEXT OF E-LEARNING

Matthew Pietrowski, Roopa Sanwardeker, and David Witkowski
Deloitte Consulting

ABSTRACT

Until recently, the methods available for evaluating learning were consistent as organizations have relied on different variations of Donald Kirkpatrick's method as their approach to learning evaluation since its origin in the mid-20th century. While this model and subsequent related models have been effective in the past, technological advances and the emergence of e-learning has transformed the training and educational landscape. This chapter seeks to evaluate contemporary approaches to learning evaluation specifically in regards to e-learning programs. After providing a brief overview of the history of learning evaluation the chapter will explore leading contemporary learning evaluation methods in depth. Specifically, it will explore Bloom's taxonomy; Kirkpatrick's four levels; Phillips' return on investment (ROI); time to competency; and the concept, input, reaction, and outcome (CIRO) evaluation approach to learning evaluation, weighing the inherent strengths

Data Analytics and Psychometrics, pages 205–229

and weaknesses of each framework from an objective standpoint. The chapter will then evaluate these existing frameworks specifically in the context of e-learning to determine the most effective models for evaluation in a virtual education environment. Ultimately, it is concluded that there are effective elements for evaluating e-learning in several of the contemporary frameworks; namely the first and fourth levels of Kirkpatrick's model, the cost optimization framework developed off of Phillips' ROI model, and the "input" stage of the CIRO framework.

HISTORICAL CONTEXT OF LEARNING EVALUATION

Gusky (2000) defines evaluation as a systematic process used to determine the merit or worth of a specific program, curriculum or strategy in a defined context. Evaluation, however, does not necessarily take place at one stage of the learning process, such as upon the completion of a training or development program; instead, the learning and the evaluation process are aligned through the construction and execution of the program. Without considering evaluation as the crux of learning, the vital process of ensuring the continuous improvement in the quality of the content and delivery of the learning experience is lost. Therefore, it is imperative to understand and develop the available frameworks for learning evaluation to ensure optimal learning capacity.

Historical accounts of learning evaluation date back to the informal methods of evaluation utilized thousands of years ago; however the field of evaluation has matured greatly over the past 50 years. As Scriven (1996) notes, "evaluation is a very young discipline—although it is a very old practice" (p. 395). Madaus, Stufflebeam, and Kellaghan (2000) provide an account of the seven development periods of program evaluation starting prior to 1900 and progressing into present day. The characterizations of each time period he describes are relatively similar up until recent past.

CATEGORIES OF EVALUATION

Since the 1930s, many evaluation approaches have emerged across a range of disciplines. Before evaluating specific evaluation approaches, it is helpful to understand the broader contextual approach frameworks. Worthen, Sanders, & Fitzpatrick (1997) classified the different approaches into six categories: (a) objectives-oriented, (b) management-oriented, (c) consumer-oriented, (d) expertise-oriented, (e) adversary-oriented, and (f) participant-oriented evaluation approaches. *Objective-oriented* evaluation approaches focus on delineating the specific objectives of a given learning program as a prerequisite to evaluation and then measuring the extent to which the goals are attained. While this approach is regarded as logical and readily usable, critics claim that not all learning objectives can be evaluated and the process by which objectives are selected is open to bias (Stufflebeam & Shinklefield, 1985). *Management-oriented* evaluation approaches intend to serve organizational leaders by meeting the informational needs of managerial decision makers (Hogan, 2007). This model is useful in determining the social acceptability, cultural relativity, and technical adequacy of the program; however its weakness can occur from evaluators giving partiality to top management. *Expertise-oriented* approaches rely on experts to judge the effectiveness of a program and make recommendations accordingly; while this approach helps improve the structure and organizational design of the program, it is limited by the externality of the evaluator who might not understand the objectives completely. An *adversary-oriented* approach to learning evaluation utilizes a judicial process to examine a program, operating under the assumption that debate will expose learning outcomes. Finally, *participant-oriented* evaluation frameworks focus on the participant's first hand experiences with the learning experience and collaborate to improve the program in the future by jointly assessing the programs strengths and weaknesses. While this helps to improve the learning experience, its reliance on individual opinion makes it more subjective and excludes the value of group data (Worthen et al., 1997). Most contemporary frameworks are a hybrid between several of these approaches; however participant-oriented evaluation has become increasingly dominant in the learning evaluation field—especially in regards to e-learning. Most of the contemporary frameworks evaluated below are primarily participant, management, and expertise-oriented.

CONTEMPORARY EVALUATION FRAMEWORKS

While Donald L. Kirkpatrick's four level methodology for evaluating training programs has historically been the leading framework in the field, contemporary learning evaluation experts have built upon the weaknesses in the Kirkpatrick model to create new methodologies. This section will first describe Bloom's taxonomy of education objectives which set the stage for learning evaluation methodology development. Then it will lay out Kirkpatrick's (1959) four levels of evaluation and address the most frequent critiques the model faces. Next, it will explore the fifth level that Phillips (1996b) proposed adding to Kirkpatrick's model, return on investment (ROI). Finally, this section will provide an overview of two other alternative evaluation methods—time to competency and CIRO evaluation. Once an understanding of existing contemporary evaluation frameworks are established, the paper can proceed in exploring the value of these evaluation methods in the context of e-learning.

Bloom's Taxonomy

One of the oldest learning evaluation frameworks that still remains relevant today was developed in the mid-20th century by a committee subset of the American Psychological Association (APA). Throughout 1949–1953, the committee conducted a series of meetings to eventually publish a *Taxonomy of Educational Objectives* (Bloom et al., 1956). These objectives were designed to improve communication between educators on the design of curricula and learning evaluations by providing a way to classify the levels of behavior that are important to learning. Each volume of the taxonomy published represents a major area of learning behavior: *cognitive* (knowledge), *affective* (attitude), and *psychomotor* (skills). While the committee collectively devised this taxonomy, it has been largely known as Bloom's taxonomy, after the leader of the committee Benjamin Bloom. This section will explore the three levels of Bloom's taxonomy by explaining the hierarchical structure within each learning area. While this framework is not used in its entirety today, it continues to provide a useful theoretical lens for learning evaluation.

Cognitive

Within the cognitive, or knowledge, domain, Bloom's taxonomy focused on six levels of learning ranging from the simple recollection of facts at the lowest level to the ability to apply knowledge and evaluate personal success at the top of the rank. Figure 8.1 shows the complete hierarchy Bloom developed for the cognitive domain. At the lowest levels, *knowledge* shows the learners basic ability to recall what they have learned, while a step above, *understanding*, is the learner's ability to summarize, explain and interpret what they have learned. *Application* is the learner's ability to apply the knowledge acquired to a scenario outside of the learning evaluation environment; while *analysis* is the learners ability to break down the information learned to identify relationships, make inferences and find evidence to support generalizations. Within the top levels, *synthesizing* is the learner's ability to add value in response to the learning experience. This can be done either by demonstrating how to apply the knowledge in a unique plan or set of operations or by improving upon past knowledge. The final level, *evaluation*, involves presenting and defending opinions by making judgments about the information learned based off the criteria explained. To demonstrate the actions required at each level of learning, it is helpful to reference the series of thinking skills Bloom articulates within each level. The bullets below the level titles in Figure 8.2 are ranked in order of criticality.

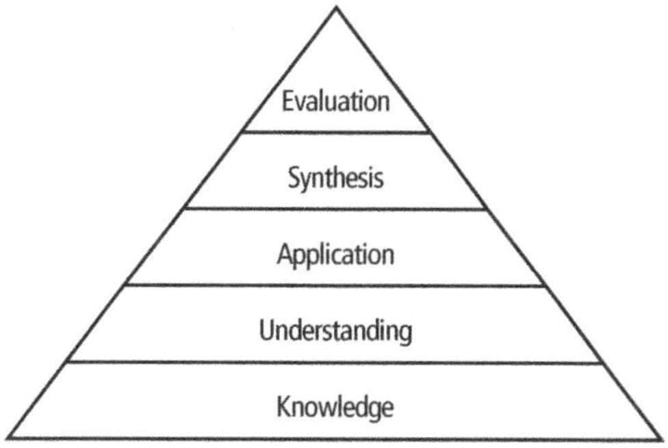

Figure 8.1 Cognitive domain hierarchy of Bloom's taxonomy.

Knowledge	Comprehension	Application	Analysis	Synthesis	Evaluation
• List Name • Identify • Show • Define • Recognize • Recall • State • Visualize	• Summarize • Explain • Interpret • Describe • Compare • Paraphrase • Differentiate • Demonstrate • Classify	• Solve • Illustrate • Calculate • Use • Interpret • Relate • Manipulate • Apply • Modify	• Analyze • Organize • Deduce • Contrast • Compare • Distinguish • Discuss • Plan • Devise	• Design • Hypothesize • Support • Schematize • White • Report • Justify	• Evaluate • Choose • Estimate • Judge • Defend • Criticize

Figure 8.2 Bloom's taxonomy ranking of thinking skills.

Affective

The five levels in the affective domain range from a passive reception of information to the building of abstract knowledge. The levels are shown in Figure 8.3.

The first level, *receiving*, is the most basic act of the learner paying attention enough to recognize the information being taught. At the next level, the

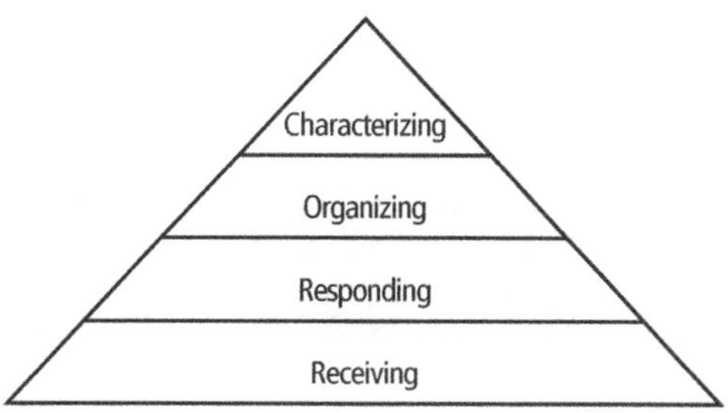

Figure 8.3 Affective domain hierarchy of Bloom's taxonomy.

student actively participates in the learning process and reacts to some extent by showing some new behavior as a result of the learning. The third level is a step beyond *responding* in that the learner attaches some *value* to the information received. Then at the fourth level, the student puts together the different values of information to compare and *organize* their new knowledge. Finally, the student *characterizes* the information to build abstract knowledge of the subject and acts consistently with the information learned.

Psychomotor

The psychomotor, or skills, domain deals with the learner's ability to physically manipulate a tool or instrument. Just as in the cognitive domain, Bloom's taxonomy ranks the psychomotor abilities across six levels ranging from innate reflex movements to nondiscursive movements. For the purposes of this paper, specific levels of psychomotor learning are less relevant; however see Appendix A for details.

In practice, Bloom's taxonomy of learning domains is helpful for categorizing learning objectives. Often times, the levels of each domain can be grouped across fewer units to help categorize cognition.

As demonstrated in Figure 8.4, categorization is a helpful way to initially assess learning impacts; however, additional criteria is required to add value to a learning evaluation. Therefore it is no surprise that Kirkpatrick's evaluation method originated shortly behind Bloom's taxonomy.

Kirkpatrick's Four Levels of Evaluation

In 1959 Donald L. Kirkpatrick defined the most widely used and popular method for learning evaluation. Kirkpatrick's four levels of learning

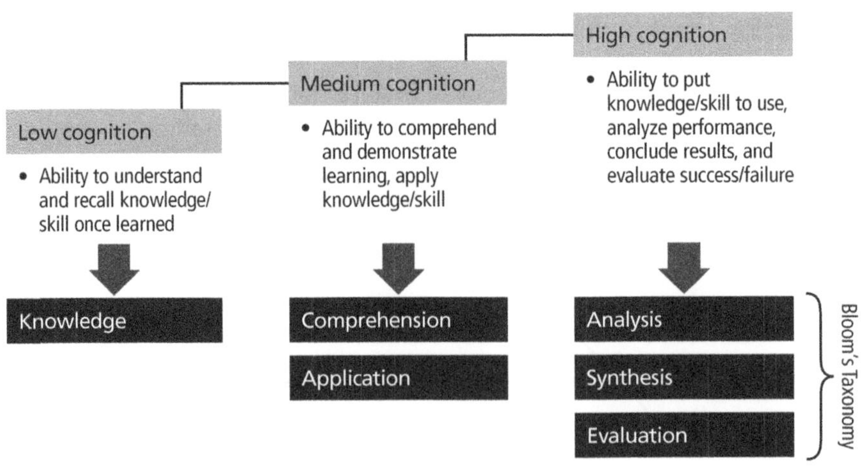

Figure 8.4 Bloom's taxonomy categorization.

evaluation first appeared in the *U.S. Training and Development Journal*, but the model was refined in 1998 when he published the second edition of *Evaluating Training Programs: The Four Levels*. The model is structured so that the degree of evaluation difficulty increases at each level just as the amount of knowledge learned about the effectiveness of the training program increases. The levels can be summarized as (a) reaction, (b) learning, (c) behavior, and (d) results.

Before addressing the specific levels of the method, it is valuable to understand why the method has served as the primary organizing design for training evaluation organizations for over thirty years. For starters, the method was the first to address the need of training professionals to understand training evaluation in a systematic way (Shelton & Alliger, 1993). Before Kirkpatrick's method, there was no system or language available to assess the extent to which training programs were successful. Secondly, the model is organized such that the fourth and final level provides critical bottom-line business insights. Additionally, the popularity of the model can be attributed to its ability to simplify such a complex process by providing a straightforward guide for the post-training questionnaires. Lastly, the model reduces the amount of information needed for training evaluation by focusing strictly on post-learning outcomes.

Level 1: Reaction

The first level of Kirkpatrick's methodology, *reaction*, measures the learner's reaction to the training program, specifically focusing on their experience, rather than the content learned. This level garners feedback on the learners satisfaction with the material and evaluates whether they consider the information relevant and useful for their job. Kirkpatrick outlines eight critical guidelines necessary for success at the first level:

1. Determine what you want to find out.
2. Design a form that will quantify reactions.
3. Encourage written comments and suggestions.
4. Get a 100% immediate response.
5. Get honest responses.
6. Develop acceptable standards.
7. Measure reactions against standards and take the appropriate action.
8. Communicate reactions as appropriate.

The results derived at this level do not concern the success of the learner's competency or the program structure more generally, it is only concerned with the learner's experience; which subsequently effects the learning evaluation at the higher levels.

Level 2: Learning

Kirkpatrick defines the second level, *learning*, "as the principles, facts, and techniques that are understood and absorbed by trainees" (Strother, 2002, p. 5). This level measures the extent to which participants attitudes change and knowledge increases as a result of the program (Kirkpatrick, 1994). This level is inherently more rigorous than the first level as it requires measuring change, which cannot be assessed through a simple reaction survey. While there are several ways to measure the difference in learning before or after the training program, Kirkpatrick recommends either using a control group or administering a pretraining evaluation to evaluate knowledge, skills, and attitudes before the program and repeating it after the program.

Level 3: Behavior

Level 3 is defined as the extent to which change in behavior has occurred as result of a training program. Strother (2002) notes that "changed on-the-job behavior is certainly the main goal of most corporate training programs, but measuring this change is a more complex task than eliciting trainees' feelings or measuring their direct learning through test scores" (p. 7). Kirkpatrick notes four prerequisites that must be present in order for a change in behavior to occur:

1. desire to change,
2. must know what to do and how to do it,
3. work in the right climate, and
4. rewarded for change.

In order to evaluate behavior, Kirkpatrick recommends using a control group when it is practical or evaluating both before and after the training. Surveys are also an effective way to measure behavioral change, especially when administered to the trainees in coordination with their immediate supervisors, their subordinates, and others who often observe their behavior. While the amount of time it takes for a behavioral change to solidify varies depending on the learning initiative, Kirkpatrick recommends allowing ample time for a behavioral change to take place; repeating the evaluation intermittently is helpful in this capacity.

Level 4: Results

The final level of Kirkpatrick's method for evaluating training programs involves measuring the final changes that occurred as a result of the training program in direct relation to the organization's bottom line. Variables measured at this level include increased production, improved work quality, reduced turnover, and so on. While every training program attempts to improve efficiency and reduce costs, it is inherently difficult to isolate training results, as critics of the framework are quick to note. As proceeding sections will address, many learning evaluation experts have built upon Kirkpatrick's fourth level framework to develop separate evaluation methods considering business results.

Limits to Kirkpatrick's Four Levels of Evaluation

While Kirkpatrick's methodology has certainly led training evaluation practices since its origin, it is not without its limitations. Bates (2004) identifies three core limitations of the model that have been widely cited throughout learning evaluation literature: incompleteness, the assumption of causal linkages, and incremental importance of information.

Model is Incomplete

The first critique that Kirkpatrick's model is incomplete rests on the premise that the four level model provides an oversimplified view of training effectiveness by ignoring the contextual and individual factors that influence training evaluation. Throughout the 1990s, training evaluation research identified the plethora of organizational, individual, training design and delivery factors that influence training effectiveness and evaluation outcomes. As a result, Cannon-Bowers, Salas, Tannenbaum, and Mathieu (1995) set a new precedent for training evaluation effectiveness that considers "characteristics of the organization and work environment and characteristics of the individual trainee as crucial input factors" (p. 143). Specifically, contextual factors for consideration were:

1. the learning culture of the organization (Tracy, Tannenbaum, & Kavanaugh, 1995);
2. the goals and values of the organization (Ford, Quinones, Sego, & Sorra, 1992);
3. the presence of interpersonal support in the workplace in regards to skill acquisition and behavior change (Bates, Holton, Seyler, & Carvalho, 2000);
4. the climate for learning transfer (Rouiller & Goldstein, 1993); and
5. the adequacy of material resources such as tools, equipment, and supplies shown to influence the effectiveness of training outcomes.

As it stands, Kirkpatrick's model does not include an examination of these factors that have now been established essential for effective evaluation. To address these shortcomings, learning evaluation experts have devised technical frameworks for evaluating learning evaluation empirically which will be discussed further on in the paper.

The Assumption of Causal Linkages

The second limitation inherent to Kirkpatrick's model implies a simple causal relationship between the levels of evaluation such that positive reactions leads to greater learning, which in turn, causes greater information transfer and subsequent positive organizational results. While Kirkpatrick does not speak explicitly about the causal linkages between training outcomes at each level, the method implies that the relationship exists (Holton, 1996). Kirkpatrick (1994) states "if training is going to be effective, it is important that trainees react favorably" and that "without learning, no change in behavior will occur" (p. 51); however research has failed to confirm such causal linkages (Bates, 2004). In fact, two training evaluation studies employing Kirkpatrick's model found little evidence of a correlation between measures at different outcome levels and the causal relationship Kirkpatrick suggests between the levels of evaluation.

Incremental Importance of Information

The final limitation to Kirkpatrick's model that Bates (2004) articulates concerns the assumption that the information garnered at each level is increasingly important. This assumption has led to the false conclusions by training evaluators that the fourth level will provide the most useful information about training program effectiveness.

While Bates' articulated limitations are not entirely comprehensive of the specific critiques of Kirkpatrick's model, they best encapsulate the thematic areas of limitation. The limitations expressed above are issues fundamental to Kirkpatrick's model, not application issues.

General Critiques

Bates provides three clear limitations to Kirkpatrick's model, whereas other critiques are even more general and concern the outdatedness of the model. Paul Berthal, the manager of research at Development Dimensions International, articulates the widespread sentiment towards Kirkpatrick's (1995) model noting:

> Kirkpatrick's classic model has weathered well. But it has also limited our thinking regarding evaluation and possibly hindered our ability to conduct meaningful evaluations... Too often, trainers jump feet first into using the model without taking the time to assess their needs and resources, or to determine how they'll apply the results... The simplicity and common sense of Kirkpatrick's model imply that conducting an evaluation is a standardized, prepacked process. But other options are not spelled out in the model. (p. 20)

Berthal goes on to explain how Kirkpatrick's model is made most effective when trainers "borrow evaluation forms, procedures, designs, approaches, techniques, and methods" and apply them to the approach (p. 20). Berthal's critique encapsulates the general sentiment among evaluation professionals which is made evident by the notable trend in supplementing Kirkpatrick's model that has occurred.

Phillips Evaluation Approach

Several learning evaluation experts have sought to address the shortcomings of Kirkpatrick's model to improve the method rather than devising a completely new evaluation approach. The founder of Performance Resources Organization, Jack J. Phillips, suggested adding ROI as a fifth level to Kirkpatrick's four level evaluation approach to help training professionals measure the financial impacts of training on the organization. Phillips (1996) provides a framework for measuring ROI to monetize the results of training from both a human and business outcome perspective.

Phillips (1991) notes:

> The common thread among most evaluation experts is that emphasis should be placed on the ultimate outcome, which results in improved group or organization performance. It is the most difficult to obtain, document, organization, and measure. The other three levels will not suffice in an ultimate evaluation. There is evidence in studies to indicate that the fourth level, a results orientation, is a method most desired and receives the most support. (p. 51)

Given the demand for a results-oriented training and learning evaluation, Phillips' ROI methodology has received much attention since its conception. The two most cited advantages to this evaluation approach are (a) to gain a better understanding of the factors influencing training effectiveness and (b) to determine the monetary value of specific training initiatives. (Hogan, 2007).

To best analyze training results, Phillips (1996) recommends dividing training results between hard and soft data. Hard data is the objective, traditional measure of organizational performance that are easy to measure and transfer into monetary values; whereas soft data is subjective and the measurement of softer skills such as communication, that are inherently harder to transfer into monetary value. To organize the data between hard and soft data, Phillips provides a complete checklist for each category. Hard data is organized by *outputs* such as tasks completed, *quality* such as rework, *time* such as training time and time to complete projects and *cost* such as overhead. Soft data, on the other hand, is organized into categories such as *work habits and climate, work attitudes* such as perceived changes in performance, *new skills* such as frequency in using new skills and *initiative* which includes items such as implementation of new ideas and number of employee suggestions. By organizing results in this way, organizations can have a comprehensive framework for evaluation. See Appendix B for the complete checklist provided in Phillip's book, *How Much is the Training Worth?*

Limitations

Despite the clear advantages of the ROI evaluation method in a learning and training evaluation context, critics highlight the challenges with applying the framework. Ultimately, it proves difficult to measure the effects of the training and learning initiative in isolation. Shelton and Alliger (1993) highlight the difficulties in applying ROI because some items cannot and should not be monetized. Phil Rutherford of the University of New England has a similar opinion on the matter claiming that anything above Kirkpatrick's first level of training evaluation "is evaluating the application of certain skills and knowledge and, as we all know, these could come from anywhere, not just training" (Abernathy, 1999, p. 23). Thus he recommends focusing on the application of competencies in the workplace that influence change at the first level.

Furthermore, monetizing intangible values is inherently difficult. Kaplan and Norton (1996), authors of *The Balanced Scorecard* claim that while financial measurements of evaluation worked fine in the industrial era, they are now out of sync with the skills and competencies that companies measure (Abernathy, 1999). Daniel Mclinden of Andersen Consulting and William Trochim, a professor at Cornell University, concur with Kaplan and Norton, noting that "it has become apparent that education evaluation must encompass methods that can deal with the psychological and sociological complexity of the education enterprise" (McLinden & Trochim, 1998, p. 288). They recommend that evaluation methods move beyond financial impact to measure the value in the development and delivery of the program rather than the evaluation of the program. General Electric (GE) benefited from this strategy in the early 2000's by emphasizing training, not its measurement. In doing this, GE saw increased consumer satisfaction and improved career development (Abernathy, 1999).

Alternative Approaches

Although time to competency CIRO and customer satisfaction frameworks lack the substance to stand alone as an evaluation framework, there are specific elements unique to each that are important to consider in this review.

Time to Competency

Phillips' ROI additive level to Kirkpatrick's evaluation method provided a business lens for addressing training needs which gave way to alternative methods for addressing business elements of training. Given that contemporary economic environments do not lend themselves to training all employees equitably and to the extent needed, Rozwell (2009) proposed a business-oriented way of evaluating the success of training programs. By measuring time to competency the value of learning activities can be calculated based off of business impact—which, in turn, allows businesses to prioritize the most effective learning programs for essential roles.

The time to competency evaluation approach is designed to measure how long it takes for people performing critical businesses processes to become proficient. Before establishing a baseline measurement for the evaluation approach, the organization must examine the roles and performance objectives that need improvement. This process requires analyzing critical business drivers, investigating documented strategy and objectives, and identifying crucial job roles (for a complete framework diagram see Appendix C). There are several methods an organization might employ to determine what the training objectives might be, such as strengths, weaknesses, opportunity, and threat (SWOT) analysis; however the specific method is not crucial so long as the organization establishes clear expectations of which roles and performance objectives are critical to business operations. Once it is established which performance objectives need improvement, the first step in calculating time to competency is for an organization to record a baseline measurement of the time it takes for an employee within a particular role to achieve the desired level of performance. While many organizations have official records or anecdotal reports estimating the approximate amount of time it takes for employees in key positions to achieve a certain level of competency, it is possible to consider published benchmarking measures or develop internal baseline measurement before the training is administered. After a representative baseline time measurement is agreed upon, the learning resources can be designed with the goal of reducing time to competency and then delivered accordingly. Ultimately, the impact of the training is the difference between the time it takes an employee to become skilled in their role once the training is applied.

CIRO Evaluation

Warr, Bird, and Rackham (1970) forwarded the CIRO evaluation approach based off of four categories of data capture: concept evaluation, input evaluation, reaction evaluation, and outcome evaluation. First, the evaluation seeks to understand the *context* of the program by identifying training needs in the context of the organization's culture and climates. After developing an understanding of the context of the training, the *input* evaluation phase considers the design and the delivery of the training activity. *Reaction* evaluation is similar to Level 1 of Kirkpatrick's evaluation as it concerns the learner's reaction to the training and attempts to measure the quality of the training experience. Outcome evaluation focuses on the value gained before, during and after the training. While CIRO does not provide specific mechanisms for evaluation, it is unique in its assessment of the objectives (context) and the training equipment (Hogan, 2007). As is explained later in the paper, the implications of input evaluation are particularly relevant to e-learning initiatives.

Customer Satisfaction

Much like Kirkpatrick's fourth level and Phillips' ROI evaluation, other experts have proposed a more specific business-facing evaluation methodology. According to Bregman and Jacobson (2000) an organization's single most important business result is employee satisfaction; therefore they propose evaluating the success of a learning or training program based off the measured effect it has on employees. They recommend asking customers directly about their perceived effect of a training initiative and outline four reasons that a customer satisfaction evaluation methodology is unique and effective. First, seeking customer feedback shows a commitment to improving the organization and that the organization values the customer's patronage. Second, it shows that the organization is serious about their development. Thirdly, it communicates to employees the primary importance of customer satisfaction. Lastly, it communicates to trainers and learning providers that their work will be valued to the extent that employees do things differently to increase customer satisfaction after the training. While the scope of application for this model is clearly limited, it is worth considering the factor of customer satisfaction when reviewing the value of a training program to align customer demand and educational outcomes.

EVALUATION IN CONTEXT OF E-LEARNING

Since the early 2000's e-learning has grown to dominate the educational training arena. E-learning applications can be structured as web-based learning, virtual classrooms, and digital collaboration (Kaplan-Leiserson, 2000). Not only is e-learning cost effective and time efficient, but it is also a preferred format for training in contemporary work environments. Additionally, e-learning programs are able to engage learners across differentiating learning styles and preferences as e-learning activates all three sensory learning styles (visual, auditory, and kinesthetic). Colorado and Howell (2009) captured the appeal of e-learning claiming it is "poised to deliver course content based on individual learning differences instead of the centuries old model of one size fits all" (p. 76). While the appeal of e-learning is clear, proper program development and evaluation is less straightforward. This section will assess the appropriateness of the contemporary evaluation methods explored above in the context of e-learning and then provide information on alternative e-learning evaluation methods that have emerged in recent years. The value of e-learning will be considered in each section to conclude that the most effective frameworks for e-learning evaluation are present at Kirkpatrick's first and fourth levels as well as in some elements of CIRO and Phillip's evaluation.

Kirkpatrick Method

As explored above, the limitations of Kirkpatrick's model concern the singularity and simplification of learning evaluation variables: while these limitations are applicable to an e-learning context, the methodology is still a useful tool for e-learning evaluation. In particular, the first and fourth levels of Kirkpatrick's framework are helpful for evaluating e-learning as both learner satisfaction and business results have been proven to be valuable measurements when evaluating e-learning programs.

Level 1: Reaction

Level 1, reaction, is not difficult to measure in an e-learning context; in fact, it has been found that most learners are very enthusiastic in regards to e-learning. The Association for Talent Development Center (ASTD) tracked the preferences of their e-learning participants and found that the majority of learners prefer e-learning over classroom learning and 84% of the learners would take a similar e-course if offered again (ASTD, 2001). Of one-thousand students who responded to an e-college.com survey, the majority said they chose online learning formats because of the flexibility and convenience of the program (Strother, 2002). Specifically a learner noted, "I was able to work with my instructor, receive tremendous technical support at all hours of the day and gain the same quality content and evaluation as my peers taking the same course in a classroom" (ecollege.com, 1999). The reaction from instructors was equally positive: "Online students participate more, perform slightly better than, and are at least as satisfied as their on-campus counterparts" (Strother, 2002).

Practically speaking, collecting reaction results from e-learners is straightforward since the online format provides a great platform for incorporating a questionnaire at the end of the training session. It is important to note, however, that even though participation in the reactionary questionnaire might be higher in e-learning courses, it does not guarantee honest responses. Galloway (2005) highlights the potential factors that can affect feedback at the first level: "lack of interest in the topic, distraction by personal problems, and resentment of the time the training takes, or even the fact of required participation" (p. 70). Since the instructor cannot gauge engagement or active participation in an e-learning course, there is a risk of skewed or distracted feedback. Furthermore, several contemporary studies regarding the evaluation of e-learning stress the importance of learner satisfaction as the most important factor in e-learning evaluation. These theories will be discussed further in the section entitled "Learner Satisfaction."

Level 2: Learning

Discussions surrounding the effectiveness of e-learning evaluation at the second level are variant. Russell (1999) published *The No Significant Difference Phenomenon* which argued that there is no significant difference between the amount of content learned from a face-to-face instructor or an e-learning course. At the time, Russell's finding of no significant differences between e-learning and in-person training was a compelling factor in support of e-learning. More recent studies, however, have discovered variances in learning across the two platforms.

The dynamism in e-learning gives program developers the opportunity to survey learners to understand their learning preferences and respond accordingly. Using extensible markup language (XML), programmers can build content that is customized to specific learning styles. Furthermore, adult learning theory has shown a positive correlation between information retention and the amount of senses involved in a learning activity (Rozwell, 2009). Storytelling and virtual environment simulations are two additional elements incorporated into e-learning that have proven educational results.

Level 3: Behavior

Regardless of the format of the learning, the mechanisms available for measuring behavioral changes remains the same; therefore the same limitations persist in an e-learning context. One important difference between evaluating behavior changes in the context of e-learning versus other platforms is that e-learning results are easier to track performance results. For example, Unilever tracks the results of the e-training programs by asking course participants to join a teleconference a few months after the course and discuss how they have integrated their new skills. Research continues to assess the learning level of e-learning evaluation, but overall it has proven to be an effective platform for this mode of evaluation.

Level 4: Results

Much like the application of Level 3 in an e-learning context, the difficulties in measuring Level 4 results are still applicable to e-learning programs. On the whole, e-learning programs have been proven to reduce costs, increase training quality and productivity, and lower rates of employee turnover and absenteeism; however these results are difficult to measure as isolated effects of e-learning. As a result, some companies deferred to alternative ways to measure e-learning results. For example, Unilever measures their e-learning results for their sales force in terms of increased sales. Research in the education evaluation field resembles the shift to a business-oriented evaluation criteria. Bassi (2001) demonstrates that investment in training adds to the value of companies shares, regardless of overall market conditions; therefore subsequent research defining alternative approaches to measuring the business results of e-learning have emerged. As a result, the lines between Kirkpatrick's fourth level and Phillips' proposed fifth level of ROI have blurred and valuable frameworks have emerged at the intersection of the two. The value of this intersection in regards to e-learning is explained further in the section entitled "Phillips Evaluation Approach."

Alternative Approaches

While additional studies applying time to competency and customer satisfaction in an e-learning context are limited, recent research has built off of the strengths of CIRO evaluation in relation to e-learning. In regards to customer satisfaction, the framework Bregman and Jacobson (2000) forwarded has the same implications for e-learning as it does for any other training program; however e-learning could help to automate the process of customer feedback. Further discussion on the customer-facing and time to competency evaluation is not required, however the implications of incorporating the CIRO framework to an e-learning context is crucial.

CIRO Evaluation

As mentioned above in the discussion of CIRO evaluation framework, the largest asset of the framework is its consideration of the educational equipment that should be used based-off of training objectives. This is a particularly helpful exercise in the context of e-learning given the plethora of platforms available for e-learning programs as well as the customizable elements within each platform. Graf and List (2005) researched the "input" element of the CIRO evaluation framework to measure the adaptation capabilities of nine leading e-learning platforms based off of the programs learning objectives. Each platform was measured across eight broad categories such as communication tools, usability adaptation, course management and specific learning objectives. Within each category, there were three to seven variables measured. For example, under the category of "management of user data" variables such as "tracking" and "personal user profile" were included. Depending on the program's learning objectives, certain variables are given more weight. While the study concluded that the Moodle platform is the best platform in regards to adaptation because of the adaptive lesson feature, their results show the differing value of each platform depending on strategic learning priorities. The strength of the input step of CIRO evaluation is a crucial element of evaluating e-learning design and results. Ultimately, it enables developers to assess the platform used depending on learning priorities.

Phillips Evaluation Approach

Though most e-learning experts agree that Phillip's ROI model must be incorporated into e-learning evaluation processes, some believe it should be added to Kirkpatrick's model while others believe ROI should be the exclusive criteria for e-learning evaluation. The experts who recommend applying ROI as a supplemental part of Kirkpatrick's model emphasize "that the evaluation of effectiveness is separable from the evaluations of costs" (Levin, 1995, p. 5). This separation is "further applicable to a technology-based classroom as companies and trainers continue to seek ways of adapting the effective parts of conventional teaching to the more often cost-effective advantages of e-learning" (Galloway, 2005, p. 2). Additionally, calculating the dollars saved on e-learning is very straightforward. For example, e-learning usually reduces travel expenses, time away for the workplace, and possibly turnover—all factors that are easily monetized.

Cost Optimization

The effectiveness of e-learning can also be measured strictly from a budgeting standpoint—much like the methodology suggested at Kirkpatrick's fourth level. For example, Rozwell (2009) provides a seven point evaluation criteria for ensuring learning cost optimization and the framework is a valuable hybrid between Kirkpatrick's fourth level and Phillips proposed fifth level. The first step and the guiding principle of the theory is to "focus learning on core business processes to reduce time to competency" (p. 2). This first step involves "identifying key roles in the organization where people are performing a critical business function and a reduction in time to competency will have a demonstrable financial impact" (p. 3). Once an organization has identified the roles that are tied to strategic business priorities, training programs can be developed accordingly. The second step to supporting cost effective e-learning development is to "re-evaluate learning programs rather than cut them." Rozwell cautions against cutting learning programs across the board, claiming it is more cost effective to reduce the inclusion criteria to ensure that top performers still have access to the learning programs they need. The third step Rozwell articulates is reminiscent of the themes explained above in Kirkpatrick's first level of learning: "survey learners to understand their preferences." This step rests on the premise that the more senses that are involved in e-learning, the better the learning activity: and that the dynamic nature of e-learning platforms, specifically Web 2.0 technology, allows for some level of learner adaptability. By assessing learner preferences relative to the cost and effectiveness of learning methods, overall program effectiveness is increased. The final fourth step concerns the nuances of e-learning programs as Rozwell recommends that e-learning programs reduce costs and increase effectiveness by utilizing unique features available for e-learning programs such as simulations, story tell capabilities, and virtual collaboration communities. Ultimately Rozwell's steps align with the telos of Phillip's evaluation approach by emphasizing ROI as a critical learning evaluation criteria.

Learner Satisfaction

As mentioned above, Kirkpatrick's first level is particularly significant in regards to e-learning. Several empirical studies investigating what drives successful e-learning programs have come to the conclusion that learner satisfaction is a pivotal element. This section will explore two leading studies emphasizing the importance of learner satisfaction in e-learning evaluation and the differentiating frameworks used to draw this conclusion.

MCDM

Shee and Wang (2008) set out to create a methodology in order to support the evaluation of e-learning and maintenance to be carried out pre and post e-learning adaption, which resulted in a multi-criteria decision making (MCDM) methodology. At its most basic level, MCDM processes require the following elements: criterion set, preference structure, alternative set, and performance values. In order to develop criterion set and preference structure a hierarchical structure must first be devised to align goals and criteria.

The criteria defined in Figure 8.5 can then be evaluated and weighted to determine the effectiveness of the e-learning initiative and respond accordingly. This methodology was designed to supply "management in both education and industry with not only a less complex but also a more appropriate and flexible way to effectively analyze their currently developed web based learning system" which "allows for a higher level of e-learner satisfaction to be achieved, and in the process increases the level of system acceptance and continued use" (Shee and Wang, 2008, p. 903).

Additional studies have confirmed the importance of e-learner satisfaction by measuring a series of hypothesis about the factors that effect a learner's evaluation of an e-learning program. Sun, Tsai, Finger, Chen, & Yeh (2008) empirically confirmed the significance of the following variables in e-learner satisfaction: learner computer anxiety, instructor attitudes

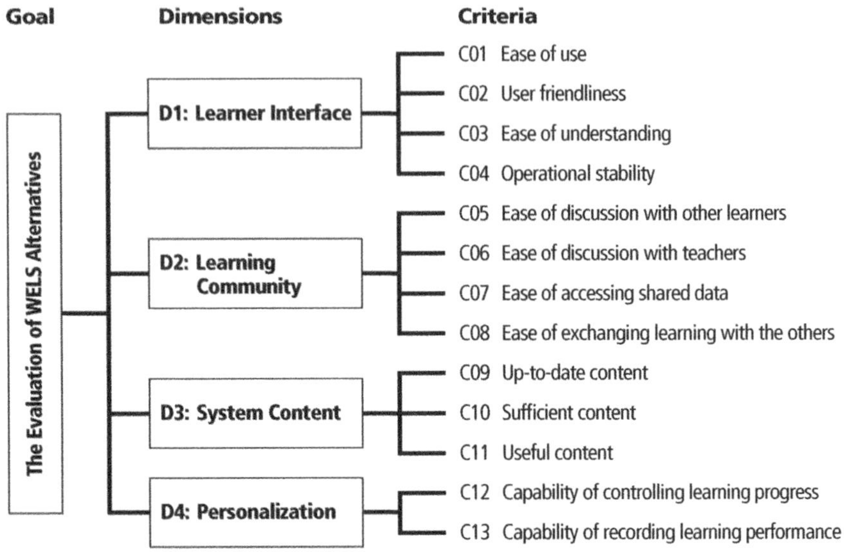

Figure 8.5 The hierarchy structure for evaluating e-learning (Shee and Wang, 2008, p. 898)

towards e-learning, e-learning course flexibility and quality, learner's perception of usefulness of the e-learning system as well as their perceived ease of use, and the diversity in the assessment. Given that these factors have a significant influence on a learner's perception of an e-learning program, it is imperative for program developers and evaluators to consider them. The research concludes that "students' initial perceived satisfaction with technology-based e-learning will determine whether they will use the system continually" (Pei-Chen et al., 2008, p. 1196); therefore the factors outlined are characterized as the *critical factors influencing e-learners satisfaction* and must continue to be considered in the evaluation of e-learning.

CONCLUSION

This paper has examined the leading contemporary frameworks for learning evaluation at a high level to provide a context for assessing their applicability in the context of e-learning. Ultimately, it was concluded that several of the contemporary frameworks prove useful in evaluating e-learning. Kirkpatrick's first level, which was previously regarded as the least important level, has come to the forefront of e-learning evaluation as learner satisfaction has proven an invaluable measure of comprehension and e-learning program success. Furthermore, critical factors influencing learning satisfaction continue to be developed and should be included in e-learning evaluations. With the emergence of MCDM index evaluation, learner satisfaction will become increasingly easy to measure and therefore continue to guide effective e-learning platforms. Kirkpatrick's fourth level and Phillips' fifth level have also been developed in the e-learning context as several cost optimization frameworks have emerged to help organizations evaluate their web-based learning platforms.

APPENDIX A
Pyschomotor Domain of Bloom's Taxonomy

PSYCHOMOTOR
Reflex movements Actions that occur involuntarily in response to some stimulus.
Basic fundamental movements Innate movement patterns formed from a combination of reflex movements.
Perceptual abilities Translation of stimuli received through the senses into appropriate movements.
Physical abilities Basic movements and abilities that are essential to the development of more highly skilled movements.
Skilled movements More complex movements requiring a certain degree of efficiency.
Non-discursive movements Ability to communicate through body movement

APPENDIX B
Phillip's (1996): Hard and Soft Data Checklist

Hard Data	Soft Data
Outputs	***Work Habits***
Units produced	Employee absenteeism
Items assembled or sold	Tardiness
Forms processed	Visits to the dispensary
Tasks completed	Safety-rule violations
Quality	***Work Climate***
Scrap	Employee grievances
Waste	Employee turnover
Rework	Discrimination charges
Product defects or rejects	Job satisfaction
Time	***Attitudes***
Equipment downtime	Employee loyalty
Employee overtime	Employee's self-confidence
Time to complete projects	Employees' perceptions of job responsibilities
Training time	Perceived changes in performance
Cost	***New Skills***
Overhead	Decisions made
Variable costs	Problems solved
Sales expenses	Conflicts avoided
	Frequency in using new skills
	Development and Advancement
	Number of promotions or pay increases
	Number of training programs attended
	Requests for transfer
	Performance appraisal ratings
	Initiative
	Implementation of new ideas
	Successful completion of projects
	Number of employee suggestions

APPENDIX C
Rozwell (2007): Diagram of Time Till Competency

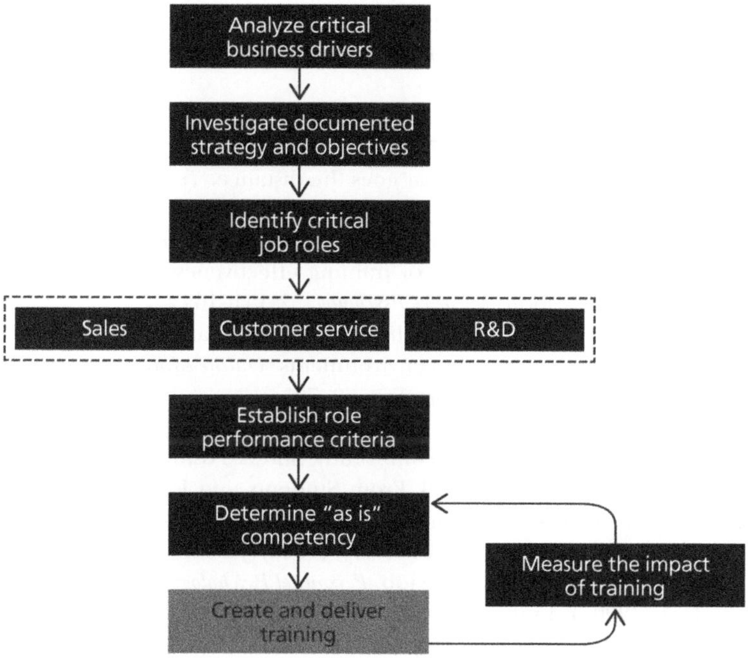

Source: Rozwell (2009) p. 3

ACKNOWLEDGMENTS

This chapter is based on a presentation at the 2016 MARC conference on Psychometrics and Data Analytics: October 29–30, 2015, at the University of Maryland, College Park.

REFERENCES

Abernathy, D. J. (1999). Thinking outside the evaluation box. *Training & Development, 53*(2), 18–24.

ASTD. (2001, February). *State of the Industry Report.* Retrieved from www.astd.org.

Bassi, L. (2001). *This Firm Bets on Training.* Retrieved from http://www.knowledgeam.com/rds.html

Bates, R. (2004). A critical analysis of evaluation practice: The Kirkpatrick model and the principle of beneficence. *Evaluation and program planning,* 27(3), 341–347.

Bates, R. A., Holton, E. F., Seyler, D. A., & Carvalho, M. A. (2000). The role of interpersonal factors in the application of computer-based training in an industrial setting. *Human Resource Development International, 3*(1), 19–43.

Bloom, B. S. (Ed.), Engelhart, M. D., Furst, E. J., Hill, W. H., & Krathwohl, D. R. (1956). *Taxonomy of educational objectives handbook I: The cognative domain.* New York, NY: David McKay.

Bregman, P., & Jacobson, H. (2000). Yes, you can measure the business results of training. *Training, 37*(8), 68–72.

Bernthal, P. R. (1995). Evaluation that goes the distance. *Training and Development, 49*(9), 41–46.

Cannon-Bowers, J. A., Salas, E., Tannenbaum, S. I., & Mathieu, J. E. (1995). Toward theoretically based principles of training effectiveness: A model and initial empirical investigation. *Military Psychology, 7,* 141–164.

Colorado, J. T., & Howell, D. (2009). The role of individual learner differences and success in the online learning environments. *Online education and adult learning: New frontiers for teaching practices,* 69–79.

ecollege.com. (1999). Survey Finds Online Education Equal to or Better than On Campus Learning: eCollege.com. Study Shows Positive Results for Online Education Based on Feedback From Students and Faculty. Retrieved from http://www.ecollege.com/company/news/stories/press_2.html

Ford, J. K., Quinones, M., Sego, D., & Sorra, J. (1992). Factors affecting the opportunity to use trained skills on the job. *Personnel Psychology, 45,* 511–527.

Galloway, D. L. (2005). Evaluating distance delivery and e-learning is Kirkpatrick's model relevant? *Performance Improvement, 44*(4), 21–27.

Graf, S., & List, B. (2005). An evaluation of open source e-learning platforms stressing adaptation issues. Retrieved from https://moodle.org/other/icalt2005.pdf

Gusky, T. R. (2000). *Evaluating professional development.* Thousand Oaks, CA: Corwin.

Hogan, R. L. (2007). The historical development of program evaluation: Exploring past and present. *Online Journal for Workforce Education and Development, 2*(4), 5.

Holton, E. F. (1996). The flawed four level evaluation model. *Human Resource Development Quarterly, 7*(1), 5–21.

Kaplan, R. S., & Norton, D. P. (1996). *The balanced scorecard: Translating strategy into action.* Boston, MA: Harvard Business School Press.

Kaplan-Leiserson, E. (2000). *e-learning glossary.* Retrieved from http://www.learningcircuits.org/glossary.html

Kirkpatrick, D. L. (1959). *Evaluation of training.* New York, NY: McGraw-Hill.

Kirkpatrick, D. L. (1994). *Evaluating training programs: The four levels.* San Francisco, CA: Berrett-Koehler.

Kirkpatrick, D. L. (1998). *Evaluating training programs: The four levels* (2nd ed.). San Francisco, CA: Berrett-Koehler.

Levin, H. M. (1995). Cost-effective analysis. In M. Carnoy (Ed.), *International encyclopedia of economic education* (pp. 381–386). Oxford, England: Pergamon.

Madaus, G. F., Stufflebeam, D. L., & Kellaghan, T. (2000). *Evaluation models: Viewpoints on educational and human services evaluation* (2nd ed.). Hingham, MA: Kluwer Academic.

McLinden, D. J., & Trochim, W. (1998). From puzzles to problems: Assessing the value of education in a business context with concept mapping and pattern matching. *Implementing Evaluation Systems and Processes, 37*, 285–304.

Pei-Chen, S., Tsai, R. J., Finger, G., Chen, Y., & Yeh, D. (2008). What drives a successful e-learning? An emperical investigation of the critical factors influencing learner satisfaction. *Computers and Education, 51*(3), 1183–1202.

Phillips, J. J. (1991). *Handbook of evaluation and measurement methods* (2nd ed.). London, England: Gulf Press.

Phillips, J. J. (1996a). *Accountability in human resource management.* London, England: Routledge.

Phillips, J. J. (1996b). How much is the training worth? *Training & Development, 50*(4), 20–25.

Rouiller, J. Z., & Goldstein, I. L. (1993). The relationship between organizational transfer climate and positive transfer of training. *Human Resource Development Quarterly, 4*(4), 377–390.

Rozwell, C. (2007). Seven smart steps for learning cost optimization. *Garnter*, 1–7.

Russell, T. L. (1999). No significant difference phenomenon. *Educational Technology and Society, 2*, 3

Scriven, M. (1996). The theory behind practical evaluation. *Evaluation, 2*(4), 393–404.

Shee, D. Y., & Wang, Y. S. (2008). Multi-criteria evaluation of the web-based e-learning system: A methodology based on learner satisfaction and its applications. *Computers & Education, 50*(3), 894–905.

Shelton, S., & Alliger, G. M. (1993). Who's afraid of level 4 evaluation? A practical approach. *Training and Development Journal, 47*, 43–46.

Strother, J. B. (2002). An assessment of the effectiveness of e-learning in corporate training programs. *The International Review of Research in Open and Distributed Learning, 3*(1). doi:10.19173/irrodl.v3i1.83

Stufflebeam, D. L., & Shinkfield, A. J. (1985). *Systematic evaluation.* New York, NY: Kluwer Nijhoff.

Sun, P. C., Tsai, R. J., Finger, G., Chen, Y. Y., & Yeh, D. (2008). What drives a successful e-Learning? An empirical investigation of the critical factors influencing learner satisfaction. *Computers & education, 50*(4), 1183–1202.

Tracy, J. B., Tannenbaum, S. I., & Kavanaugh, M. J. (1995). Applying trained skills on the job: The importance of work environment. *Journal of Applied Psychology, 80*, 239–252.

Warr, P., Bird, M., & Rackham, N. (1970). *Evaluation of management training.* London, England: Gower Press.

Worthen, B. R., Sanders, J. R., & Fitzpatrick, J. L. (1997). *Educational evaluation: Alternative approaches and practical guidelines* (2nd ed.). White Plains, NY: Longman.

CHAPTER 9

HIGH LEVEL STRATEGIC APPROACHES FOR CONDUCTING BIG DATA STUDIES IN ASSESSMENT

Manfred M. Straehle
Assessment, Education, and Research Associates

Liberty J. Munson
Microsoft

Austin Fossey
Georgetown University

Emily Kim
The Predictive Index

What is big data? What are some general approaches to conceptualizing and utilizing big data? How can this be applied to psychometric situations? These are the keynote questions that this chapter attempts to answer. The authors have divided this chapter into three parts: an introduction to big data, a psychometric approach to big data, and a carefully selected case study. First, an overview of big data is presented, along with the overall high

Data Analytics and Psychometrics, pages 231–246

level strategic big data approaches. The next part integrates the high level strategic big data approaches that could be applied to psychometric practices. The third part of this chapter illustrates the use of high level strategic approaches using a case study.

PART 1. INTRODUCTION TO BIG DATA

What Is It?

The term *big data* was first coined in the late 1990s while emerging research and interest on the topic began in earnest in the early 2000s. However, the concept of big data—gathering, storing, filtering, processing, and analyzing data—has been around for decades (Gandomi & Haider, 2015). Big data earned its place in the Oxford English Dictionary in 2013, where it is defined as "extremely large data sets that may be analyzed computationally to reveal patterns, trends, and associations, especially relating to human behavior and interactions" (Big Data, n.d.). Undoubtedly, with the mass expansion of computing and technology, big data has grown by leaps and bounds in a relatively short amount of time. In fact, as of 2016, research suggests that approximately "90% of the data in the world [sic] has been created in the past two years" ("Big Data and the Future of Privacy," 2016). With this in mind, the meaning of big data is a constantly moving target. As a result, many researchers have adopted the definition proposed by Doug Laney who defined big data by three dimensions known as the "3Vs"—volume, velocity, and variety (Laney, 2001, p. 3).

Volume refers to the size of the data set—the subjective size that many organizations consider to be big data. Today, big data is typically in the terabyte to petabyte or larger range. Some large corporations, such as Google and Walmart, can collect petabytes of data in a single day. However, Laney (2001) hypothesized that "as data volume increases, the relative value of each data point decreases proportionately" (p. 1). In other words, bigger is not always better. Organizations need to make smart decisions about indefinite storage of data because of the economic implications of the value of each successive data point.

Velocity refers to the speed of data creation and interaction—how quickly data is gathered, streamed, stored, filtered, processed, or analyzed, and if it is collected real time. Laney (2001) argues that big data velocity is "increasingly perceived as a competitive differentiator" (p. 2), and there is no reason to believe this will change in the near future.

Variety refers to the vastly differing source material and formatting of data. Data can be unstructured, semi-structured, or structured and can take the form of nearly anything—transactions, GPS, multimedia, social networks—anything we interact with can generate data. Unstructured data is information that is not organized in a database or not easily organized or interpreted such as a tweet on Twitter, video or audio clip, or a string of text (McAfee & Brynjolfsson, 2012). Structured data is the opposite; it is typically a set of easily interpretable numerical entries that fit comfortably in the scope of traditional databases. Data that can be condensed into tables of a spreadsheet would be a simple example. Estimates suggest that structured data "constitutes only 5% of all existing data" (p. 138), highlighting the nuanced heterogeneity that is usually found in big data sets (Gandomi & Haider, 2015). Semi-structured or multi-structured data operate in a gray area with imprecise delineations compared to structured and unstructured data. Some examples of semi-structured data may include XML documents or web logs.

Many individuals involved in data sciences believe there should be reasonable extensions to the 3Vs to reflect additional dimensions of big data that have become more prominent over time. For instance, researchers have made an excellent case for "veracity."

Veracity, or accuracy, a term increasingly important in today's technical landscape, indicates data uncertainty and reliability. Our level of uncertainty with data sets may be due to abnormalities, ambiguities, inconsistencies, biases, or any other types of noise. Poor quality of data, untrustworthy data, and inconsistencies with data collection, and other issues illustrate the importance of considering veracity.

Keep in mind that our definitions and understanding of each of these elements is constantly changing as technology advances. For example, what may be considered big data today may not be 10 years from now—our current definition is an ever-moving target. However, one aspect of big data that will remain unchanged is the fact that the three or four or even five Vs are generally interconnected—all must be considered in the high level strategic approaches to big data.

How to Approach Big Data

The authors believe that there are two overall strategic approaches to work with big data: exploratory and intentional. Exploratory approaches typically consist of harvesting, mining, and analyzing data with the hope that relationships may be derived from the existing variables (data). From a business perspective, this can become costly, both in terms of money and time.

Intentional approaches to big data, on the other hand, rely on searching for solutions to fully-defined, operational research questions. When organizations can clearly identify the question they are trying to answer with big data sets, time and resources can be allocated more effectively and efficiently. It should be noted that organizations of all sizes can utilize big data. However, due to the nature of small or medium sized businesses, intentional approaches may prove more prudent financially as it allows a targeted approach to data analysis and generally requires fewer resources.

Regardless if exploratory or intentional, data scientists typically follow five steps when analyzing big data.

1. *Identify goals and intentions in collecting big data.* What precisely does your organization hope to gain from big data? What insights are you hoping it will provide? Collecting data for the sake of collection can waste time and resources; a careful evaluation of the purpose of data collection will save time, money, and resources.
2. *Collect the data.* Data collection can be prepared through platforms that consume raw data and store it securely across servers that can handle big data workloads. Some examples of these data collection technology platforms include Hadoop and Cloud Computing, and popular services are available through venues such as Amazon Web Services, SAS, Microsoft, IBM, etc.
3. *Organize and manipulate the data.* These processes take place between data storage and data analysis. Managing big data can be done through "(a) acquisition and recording; (b) extraction, cleaning, and annotation; and (c) integration, aggregation and representation" (Gandomi & Haider, 2015, p. 141).
4. *Analyze the data.* Data analysis can be classified in many ways. Gandomi and Haider (2015) choose to condense the analyses into two classifications: (a) modeling and analysis and (b) interpretation. Others, such as Amazon Web Services, opt to distinguish features by three major categories: (a) descriptive analytics, (b) predictive analytics, and (c) prescriptive analytics. In general, common analytic techniques include predictive modeling, association rule learning, data mining, neural networks, regression analysis, optimization, sentiment analysis, pattern recognition, and visualization to name a few (Manyika et al., 2011).
5. *Report the data.* Data visualization is often key to effectively communicating the results of the analysis and is typically done through the creation of simple, interactive, or multimedia visuals. These visualizations can be in the form of images, diagrams, or charts. They can also include more complex arrangements, such as spatial information flows, tag clouds, history flows, and so on (Manyika et al., 2011). Organizations find it useful when the data is communicated in a way that is future-focused, providing suggestions to improve future outcomes.

In sum, big data analysis can be used to monitor and interpret data in real time to find unexpected relationships between separate data points as well as provide insights into events that may happen in the future.

Finally, and perhaps, most importantly, big data processes must maintain privacy and security of personal data. Although big data as a research tool has many benefits, it also has the potential for serious privacy and other information security risks. This concern has grown to the point that a White House Report entitled, "Big Data and Privacy: A Technological Perspective" has been written by the President's Council of Advisors on Science and Technology (PCAST) to address the matter (White House, 2014). This report highlights the risks, current research, and recommendations that relate to big data in terms of both privacy and policy. PCAST states that "as the size and diversity of available data grows, the likelihood of being able to re-identify individuals... grows substantially" (White House, 2014, p. xi). This, in and of itself, has a major impact on preserving and maintaining individual anonymization. Individuals have a right to a certain level of privacy, and with the use of big data from sources such as data brokers or other potentially unscrupulous information vendors, this sense of privacy could be violated without further consideration or perhaps even recognition that it's been done. Furthermore, "PCAST believes it is the use of data... where [unexpected] consequences are produced" (White House, 2014, p. xii) that is of greatest concern. For example, through the use of predictive analytics, big data has the potential to draw discriminatory conclusions in a way that is automated and unintentionally concealed. "Making incorrect conclusions about individuals... may affect members of certain groups disproportionately (e.g., in employment, credit, fair housing decisions)" (White House, 2014, p. xii). Another key concern is in the case of data breaches. The implications of these instances are obvious as they can lead to identity theft, exposure of personal details, and other harmful outcomes, not only to the individual but to the organization as well.

Big Data in Assessment

Now that big data has been defined and various approaches and concerns have been discussed, this next section focuses on the uses of big data in assessment. For the assessment industry, some common big data sets include registration data, programmatic marketing and financial data, test or exam data (psychometric data), exam recertification data, examinee survey data (e.g., satisfaction surveys), and other learning data, such as the number of individuals taking exam-related courses.

A more specific area includes personality testing. Many tests, such as the Sixteen Personality Factor Questionnaire (16PF) and the Minnesota Multiphasic Personality Inventory (MMPI) rely on large data sets to identify behavioral patterns that are translated into scoring that accurately classifies an individual's personality. Cattell, the developer of the 16PF, created three categories of data to describe individuals' personality: L-data, T-data, and Q-data. L-data is life data that is collected from everyday life events, such as GPA, travel history, or credit reports. T-data is experimental data typically collected in labs through the use of objective tests. Q-data is data obtained from questionnaires and other relevant tests. These dimensions of the 16PF are an accurate demonstration of large and diverse variety data sets being used to find patterns that are the basis of personality classifications.

While assessment data can take many forms, the steps to manage big data in the assessment industry apply regardless. Five steps, developed by AERE (Assessment, Education & Research Experts), are presented below.

1. *Define and operationalize the question your organization seeks to answer.* Attempt to make your interactions with big data more intentional rather than exploratory. Be specific when framing the research question and how the organization will find the answer.
2. *Involve multiple stakeholders when discussing big data (i.e., vendors, IT, subject matter experts).* Different stakeholders can provide varying perspectives in the gathering, storage, analysis, and interpretation of big data. Gaining the input of these groups can ensure all parties are on the same page from a business perspective.
3. *Identify your data sources and develop a data dictionary.* Organization is key to dealing with the massive volume of information that is inherent in big data. Developing a dictionary of terms and original sources of information will keep information clear, especially if the intention is to store data long-term.
4. *Standardize multiple data sets by using common variables (data fields).* Again, organization is paramount to successful, time-effective management of big data. For example, keeping data organized with ID numbers and demographics in a standardized way, such as by unique identifier, last name, and first name, will make it easier to merge data across multiple sources, saving time, money, and resources.
5. *Produce simple reports designed to answer the question.* Reporting results of big data is often augmented by visualization. Know who your stakeholders are and visualize the data in a way the will have the most impact for them and clearly shows the answer the question that led to the analysis in the first place.

Other Data: Small and Medium Data

While big data holds a prominent space in our current analytic infrastructure, it is equally important to note the importance of small and medium data. In contrast to big data, small data can in fact be as small as one observation. For example, Jean Piaget, the renowned child psychologist, built his theories from observing his own children. Small data is different from large data in the question being asked, the level analysis, as well as the confidence and accuracy of generalizing results. Big data may predict what is going to happen in the future, which typically involves a higher degree of analytic complexity and a larger number of differing variables. However, in the case of small data, data analysis tends to be less complex (although not always!) with a fewer number of variables (again, not always!).

The 2014 White House report on Big Data defines small data as "the collection and use of data sets by private- and public-sector organizations where the data are disseminated in their original form or analyzed by conventional statistical methods" (p. ix). The number or volume of data points alone does not dictate if you are dealing with big or small data, and one size of data is not inherently better than the other. Rather than focusing on the size of the data, it is crucial to use data in a meaningful way, based on a well-designed reach question, using the right statistical tools.

PART 2. USING BIG DATA TO SEE THE WORLD DIFFERENTLY: A PSYCHOMETRIC APPROACH

Understanding Test Taking Behaviors

In the psychometric world, big data has the potential to change the way practitioners think about assessments and learning. Clearly, in high volume exam programs, big data is a way of life as item level information gathered from each exam delivered is leveraged for the psychometric analysis that is performed to maintain the quality, validity, and reliability of exams. However, with the advances in technology and more exams being delivered via computers and online, there is greater access to even more information about test takers behaviors during the exam. We can track most interactions between the test taker and electronic assessment instruments through "clickstream data." With access to this level of information, it is possible to better understand how test takers are interacting with exam content. Are there certain item types where test takers are changing the answers to their questions more often than other item types during the exam? Are there item types where there is little to no mouse movement for longer periods of time than for other item types? Both might suggest that the item type, rather than the item, is confusing. What can you do to improve the instructions so that candidates understand what's expected of them? Ultimately, understanding and removing barriers to answering questions removes error from the evaluation process, leading to increased validity and reliability in the assessment process.

Along these lines, big data can be leveraged to better understand the effectiveness of various item types with different audiences and content domains. Do different item types differentiate test takers in different audiences more effectively than they do in other audiences? If so, different design specifications should be considered for different audiences. Do different item types provide a more valid evaluation of different content domains? Again, if so, different design specs should be considered based on the content domain. Keep in mind, though, that discrepancies that are found in terms of which groups of people are answering questions correctly or incorrectly could be related to characteristics of that group itself (e.g., questions that include a word or phrase that is more accessible to a certain group of people [i.e., race or socioeconomic status] that may confuse test takers of differing groups). While potentially discriminatory items may be identified with greater ease through the assistance of big data, it can unintentionally lead us to draw incorrect or discriminatory conclusions about certain individuals or groups of individuals, perhaps without full awareness of doing so.

Further, with advances in machine learning, it seems possible to train machines to identify anomalous and aberrant behaviors during the testing session. If this can happen effectively, it is possible that machine proctored exams may replace human proctored exams. If the machine identified aberrant behaviors, it could automatically take the action prescribed by the testing program (e.g., end the exam, warn the test taker, start displaying "junk" items to protect their IP for further exposure, etc.). Beyond that, if machines are learning, they may identify other behaviors or patterns of behaviors that humans haven't been able to see in the data that suggest aberrance. All of these ideas will only improve the validity, reliability, and fairness of the assessment process—all through the power of big data, asking the right research questions, and conducting the right statistical analysis.

How Do Learners Learn?

The insights gained from "clickstream" data may prove invaluable to our understanding of how learners learn. With a better understanding of how learners are interacting with courses through big data, we can identify points in the courses where learners are struggling or abandoning it and take the appropriate action to improve their learning experiences. We can leverage big data to build adaptive learning solutions that pinpoint learning gaps and provide learning opportunities that are targeted to fill those gaps. We can identify the elements of a course and extrapolate what course structures drive the best learning outcomes. What should the ratio of videos, reading, and formative and summative assessments be to maximize learning? We can restructure courses to better fit the needs and behaviors of our learners.

Taking this one step further, we can start linking learning behaviors with outcomes of interest, such as improvements in performance or success on exams, and identifying patterns that seem to result in the most desirable outcomes. Are learners who are ultimately more successful on the job engaging with the learning content in different ways than those who are less successful? What are they doing differently? How can you structure courses to maximize that result?

As you can see there are a lot of questions in this space that big data can help us start answering. The possibilities for how we can leverage big data to drive better assessments and learning experiences are significant, endless, and continually evolving. It is through big data that we'll make our next big breakthrough in learning and assessment.

PART 3. VALIDATION AND BIG DATA: A CASE STUDY—USING AERE'S FIVE STEPS AT THE PREDICTIVE INDEX

The Predictive Index (PI) Behavioral Assessment is a theory-based, self-report measure of normal adult work-related personality and has been developed and validated extensively and exclusively for use within occupational and organizational populations. Intended as a management tool and based largely on the personality trait theories of physiological psychologist W. Marston (1928), the PI Behavioral Assessment focuses on several core motivating needs and drives of an individual. The PI Behavioral Assessment yields quasi-ipsative measures of four personality drives: dominance, extraversion, patience, and formality. The PI Behavioral Assessment was first released in 1955, and in early 2017, PI released an updated form that includes a fifth drive: objectivity. With this new release, there was significant work in critiquing and improving the assessment psychometrically (Foster et al., 2016).

Step 1. Define and Operationalize the Question

The PI Behavioral Assessment is what Zubin (1938) called a *configural assessment,* meaning the primary interpretations about a respondent's personality are derived from the relative configuration of their scores. These have historically been reported with plots of the scores connected with zigzag lines. The configurations of possible zigzags were grouped into 47 buckets called *patterns.*

As part of the critiquing work for the new version of the PI Behavioral Assessment, the research team was tasked to improve the way to describe and group these configural patterns representing personality. Operationally, PI was wrestling with the challenges of having 47 different personality patterns as outputs from the PI Behavioral Assessment. The sheer volume of potential outcomes presented an array of validity issues in terms of supporting the interpretations of the patterns, maintaining reporting output for all 47 patterns, and demonstrating the psychometric properties of the patterns. For example, several patterns were so similar that a respondent could be expected to be assigned to as many as three patterns based only on measurement error variance.

This situation was exacerbated by the fact that there was little to no information as to how the 47 patterns were created when the PI Behavioral Assessment was first developed in the 1950s. Best practice suggested that PI provide a published rationale supporting the structure of its pattern classification system. As a result, the research team examined the big data to improve the reporting of configural personality patterns and the validity of their interpretations.

Step 2. Involve Multiple Stakeholders

For the project, stakeholders included test users (i.e., hiring managers and consultants), trainers, product designers, psychometricians, and PI's business leaders. Test users and trainers were recruited from PI's Partner Network through the use of email newsletters which asked for volunteers to provide feedback. Multiple calls for volunteers were posted in these newsletters throughout August and September 2016, and subscribers were encouraged to forward the information on to others. Many of these volunteers participated in the survey (described in the next section), although a few trainers participated in one-on-one interviews with the research team at the request of PI leadership.

PI has its own staff of product designers and psychometricians, and these stakeholders worked together throughout the research process to determine how new pattern methodology could be operationalized into PI's existing assessment software.

Finally, PI's business leaders (company executives) were also engaged to provide feedback in multiple roundtable discussions. The business leaders provided two perspectives, being both test users and also the group responsible for the company's success. Their feedback was useful for evaluating pattern concepts that would improve the PI Behavioral Assessment while also being tempered by the realities of needing a solution that could be implemented efficiently and with minimal disruption to the business.

Step 3. Identify Data Sources, Develop Data Dictionary

The research team organized the development of a new pattern methodology using the *evidence model* concept from evidence-centered design (ECD). ECD applies a broad range of assessment design resources (e.g., subject matter knowledge, software design, psychometrics, pedagogical knowledge) to the inferences that are drawn from the assessment scores (Mislevy, 2011). ECD was chosen because of its flexibility as a principled assessment development framework and because of its history of use in grouping responses into buckets on other assessments (e.g., Stevens & Casillas, 2006). In ECD, the evidence model identifies evidence data from the assessment responses and uses a measurement model to accumulate those data into an inference about the respondent (Mislevy, Behrens, Dicerbo, & Levy, 2012).

In the case of the PI Behavioral Assessment, the evidence model needed to collect data from PI Behavioral Assessment responses and scores and then assign the respondent to a meaningful personality pattern. To help support interpretive distinctions between pattern groups, the research team sought to create an evidence model that would maximize the differences between personality groups while minimizing the within-pattern differences. This would ensure that patterns were different enough to communicate meaningful differences in personality configurations, yet specific enough that two people with the same personality pattern would be expected to have similar scores on the PI Behavioral Assessment.

Based on stakeholder feedback in interviews and a working knowledge of the logic trees underlying the existing 47 patterns, the research team collected a broad range of potential evidence inputs for the evidence model. These included the PI Behavioral Assessment scores, the relative configuration of those scores (i.e., the shape of the zigzag chart), the score's relative position to the population mean score, and potentially different weightings of scores in the measurement model (e.g., giving more consideration to the dominance score in the assignment of a personality pattern).

To determine which of these potential evidence data were relevant for pattern interpretation, a survey was developed to determine how SMEs interpreted similarities and differences between 36 pairs of patterns. In this survey, SMEs were asked to rate the degree of fit between the individual scores and overall patterns pairs of PI Behavioral Assessment pattern charts. To create these pairs, real personality patterns were randomly selected from the PI Behavioral Assessment database. These patterns served as the reference patterns for the study. They were then manipulated to create similar yet different comparison patterns. As a result of these manipulations, pattern scores were stretched, subjected to sign changes, or adjusted to change their relative position to the population mean, thus providing a sufficient domain of pattern comparisons to evaluate which evidence data were relevant to SMEs when making a decision about the similarity of patterns.

Thirty-six SMEs responded to the survey, representing a mix of test users and test trainers with varying years of experience using the PI Behavioral Assessment; however, three SMEs could not complete the survey. In interviews, these three volunteers explained that they struggled with the concept of evaluating similarities between patterns from the assessment. One other result was discarded because the respondent only rated three of the pattern pairs, and these ratings were vastly different from the group mean ratings. This may have been a volunteer exploring the survey and testing it out. Fit ratings for the individual factor scores and overall pattern pairs were collected from the remaining 32 SMEs, along with their comments about how they made their decisions.

Regression analyses showed that the average SMEs fit ratings of similarities between the individual PI Behavioral Assessment scores in a pair of patterns explained 86% of the variance in the average SME fit ratings of differences between patterns. Based on these findings, the research team elected to use only the PI Behavioral Factor scores in the evidence identification part of the evidence model.

Step 4. Standardize Multiple Data Sets

The research team was tasked to identify a measurement model to improve upon the existing pattern identification rules. In the absence of a theoretical foundation for the structure of pattern groups or the number of pattern groups that would be the most interpretable, the research team decided to use an exploratory, empirically-based approach to defining the measurement model (Bejar & Braun, 1994). For the application of defining groups of similar personality patterns, the research team chose to use clustering algorithms that have been used for similar exploratory grouping assignments in other assessments and evaluation studies (e.g., Stevens & Casillas, 2006; Kerr & Chung, 2012; Stevens et al., 2012; Xu, Recker, Qi, Flann, & Ye, 2013; Corrigan et al., 2014).

Because this was an exploratory approach, best practice suggested that two competing clustering algorithms be used to validate each other's solutions in terms of cluster assignments, fit, and most importantly interpretability (Kriegel, Kröger, & Zimek, 2009; Xu et al., 2013). For this study, the research team selected the self-organizing maps (SOM) clustering algorithm and the fuzzy clustering algorithm from R (Wehrens & Buydens, 2007; Maechler, Rousseeuw, Struyf, Hubert, & Hornik, 2016; R Core Team, 2015). These two algorithms were selected based on the following requirements identified by the research team and the product designers:

- The algorithms had to function with non-spherically distributed data like the PI Behavioral Assessment scores.
- The algorithms had to yield cluster assignments that could be compared across both algorithms.
- Clustering solutions had to provide a way to evaluate clustering solutions that were similar to each other so that the product developers could aggregate clusters further into categories (e.g., "socially-driven personality patterns").

Finally, the product designers requested that the research team identify a clustering solution with a number of clusters that could be represented as a square or rectangular grid on a report. There was no measurement rationale for this—the product designers simply wanted to represent the patterns as a grid to stakeholders.

Based on the request from the product designers, SOM and fuzzy clustering solutions were created using 9, 12, 16, 20, and 25 clusters. In addition to varying the number of clusters, the parameters for the two clustering algorithms were varied to produce competing solutions. The research team tried alternative values for the alpha learning rate in the SOM algorithm and the fuzzy parameter in the fuzzy clustering algorithm. The evidence inputs for the models were also varied: The research team conducted one set of analyses with the unadjusted factor scores from the PI Behavioral Assessment and another set of analyses with standardized scores that were multiplied by a constant wherein the most extreme score in a person's pattern configuration was always equal to the same value. This was based on stakeholder recommendations that the shape of a person's pattern zigzag might be more meaningful than the magnitude or width of that zigzag pattern. This adjustment had the effect of standardizing the width of everyone's configural pattern chart.

Because this was both an empirically based approach and a configural assessment, two clustering algorithms were used to identify the best set of patterns in the data: SOM and fuzzy clustering. Both algorithms could accommodate the data structures, and both yielded comparable cluster solutions, making it easier to identify the better model. SOM provides a two-dimensional grid of clusters that shows which patterns are more similar to each other. Fuzzy Clustering, on the other hand, yields a cluster score that identifies the probability of a result belonging to any given cluster and is useful for grouping similar clusters.

All told, 160 different clustering solutions were produced using a dataset of 10,424 results from the development of PI's new form of the assessment. Cluster assignments for all 160 solutions were re-coded for standardized comparison. For example, if 250 respondents were assigned to Cluster 1 in one solution and the same 250 respondents were assigned to Cluster 9 in another solution, those cluster labels were re-coded to reflect the fact that it was the same group of patterns. Each solution's fit was measured using the Davies-Bouldin index (Davies & Bouldin, 1979).

Step 5. Produce Simple Reports

The best-fitting solutions (as measured with Davies-Bouldin index) for the varying number of clusters were selected to be presented at roundtable discussion groups with SMEs, product designers, and PI's business leaders to evaluate the interpretability of the solution. Reports were created to showcase the final competing solutions along with other informative impact data, such as frequency distributions and comparisons to the existing 47 pattern logic. To help guide the roundtable discussions around the interpretability of each solution, the mean scores for each cluster in a solution were plotted with the zigzag charts that were familiar to the stakeholders. This helped the stakeholders evaluate when a solution did not provide enough variety in pattern assignments or when two pattern clusters were too similar for practical purposes.

PI's Future Steps

As of this writing, PI continues to finalize their preferred clustering solution, but this research has provided PI with sound validity evidence to support their decision and the use of pattern labels. The use of the PI Behavioral Assessment factor scores as the sole evidence data in the evidence model was validated through the SME fit survey and the regression analyses demonstrating where SMEs evaluated the similarities of patterns based on comparisons of factor scores alone. The use of exploratory clustering algorithms for measurement models is validated through the comparison of two algorithms, varying parameters, and SME feedback about the interpretability of varying solutions. This research is valuable for PI as they replace their pattern assignment evidence model and update how they communicate personality patterns to their stakeholders. In reflecting on the project, its success was based upon several key elements. First was the willingness of the team to acknowledge that the existing patterns may not be valid and the support to investigate how the assessment could be improved. Second was the stakeholder involvement throughout the process—their feedback was instrumental in terms of updating assumptions and describing similarities. Finally, in identifying a new evidence mode, the research team cast a broad net that captured all the nuances required for the appropriate data analysis and interpretation. Multiple algorithms were used, and measures were preemptively set to effectively evaluate solutions and provide a defensible rationale for the final product.

PART 4: CONCLUSION

In conclusion, this chapter sought to answer core questions regarding big data in the scope of the assessment community. The first section briefly describes the nature of big data, approaches to big data, and the use of big data in assessments and psychometrics. The second section delved into the application of big data in psychometric practices such as test taking behaviors and how learners learn. Finally, the third section was a case study that provided an example as to how big data can be applied at an organizational level using the general high-level strategic steps mentioned earlier in the chapter. In sum, the strategic approaches to big data should provide guidance on assessment endeavors.

REFERENCES

American Educational Research Association, American Psychological Association, & National Council on Measurement in Education. (2014). *Standards for educational and psychological testing.* Washington, DC: AERA.

Bejar, I. I., & Braun, H. I. (1994). On the synergy between assessment and instruction: Early lessons from computer-based simulations. *Machine-Mediated Learning, 4*(1), 5–25.

Big Data. (n.d.). In *Oxford English Dictionary online dictionary.* Retrieved from https://en.oxforddictionaries.com/definition/big_data

Big Data and the Future of Privacy. (2016). Retrieved from https://epic.org/privacy/big-data/

Corrigan, S., Stephenson, S., Makany, T., Frenz, M., Hoffman, E., Bauer, M., . . . Menon, U. (2014, April). *Combining fun, learning, and measurement: Game development in the classroom and beyond.* Workshop presented at the Annual Meeting for the National Council on Measurement in Education, Philadelphia, PA.

Davies, D. L., & Bouldin, D. W. (1979). A cluster separation measure. *IEEE Transactions on Pattern Analysis and Machine Intelligence, 1*(2), 224–227.

Foster, D., Maynes, D., Miller, J., Chernyshenko, S., Mead, A., Drasgow, F., . . . Drazewski, P. (2016). *The predictive index behavioral assessment technical manual* [Technical report]. Westwood, MA: The Predictive Index.

Gandomi, A., & Haider, M. (2015). Beyond the hype: Big data concepts, methods, and analytics. *International Journal of Information Management, 35*(2), 137–144.

Kerr, D., & Chung, G. (2012). Identifying key features of student performance in educational video games and simulations through cluster analysis. *Journal of Educational Data Mining, 4*(1), 145–182.

Kriegel, H.-P., Kröger, P., & Zimek, A. (2009). Clustering high-dimensional data: A survey on subspace clustering, pattern-based clustering, and correlation clustering. *ACM Transactions on Knowledge Discovery from Data, 3*(1), 1–59.

Laney, D. (2001). *3D data management: Controlling data volume, velocity, and variety* (Report No. 949). Stamford, CT: META Group.

Maechler, M., Rousseeuw, P., Struyf, A., Hubert, M., & Hornik, K. (2016). Cluster: Cluster analysis basics and extensions [Software version 2.0.4]. Available from https://cran.r-project.org/web/packages/cluster/index.html

Manyika, J., Chui, M., Brown, B., Bughin, J., Dobbs, R., Roxburgh, C., & Byers, A. H. (2011). *Big data: The next frontier for innovation, competition, and productivity.* The McKinsey Global Institute. Retrieved from https://www.mckinsey.com/business-functions/digital-mckinsey/our-insights/big-data-the-next-frontier-for-innovation.

Marston, W. (1928). *The emotions of normal people.* New York, NY: Harcourt, Brace and Company.

McAfee, A., & Brynjolfsson, E. (2012, October). Big data: The management revolution. *Harvard Business Review.* Retrieved from https://hbr.org/2012/10/big-data-the-management-revolution

Mislevy, R. J. (2011). *Evidence-centered design for simulation-based assessment* (CRESST Report 800). Los Angeles, CA: University of California, National Center for Research on Evaluation, Standards, and Student Testing.

Mislevy, R. J., Behrens, J. T., Dicerbo, K. E., & Levy, R. (2012). Design and discovery in educational assessment: Evidence-centered design, psychometrics, and educational data mining. *Journal of Educational Data Mining, 4*(1), 11–48.

R Core Team. (2015). R: A language and environment for statistical computing [Software version 3.2.0]. Vienna, Austria: R Foundation for Statistical Computing. Retrieved from http://www.R-project.org/

Stevens, R. H., & Casillas, A. (2006). Artificial neural networks. In D. M. Williamson, R. J. Mislevy, & I. I. Bejar (Eds.), *Automated scoring of complex tasks in computer-based testing* (pp. 259–312). Mahwah, NJ: Erlbaum.

Stevens, R., Galloway, T., Wang, P., Berka, C., Tan. V., Wohlgemuth, T., . . . Buckles, R. (2012). Modeling the neurodynamic complexity of submarine navigation teams. *Computational and Mathematical Organization Theory, 19,* 346–369.

Wehrens, R., & Buydens, L. M. C. (2007). Self- and super-organizing maps in R: The Kohonen package. *Journal of Statistical Software, 21*(5), 1–19.

White House. (2014). *Big data and privacy: A technological perspective.* Washington, DC: Executive Office of the President, President's Council of Advisors on Science and Technology.

Xu, B., Recker, M., Qi, X., Flann, N., & Ye, L. (2013). Clustering educational digital library usage data: A comparison of latent class analysis and k-means algorithms. *Journal of Educational Data Mining, 5*(2), 38–68.

Zubin, J. (1938). A technique for measuring like-mindedness. *Journal of Abnormal and Social Psychology, 33,* 508–516.

CHAPTER 10

INTEGRATING SURVEY AND LEARNING ANALYTICS DATA FOR A BETTER UNDERSTANDING OF ENGAGEMENT IN MOOCs

Evgenia Samoilova
University of Mannheim

Florian Keusch
University of Mannheim

Frauke Kreuter
University of Maryland and University of Mannheim

While the popularity of massive online open courses (MOOCs) is increasing among both traditional and nontraditional university students, relatively low completion rates are often mentioned as a key point of criticism (Bates, 2012). Despite the prevalence of these unfavorable views, there is a growing

Data Analytics and Psychometrics, pages 247–261

body of research that explicitly focuses on the heterogeneity of learners that goes beyond an oversimplified categorization of participants into completers and non-completers (Koller, Ng, Do, & Chen, 2013; Kizilcec, Piech, & Schneider, 2013). Given different backgrounds, intentions, skill levels, and constraints of learners, one of the prerequisites for further improvement of MOOCs is a better understanding of how different subpopulations of learners interact with course components (Kizilcec et al., 2013) and what accounts for observed behavioral differences. To address this problem, researchers and practitioners use two main types of data: learning analytics (see Long & Siemens, 2011) and survey data. Although learning analytics provides new and innovative ways of measuring learning behavior, measurements of subjective states (e.g., believes about teaching and learning or course satisfaction) are still primarily based on survey data. For example, learner intention[1] (Koller et al., 2013; Reich, 2014; Kizilcec & Schneider, 2015) is considered to be one of the key pieces of information needed to understand retention and engagement in MOOCs. This construct is currently measured via web-based surveys of registered MOOC participants. The major challenge of using survey data to study MOOCs are very high unit nonresponse rates. Depending on whether the survey is conducted at the beginning or at the end of the course, papers report response rates in the range between 4 and 30% (Breslow et al., 2013; Reich, 2014; Kizilcec & Schneider, 2015). Such response rates are potentially problematic, as survey methodologists warn that low response rates might lead to nonresponse bias (see Groves & Peytcheva, 2008). While quality and interpretation of learning analytics data has been receiving some attention in the literature (DeBoer, Ho, Stump, & Breslow, 2014), survey data in MOOCs are often taken at their face value.

Drawing on data from the first session of the Coursera MOOC Questionnaire Design for Social Surveys, this chapter aims to demonstrate the importance as well as potential challenges of complementing learning analytics with survey data in studying engagement in MOOCs. Using activity logs and data from the pre- and post-course survey of 16,846 registered course participants, we examine the relationship between participation in course evaluation surveys and student behavioral engagement in the course. The findings suggest that for the given Coursera course the vast majority of our survey data stems from the most engaged students. The post-course survey data is almost entirely limited to most engaged students. In other words, our knowledge about the student subgroups who might need more support to successfully participate in the course is scarce. In the discussion section, we address possible approaches to collect relevant data on less engaged learners, in order to understand their challenges. In addition, we also discuss how in future engagement research, survey response rate can be used as a predictor to better understand engagement.

MEASURING SUCCESS OF MOOCS

In the first years of their existence MOOCs were praised for their potential to democratize education (Koller, 2013). Most MOOCs are courses in various disciplines and of various levels administered online and open to everybody without formal restrictions. Easy accessibility of such courses as well as high involvement from world leading universities in offering MOOCs raised hopes that this recent innovation can help reduce education gap. One of the most cogent criticism however that MOOCs faced in the first years of their advancement included very low completion rates (Koller et al., 2013). While thousands of students could join a single course at the same time, average completion rates are currently about 15% (Jordan, 2015).

These low completion rates are indeed alarming when viewed within the traditional education framework (Koller et al., 2013). Yet, MOOCs can hardly be measured against traditional standards, as they take place within much less formal settings (see Sefton-Green, 2010 for more on informal education). Increasing spread of Internet access paired with increasing online learning offers made informal (out-of-school) learning more widespread (Means, Bakia, &, Murphy, 2014). As Collins and Halverson (2009) argued, this type of learning enabled by new technologies can be characterized (among other features) as interest-driven. Means et al. (2014) further described this type of learning as "self-directed" and "self-initiated" (p. 73). The authors have also identified at least five possible intentions associated with out-of-school learning: "episodic learning to satisfy curiosity; learning as entertainment; learning to enable better living; learning for professional advancement; and learning to reinforce or substitute for formal instruction" (p. 73). While all five categories can be thought of as intentions to prompt MOOCs learners to start and/or persists in a course, the main intention in traditional formal education is usually reduced to acquiring a degree. Consequently, using traditional metrics such as completion rates to evaluate success of MOOCs is clearly not tenable and should be replaced with better fitted measures (Breslow et al., 2013; Koller et al., 2013).

Acknowledgment of the vast learner diversity as well as the informal setting in MOOCs is mostly reflected in research on engagement. Engagement has been one of the central topics in studying learning in traditional as well as online classrooms. Although engagement is often defined in different ways (see Ainley, 2012; Skinner & Pitzer, 2012), this concept is primarily used to refer to one's interactions with the learning environment (Järvelä & Renninger, 2014). In this chapter, we follow one of the most commonly used definitions of this construct in learning literature that acknowledges behavioral, cognitive, and affective aspects of engagement (Fredricks, Blumenfeld, & Paris, 2004).

Most empirical studies on this subject focused on behavioral patterns of engagement aiming to problematize a dichotomous (completer versus non-completer) description of the MOOC learners. One of the most influential papers on behavioral engagement in MOOCs (Kizilcec et al., 2013) analyzed data from three of Stanford's courses in computer science and identified four main groups of learners: completers, disengaging, auditors, and samplers. Completers were similar to common expectations with regards to traditional students. Although they had different levels of performance they all at least tried to engage with all of the course assignments. Disengaging students first showed the same patterns as completers, but then disengaged or completely disappeared from the course. While auditors engaged with lecture videos throughout the whole course period, samplers watched only few lectures. Anderson, Huttenlocher, Kleinberg, and Leskovec (2014) looked at three courses in a large scale quantitative analysis on one of the most popular MOOC platforms Coursera. They identified a slightly different pattern with five groups including viewers (same as auditors described above), solvers (students who engage in the assignments such as for example quizzes but do not engage in lecture videos), collectors (students who primarily download videos), all-rounders (those who equally engage in both lecture videos and assignments), and bystanders (participants who disappear after having registered for the course). Yet another approach to categorize behavioral engagement focused on the amount of time that learners use for various activities (Breslow et al., 2013).

While a taxonomy of behavioral engagement is clearly a better way to evaluate the quality of MOOCs when compared to course completion rates, we know very little about subgroups of learners involved in the identified patterns of engagement. In other words, given a possibility of various intentions and backgrounds of the learners, especially in informal settings, interpreting a particular engagement or disengagement pattern as alarming is not a straightforward process. In other words, limited engagement in MOOCs for certain subgroups does not necessarily mean lower satisfaction and a need for improvement. In order to fully understand engagement in MOOCs, research needs to consider nonbehavioral aspects of engagement as well as learners' indentions that are closely intertwined with their behavior.

MEASURING ENGAGEMENT AND STUDENTS' INTENTION IN MOOCS

Most data used to measure behavioral engagement in MOOCs come from activity logs collected during the course. Activity logs can include (yet are not limited to) clickstream data, text data from discussion forums, as well as log files with achievement results (e.g., grades). Such "pre-existing, machine-readable data" (Ferguson, 2012, p. 305) lead to the emergence of the entirely new field of learning analytics. The 1st International Conference on Learning Analytics and Knowledge defined learning analytics as "the measurement, collection, analysis and reporting" of learners' data (as cited in Long & Siemens, 2011, p. 34). Learning analytics data—considered a form of *found* (Japec et al., 2015) or *organic* data (Groves, 2011a; Groves, 2011b) in survey and data research communities—proves not only to help answering existing research questions, it also enables educational researchers to approach new ones. The research on typologies of behavioral engagement in MOOCs described above can hardly be imagined without available learning analytics data. Nevertheless, these sources of data are not well-suited (at least at the moment) to tackle measurement of subjective (nonbehavioral) states. Therefore, survey data (when collected and analyzed properly) can provide higher quality measures for research questions concerned with learner intention or nonbehavioral engagement. It is hence not surprising that the few existing attempts to collect data on intentions in MOOCs use survey instruments (Reich, 2014; Ho et al., 2015; Kizilcec & Schneider, 2015).

The major challenge of using survey data to study MOOCs are very high unit nonresponse rates, that is, students not participating in course evaluation surveys. For example, in the above mentioned studies of intention Reich (2014) reports a survey response rate of 27%, while Kizilcec & Schneider (2015) conducted surveys with less than 7%. The survey response rate is an important indicator of survey data quality, as high nonresponse rates can indicate a potential nonresponse bias, defined as the difference between the estimate obtained from the data of respondents and the "true value" in the entire sample including nonrespondents (Groves et al., 2009). In other words, nonresponse is a problem when nonrespondents systematically differ from the respondents in the variables of interest. In the following two sections, we describe the use of the data from a social science Coursera MOOC to study the relationship between survey response rates and students' behavioral engagement.

METHODOLOGY

The data for this study come from the first session of the Questionnaire Design for Social Surveys MOOC taught by faculty of the University of Michigan in Summer 2014. Overall, 16,846 international participants were enrolled in the course. The course is aimed at students and professionals from various disciplines involved in primary data collection. Topics covered in the course include the basic elements of designing and evaluating questionnaires. The course was composed of six unit weeks. Each unit contained a number of short prerecorded video lectures, recommended readings, and quizzes addressing the unit content. The final exam was placed at the end of the sixth week and was aimed to cover content of the entire course. In addition to the quizzes, students had to engage in a peer-review project. Out of 16,846 participants, 48.6% engaged in at least one of the course activities; 51.4% did not attempt to start any videos, did not submit any of the quizzes, and did not participate in the peer-review project. Of the people enrolled, 0.3% ($n = 50$) received a passing grade at the end of the course for finishing all required assignments (quizzes, final exam, and peer-review project).

Available learning analytics data included activity logs of the learners. Activity logs are comprised of submission data for the weekly quizzes and final exam, the peer review assignment, as well as data indicating whether the students attempted to view a video (i.e., downloaded or started streaming). It is important to note that in 2014, no detailed clickstream data for video watching were available, which would allow specific behavior such as for example pausing or percentage of the played material.

The survey data came from the pre- and post-course surveys. Both surveys were based on self-administered online questionnaires. The pre-course questionnaire included 15 questions mostly focused on the demographic questions of the user. The invitation for the survey was sent via email at the start of the course, which means that students could participate in the survey any time and not necessarily before they started working on the course material. The post-course questionnaire comprised 20 questions addressing various aspects of learners' course experiences. The invitation for the survey was sent after the course ended to all of the participants regardless of their engagement level.

Both learning analytics and survey data included secondary data collected and anonymized by a Coursera team. Linking data was possible due to an existing ID assigned to each participants. The study was reviewed and considered as exempt by the Health Sciences and Behavioral Sciences Institutional Review Board (IRB-HSBS) of the University of Michigan.

Although it is tenable to expect a higher response rate for the pre-course survey, the observed differences in the response rates for the two surveys are very large. While only 2.4% ($n = 406$) of the enrolled students responded to the post-course survey, the response rate for the pre-course survey is 31.4% ($n = 5{,}282$). The post-course survey participants are not a complete subset of the pre-course survey participants, 75.3% ($n = 305$) of those who responded to the post-course survey also responded to the survey at the start of the course. The distribution of the key demographic variables of the post-course respondents (based on their pre-course survey responses) is very similar to that of the pre-course survey respondents. As Table 10.1 demonstrates, the demographic characteristics of the learners suggests that the MOOC audience is highly educated, older than traditional university

TABLE 10.1 Learner Characteristics Based on the Pre-Course Survey (N = 5,282)

	Mean/%	Median	SD
Gender			
Female	52.5%		
Male	46.6%		
Other	0.3%		
Age	35.3	33.0	11.2
Highest level of schooling			
No high school degree	0.9%		
High school degree	8.5%		
Associate degree	2.2%		
Bachelor's degree	28.4%		
Master's or professional degree	47.0%		
Doctorate degree	10.0%		
Involved in an educational program:			
Full-time student	13.5%		
Part-time students	22.1%		
Employment status			
Employed full-time (incl. self-employed)	59.9%		
Employed part-time (incl. self-employed)	13.7%		
Not employed	4.0%		
Unemployed	6.0%		
U.S.-based	24.0%		

students, with a strong representation of students from the United States, and has more women than men. Only 6.0% (n = 317) of students reported to be unemployed, while not being involved in any educational program.

The post-course survey (see Table 10.2) shows that most of the respondents reported to have a strong desire to take the course, rated the course highly, and had learned a lot.

TABLE 10.2 Selected Items From the Post-Course Survey. N = 406 (1–strongly disagree, 2–disagree, 3–neither agree nor disagree, 4–agree, 5–strongly agree)

Items	Mean	Median	SD
I had a strong desire to take this course	4.1	4	0.8
Overall this was an excellent course	4.1	4	0.9
I learned a great deal in this course	3.6	3	1.0

In order to investigate existing learning patterns beyond a binary indicator of completion, we draw upon a parsimonious approach to categorize learning behavior across units applied by Kizilcec et al. (2013). In the first step, we differentiate between active and non-active students. 8,660 *non-active* students disappear from the course after registration, as opposed to 8,186 *active* students who engaged in one of the course activities at least once. Next, we differentiate the sample of active students further by describing each student's behavioral engagement across the six course unit-weeks. For each unit-week, the participants were assigned one of the following labels: at least 50% of the videos were started and the quiz was submitted (3); less than 50% of the videos were started and the quiz was submitted (2); only watching videos without submitting the quiz (1); no engagement (0). For example, if a learner started all of the videos in the first week and submitted the quiz but then only started videos during the other weeks without submitting the quizzes, she or he would be assigned the following six values: 3, 1, 1, 1, 1, 1. Clustering was performed on the sample of active students only, i.e., students who engaged with at least one of the videos or quizzes during the course. The peer-review activity logs were only used to describe the cluster solutions. To cluster the data we used a robust alternative to a k-means cluster analysis, Partitioning Around Medoids (PAM). Similar to Kizilcec et al. (2013) Manhattan distance was used. The identified clusters are compared based on the survey response rates. The comparison is based on descriptive statistics, the Chi Square and exact Fisher's tests, and odds ratios.

RESULTS

The elbow method and the average silhouette approach suggested a three cluster solution for active students based on the PAM algorithm. The Silhouette test indicates a reasonable structure of the clusters (average silhouette score = 0.6). Table 10.3 summarizes behavioral patterns of the three cluster groups:

- *Diligent* students ($n = 1{,}395$) constitute 17.0% of the students who engaged with the course material at least once (active students) and 8.3% of all course participants. This group of students engaged with most of the course videos and submitted quizzes throughout all of the 6 weeks. Of the diligent students, 61.6% also submitted the peer-review project.
- *Auditors'* ($n = 1{,}580$) engagement with videos highly resemble the diligent students. While auditors start most of the videos during the whole durations of the course, only a small proportion of the students submit videos in the first three weeks. In the rest of the weeks,

TABLE 10.3 Summary of Learning Behavior of Active Student Clusters

	Diligent		Auditors		Browsers	
Average % of videos started by students	week 1	93.08	week 1	95.29	week 1	62.25
	week 2	91.49	week 2	93.16	week 2	18.23
	week 3	88.21	week 3	91.61	week 3	6.54
	week 4	84.12	week 4	89.41	week 4	0.55
	week 5	62.93	week 5	66.85	week 5	0.23
	week 6	65.16	week 6	70.83	week 6	0.24
% of students who submitted quizzes	week 1	99.21	week 1	18.28	week 1	33.60
	week 2	99.57	week 2	11.01	week 2	12.95
	week 3	98.78	week 3	4.62	week 3	3.82
	week 4	92.7	week 4	3.92	week 4	0.15
	week 5	85.23	week 5	2.41	week 5	0.06
	week 6	71.76	week 6	0.75	week 6	0.04
% of students who submitted a peer review project	61.6		1.7		2.2	
Total	1,395		1,580		5,211	

percentage of students who submit a weekly quiz approaches zero. Of the active participants, 19.3% and 9.4% of all participants are auditors. It is not surprising that only 1.7% of auditors submitted the peer-review project.

- *Browsers* ($n = 5{,}211$) are learners who browse through the course materials before completely disengaging from the course by the fourth week. Active students are mostly comprised of browsers (63.7%). Browsers also constitute 30.9% of all course participants. Only 2.2% of these learners took part in the peer-review project.

Table 10.4 shows response rates for the course participants by their level of behavioral engagement.

First we differentiate between active and non-active students. Given the response rate for all of the learners (31.4% for the pre-course survey and 2.4% for the post-course survey), it is clear that the response rate is notably higher among active learners compared to the non-active ones for both instruments. Among students who did not engage with the course after enrollment 20.4% responded to the pre-course survey, compared to 42.8% among the active students. Further delineation of active learners based on the three clusters provides more fine-grained information.

Diligent students have the highest response (63.1%) rate followed by browsers (40.4%) and auditors (32.8%). For the post-course survey, differentiating between various clusters is especially important, as responses are

TABLE 10.4 Response Rates for the Pre- and Post-Course Surveys by the Level of Students' Behavioral Engagement

Response Rate	Non-active	Active		
Pre-course survey	20.40%	42.82%		
		Diligent	Browsers	Auditors
		63.08%	40.43%	32.78%
Post-course survey	Non-active	Active		
	0.28%	4.65%		
		Diligent	Browsers	Auditors
		21.13%	0.79%	2.78%
Total	8,660	1,395	5,211	1,580

almost entirely limited to the diligent students. Response rates for the non-active students, browsers, and auditors are extremely low. In the diligent cluster, 21.1% of the learners participated in the post-course survey.

Given that the number of responses for the post-course survey is very small, we will look at the odds ratio only for the pre-course survey. Figure 10.1 reports odds ratios for the association between responding to a

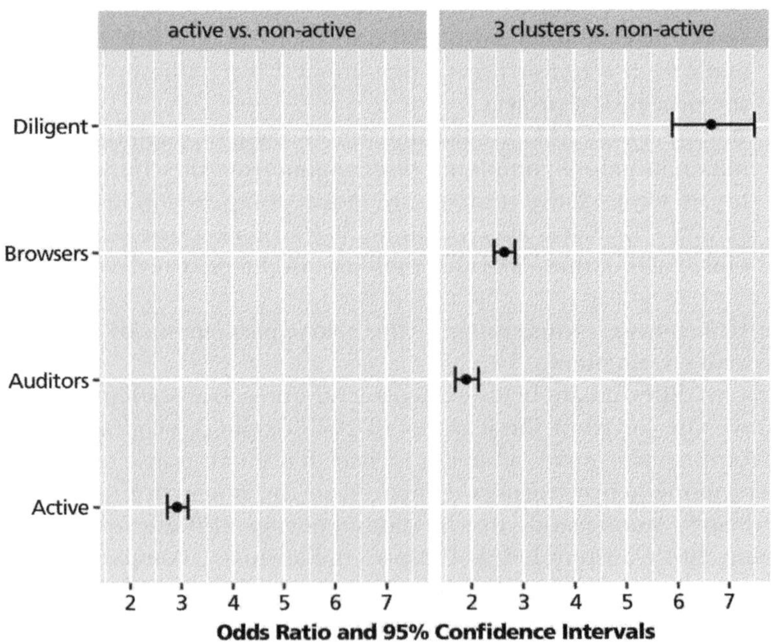

Figure 10.1 Estimated odds ratios and 95% confidence intervals of pre-course survey participation for engagement clusters.

pre-course survey and membership in one of the identified engagement groups (active, diligent, browsers, and auditors with non-active students serving as the reference group). As expected, for all of the engagement groups, odds ratios are higher than 1, indicating a positive association between the pre-course survey response and engagement. Moreover, Figure 10.1 demonstrates that lumping the three clusters (diligent, browsers, and auditors) together into one *active* student group obscures this relationship. Diligent students are 6.7 times more likely to have participated in the pre-course survey than non-active students. Estimated odds for browsers and auditors are 2.7 and 1.9, respectively. The difference in the likelihood to have participated in the pre-course survey is statistically significant (at the 5% level) between all engagement groups (each of these clusters was chosen as a reference category).

The above described differences in response rates across the identified clusters help interpret results of the pre- and post-course surveys. Table 10.5 illustrates some of the findings of the pre- and post-course survey by level of students' behavioral engagement. One of the most interesting differences is the over-representation of female respondents in the diligent cluster

TABLE 10.5 Selected Items for the Pre- and Post-Course Surveys by the Level of Students' Behavioral Engagement. Percentage of the Respondents for the Respective Cluster/Mean, Median, and SD

	Non-active	Auditors	Browsers	Diligent
Pre-course survey				
Female students	54.6%	36.6%	54.1%	84.3%
At least Master's or professional degree	51.6%	64.6%	57.3%	62.5%
Full-time students	25.4%	19.2%	21.8%	17.3%
Full-time (self-)employed	55.8%	61.5%	59.1%	63.5%
U.S.-based	21.2%	14.6%	20.4%	22.5%
Total	1,767	522	2,107	886
Post-course survey				
I had a strong desire to take this course	Mean = 4.7 Median = 5.0 SD = 0.5	Mean = 4.4 Median = 4.0 SD = 0.6	Mean = 4.1 Median = 4.0 SD = 1.0	Mean = 4.1 Median = 4.0 SD = 0.8
Overall this was an excellent course	Mean = 4.4 Median = 5.0 SD = 0.7	Mean = 4.2 Median = 4.0 SD = 0.9	Mean = 4.2 Median = 4.0 SD = 0.7	Mean = 4.1 Median = 4.0 SD = 0.8
I learned a great deal in this course	Mean = 4.0 Median = 4.0 SD = 0.8	Mean = 4.0 Median = 4.0 SD = 0.8	Mean = 3.8 Median = 4.0 SD = 1.0	Mean = 4.1 Median = 4.0 SD = 0.8
Total	**25**	**44**	**41**	**296**

compared to the other clusters. From the available data, it is not clear whether the high proportion of female respondents is due to gender differences in the response rate to the pre-course survey (see Keusch, 2015 for more information on higher response rates among women in web surveys), "true" gender differences across the engagement groups, or a combination of both.

DISCUSSION AND CONCLUSION

By using data from a social science course on the Coursera platform, we aimed to investigate the association between survey response and engagement, a relationship that was under-investigated in previous studies. In addition to comparing students who did not show any engagement with course materials against those who engaged in at least one activity, we categorized active students into three different clusters based on their engagement with the learning materials: diligent, browsers, and auditors. Although the study is limited to data from a single MOOC within a specific context on the Coursera platform, the findings confirm reports in previous research (Kizilcec et al., 2013; Reich, 2014). The results show that most of the survey data (especially with regards to the post-course evaluation) stems from the most engaged MOOC students. This is problematic, as we know very little about learners who were less engaged in the course and thus might need more support to successfully finish it. The possibility of nonresponse bias questions some of the established theses in the MOOC literature. For example, do students with nontraditional engagement patterns (i.e., auditors) really have high levels of satisfaction, as proposed by Kizilcec et al. (2013)? While this might just be the case, more data on non-respondents to the post-course satisfaction survey from these groups is needed to verify this claim.

The findings also demonstrate that activity logs can tell us a lot about learners' behavior but they are not enough to sufficiently understand students' engagement. To increase understanding, two possible approaches could be implemented in future projects. The first approach concerns improvement of the currently used data collection, including improvements to the instruments and the process with which the data are collected. Pre-course surveys could include questions about students' intention for the course, to allow subsetting analyses of activity logs and other learning metrics to those students that intended to engage in the course. Likewise one can filter out those that knew from the beginning that they won't have the time to finish the course or just wanted to take a peek. To gain more insight out of both pre- and post-course surveys, one could focus on improving response rates (Keusch, 2015). One option could include explicitly targeting non-respondents classified as non-diligent students for the purpose of investigating reasons for their learning behavior. This approach could be combined with using incentives (Singer & Ye, 2012) to motivate response among the least engaged as well as qualitative approach, such as online focus groups, to study these subgroups and their intentions in more depth.

Alternatively, one could empirically investigate a possibility of using behavioral measures (for example, participation in the pre-course survey) as a proxy for measuring subjective states, primarily learners' intention. Given that topic salience is one of the strongest predictors of survey participation (Adams & Umbach, 2012; Groves, Presser, & Dipko, 2004), we could hypothesize that respondents to the pre-course survey are more interested in the course topic than non-respondents. Since those who are more interested in the topic are more likely to be motivated and committed to finish the course at its start, the use of such a proxy is tenable. While some authors already suggested using behavioral measures obtained via learning analytics to study subjective aspects of learners' behavior (Koller et al., 2013), they did not go further than suggesting to use variables indicating students' engagement with the course material. Such an approach was rightfully criticized for "circular" reasoning (Ho et al., 2015). In contrast, survey response is different from engaging with the learning material. In addition, if participation in the pre-course survey (at best combined with other existing data, such as, for example, learner's location measured via IP address) could help predict learners' intentions for participation, one could implement interventions at an early stage of the course.

The accessibility of unobtrusive measures of actual behavior in online learning opens new opportunities for empirical research. Survey and learning analytics approaches could be used in a complementary manner, to increase our knowledge about the relationship between traditional self-reports and their possible proxies obtained via new sources of data. Integrating traditional data sources such as survey data with newly emerging organic types of data can result in a much more informative picture of learning experiences than if exclusively relying on one source of data (Samoilova, Keusch, Wolbring, 2017). Consequently, development of effective strategies of data integration are highly relevant for the advancement of MOOC research and practices.

NOTE

1. While some authors use "intention," "motivation," and "goals" to refer to the same concept of participants' intentions of participating in a course, we prefer to use "intention," as the other two constructs are much broader than their use in the context of engagement.

REFERENCES

Adams, M. J. D., & Umbach, P. D. (2012). Nonresponse and online student evaluations of teaching: Understanding the influence, fatigue, and academic environments. *Research in Higher Education, 53*(5), 576–591.

Ainley, M. (2012). Students' interest and engagement in classroom activities. In S. L. Christenson, A. L. Reschly, & C. Wylie (Eds.), *Handbook of research on student engagement* (pp. 283–302). New York, NY: Springer International.

Anderson, A., Huttenlocher, D., Kleinberg, J., & Leskovec, J. (2014, April). *Engaging with massive online courses.* Paper presented at WWW '14, Seoul, South Korea. Retrieved from http://cs.stanford.edu/people/ashton/pubs/mooc-engagement-www2014.pdf

Bates, T. (2012). What's Right and What's Wrong About Coursera-style MOOCs? [Web log comment]. Retrieved from http://www.tonybates.ca/2012/08/05/whats-right-and-whats-wrong-about-coursera-style-moocs/.

Breslow, L., Pritchard, D. E., DeBoer, J., Stump, G. S., Ho, A. D., & Seaton, D. T. (2013). Studying learning in the worldwide classroom research into edX's first MOOC. *Research and Practice in Assessment,* 8, 13–25.

Collins, A., & Halverson, R. (2009). *Rethinking education in the age of technology: The digital revolution and the schools.* New York, NY: Teachers College Press.

DeBoer, J., Ho, A. D., Stump, G. S., & Breslow, L. (2014). Changing "course": Reconceptualizing educational variables for massive open online courses. *Educational Researcher, 43*(2), 74–84.

Ferguson, R. (2012). Learning analytics: Drivers, developments, and challenges. *International Journal of Technology Enhanced Learning, 4*(5/6), 304–317.

Fredricks, J. A., Blumenfeld, P. C., & Paris, A. H. (2004). School engagement: Potential of the concept, state of the evidence. *Review of Educational Research,* 74(1), 59–109.

Groves, R. M. (2011a). Three Eras of Survey Research. *Public Opinion Quarterly, 75*(5), 861–871.

Groves, R. M. (2011b). *Designed Data and Organic Data* [Web log comment]. Retrieved from http://1.usa.gov/15NDn8w

Groves, R. M., Fowler, F. J., Couper, M. P., Lepkowski, J. M., Singer, E., & Tourangeau, R. (2009). *Survey methodology* (2nd ed.). Hoboken, NJ: John Wiley & Sons.

Groves, R. M., & Peytcheva, E. (2008). The impact of nonresponse rate on nonresponse bias: A meta-analysis. *Public Opinion Quarterly,* 72(2), 167–189.

Groves, R. M., Presser, S., & Dipko, S. (2004). The role of topic interest in survey participation decisions. *Public Opinion Quarterly, 68*(1), 2–31.

Ho, A. D., Chuang, I., Reich, J., Coleman, C. A., Whitehill, J., Northcutt, C. G., & Williams, J. J. (2015). *HarvardX and MITx: Two years of open online courses Fall 2012–Summer 2014.* HarvardX Working Paper.

Japec, L., Kreuter, F., Berg, M., Biemer, P., Decker, P., Lampe, C., . . . Usher, A. (2015). Big data in survey research. AAPOR Task Force Report. *Public Opinion Quarterly, 79*(4) , 839–880.

Järvelä, S., & Renninger, K. A. (2014). Designing for learning: Interest, motivation, and engagement. In R. K. Sawyer (Eds.), *The Cambridge Handbook of the learning sciences* [Kindle Edition]. New York, NY: Cambridge University Press.

Jordan, K. (2015). *MOOC completion rates: The data* [Web log post]. Retrieved from http://www.katyjordan.com/MOOCproject.html

Keusch, F. (2015). Why do people participate in Web surveys? Applying survey participation theory to internet survey data collection. *Management Review Quarterly, 65*(3), 183–216.

Kizilcec, R. F., Piech, C., & Schneider, E. (2013, April). Deconstructing disengagement: Analyzing learner subpopulations in massive open online courses. In *Proceedings of the Third International Conference on Learning Analytics and Knowledge, LAK 2013.* Leuven, Belgium. Retrieved from: http://rene.kizilcec.com/wp-content/uploads/2013/09/Kizilcec-Piech-Schneider-2013-Deconstructing-Disengagement-Analyzing-Learner-Subpopulations-in-Massive-Open-Online-Courses.pdf

Kizilcec, R. F., & Schneider, E. (2015). Motivation as a lLens to uUnderstand oOnline lLearners. *ACM Transactions on Computer-Human Interaction (TOCHI), 22*(2). Retrieved from http://dl.acm.org/citation.cfm?doid=2744768.2699735

Koller, D. (2013, December 31). MOOCs can be a significant factor in opening doors to opportunity. *EdSurge.* Retrieved from https://www.edsurge.com/news/2013-12-31-daphne-koller-moocs-can-be-a-significant-factor-in-opening-doors-to-opportunity

Koller, D., Ng, A., Do, C., & Chen, Z. (2013). Retention and intention in massive open online courses: In depth. *Educause Review.* Retrieved from http://er.educause.edu/articles/2013/6/retention-and-intention-in-massive-open-online-courses-in-depth

Long, P., & Siemens, G. (2011). Penetrating the fog: Analytics in learning and education. *EDUCAUSE Review, 46*(5), 31–40.

Means, B., Bakia, M., & Murphy, R. (2014). *Learning online: What research tells us about whether, when and how.* New York, NY: Routledge.

Reich, J. (2014). MOOC completion and retention in the context of student intent. *Educause Review.* Retrieved from http://er.educause.edu/articles/2014/12/mooc-completion-and-retention-in-the-context-of-student-intent

Samoilova, E., Keusch, F., & Wolbring, T. (2017). Learning analytics and survey data integration in workload research. Zeitschrift für Hochschulentwicklung. *Special Edition: Learning Analytics: Implications for Higher Education, 12*(1), 65–78. Retrieved from: https://www.zfhe.at/index.php/zfhe/article/view/991

Singer, E., & Ye, C. (2013). The use and effects of incentives in surveys. *Annals of the American Academy of Political and Social Science, 645*(1), 112–141.

Sefton-Green, J. (2010). *Learning at not-school: A review of study, theory, and advocacy for education in non-formal settings.* Cambridge, MA: MIT Press.

Skinner, E. A., & Pitzer, J. R. (2012). Developmental dynamics of student engagement, coping, and everyday resilience. In S. L. Christenson, A. L. Reschly, & C. Wylie (Eds.), *Handbook of research on student engagement* (pp. 21– 44). New York, NY: Springer International.

Printed and bound by CPI Group (UK) Ltd, Croydon, CR0 4YY

15/09/2026

14962335-0003